MODERN MONETARY THEORY

By the same author

MONEY

ECONOMIC THEORY: Equilibrium and Change

NEW DIRECTIONS IN ECONOMIC POLICY

THE COST OF TRUCKING: Econometric Analysis (*with others*)

RESOURCE ALLOCATION AND ECONOMIC POLICY
(*editor with Michael Allingham*)

MODERN MONETARY THEORY

M. L. BURSTEIN

'Mais nous nous representons l'avenir comme un reflet du présent projeté dans un espace vide, tandis qu'il est le résultat, souvent tout prochain, de causes qui nous échappent pour la plupart.'—Marcel Proust, *À la Recherche du Temps Perdu*, Vol. xii, *La Prisonière* (Paris: Gallimard, 1923) p. 146.

M
MACMILLAN

First published 1986

Published by
THE MACMILLAN PRESS LTD
Houndmills, Basingstoke, Hampshire RG21 2XS
and London
Companies and representatives
throughout the world

British Library Cataloguing in Publication Data
Burstein, M. L.
Modern monetary theory.
1. Money
I. Title
332.4'01 HG221
ISBN 0-333-33155-9

Reprinted and bound 1994
in Great Britain by
Antony Rowe Ltd, Chippenham, Wiltshire

For Milka

Why with time do I not glance aside
To new-found methods and to compounds strange?
Why write I still all one, ever the same
And keep invention in a noted weed,
That every word doth almost tell my name,
Showing their birth and where they did proceed?
. . . . . .
So all my best is dressing old words new,
Spending again what is already spent;
(*Shakespeare, Sonnet LXXVI*)

Contents

Preface: Apologia

A living science practises creative destruction. Modern developments are recombinations of old ones, infused with drawings from expanding technical possibilities. Yesterday's economics disappears; and continues. This book is meant to supply an example.

English economics is in my bones. I began to read the *General Theory* in 1941; and will die reading it. I tried to explain in 1975 (in *Economic Inquiry*) why the book, and its author, have fixed my star. But I have not before acknowledged how much I owe to Roy Harrod and Joan Robinson for the many hours they indulged me in Evanston; I have a special feeling for the 'Circus' too.

I began to read Marshallian economics in Wisconsin forty-five years ago. When I first came up to the University of Chicago, its leading figure, for a seventeen year old, and an avid reader of the press, was Henry Simons. Simons, a fascinating and kind man, and, of course, a practitioner of Marshallian economics, gave me a lot of his time. By the time I entered Chicago's graduate-economics programme, twelve years later, Marshallian economics was being expounded there with brilliant lucidity by Milton Friedman, an exemplary teacher. The book will show that I have been as thoroughly infected by Friedman's price theory, including its applications to monetary economics, as perhaps resistant to monetarism.

The flow of the narrative must be interrupted to note the influence of a remarkable, wonderfully American, economist and philosopher, Frank Knight, the most revered of my many great teachers. Mr Knight cannot be pigeon-holed. He requires and deserves a special paragraph. (Chapter 6 displays his influence, as does Chapter 8.) To have known and loved Knight grants immunity against viruses that would transform economics into petty engineering.

It became necessary to assimilate the analytical apparatus that might be called MIT economics. I single out the work of Paul Samuelson: partly because it is colossal; partly because Samuelson, along with W. A. Mozart, S. S. van Dine, T. S. Eliot, Marcel Proust *et al.*, belongs to a gaggle of geniuses, personally unknown to me, who are exceptionally salient in my mind. He, along with Debreu, Gale and his co-workers Dorfman and Solow (see *Linear Programming and Economic Analysis*) and, recently, Arrowsmith and Place, developed for me a sense of mechanism that in time led to a quite complete turnover of my stock of images of the macroeconomy.

Formal, more-or-less mathematised, economic theory has at least three commanding virtues.

It makes it possible to strip one's reasoning to essentials; and to find that Beauty which informs Truth.

It communicates with physics.

It supplies a language permitting efficient communication within and between generations of students of economics, incidentally making it much easier to discover Error.

Whatever its virtues *en général*, the more formal economics (which one would be tempted to call continental in inspiration if Hicks's *Value and Capital* were not so important to it) has led to paradigms that have revived the corpse of monetary theory. Inevitably, then, a discriminant identifying *modern* monetary theory is a degree of formalism. The success of the resulting synthesis owes much to James Tobin, as the book will make clear.

From the beginning, monetary theorists have quarrelled – they love to quarrel – about *What is money?* The book suggests that the question has no useful answer: monetary theory may not be about money!

The formal analysis is based on two paradigms:
(1) Statics are nested in properties of rest points of dynamic systems, e.g.

$$\dot{x} = f(x)$$

(2) Comparative statics are extracted from linear systems obtained by differentiation in neighbourhoods of equilibria:

$$A(d\bar{x}) = B(d\alpha)$$

M. L. BURSTEIN

Part I
The Ontology of Money

1 The Essential Properties of Money

1.1 INTRODUCTION: THE STATE THEORY OF MONEY REFUTED

Everyone knows that indirect exchange is more productive than barter – see, for example, Clower (1967), Niehans (1978) and Ostroy (1973). But it is not widely understood that indirect exchange, while entailing *money of account*, does not entail a unique dedicated substance, *money*. Monetary functions are ontologically distinct from things that may be called money.

Perhaps the most egregious, and surely the most influential, example of confusion of monetary functions with money-stuff is the *State Theory of Money* – associated with Knapp (1924) holding that money is peculiarly a creation of the state. Thus Keynes (1930, pp. 3–4) wrote: 'Money of account is the *description* or *title* and money is the *thing* which answers to the description . . . The difference is like that between the King of England . . . and King George . . . It is for the State to declare, when the time comes, who the King of England is.'

Keynes was inconsistent on the point. In the following passage (Ibid., pp. 4–5) he correctly implies that the state has usurped monetary powers but is not intrinsically dominant in the domain of money. 'The Age of Chartalist or State Money was reached when the State claimed the right to declare what thing should answer as money to the current money-of-account – when it claimed the right not only to enforce the dictionary but also to write the dictionary.' (See also von Mises, 1953; and Mann, 1953, 1971.)

Hayek (1976, pp. 30–4) shows that the State Theory of Money was engendered by faulty understanding of *legal tender* – 'a kind of money a creditor cannot refuse in discharge of a debt due to him in money issued by the government'. Hayek (pp. 30–1) continues:

> The term 'legal tender' has come to be surrounded by a penumbra of vague ideas about the necessity of the state to provide money – a

> survival of the medieval idea that it is the state which somehow confers value on money . . . [probably originating] in the naive belief that . . . money must have been invented . . . This belief has been wholly displaced by our understanding of the spontaneous generation of . . . undesigned institutions by a process of social evolution.

The medieval doctrine, suggestively called *valor impositus*, was received by Knapp, who exercised great, mostly pernicious, influence. The correct view reminds us that the theory of value and the idea of the nation state do not intersect. (See Breckenridge, 1903; Farrer, 1898; Mann, 1971; and Nussbaum, 1957.)

1.2 MONEY OF ACCOUNT

1.2.1 Foundations

Hawtrey (1947, p. 2) writes: 'We have to find not the historical but the logical origin of money.' He continues (pp. 7–8):

> The idea of money is dependent on that of a debt, while that of a debt is not dependent on that of money . . . A sovereign is a coin but a pound is not. The coinage acts valued a sovereign at a pound . . . A debt of a pound could be discharged with a sovereign . . . The word 'shilling' is ambiguous, meaning equally a twentieth part of a pound and the coin with which a debt of that amount may be paid . . . The money of account must exist before the money.

And Einaudi (1952) shows that European trade in the fourteenth and fifteenth centuries, organised outside a nation-state context, was metricised by a spontaneously generated institution Einaudi calls *imaginary money*.

Toynbee (1954) correctly treats money of account as part of a system of weights and measures – as does the Constitution of the United States, Article I, Sec. 8§§5: 'the Congress shall have the power to coin money, regulate the value thereof, and of foreign coin, and fix the standard of weights and measures'. There presses upon the simplest cultures the necessity of maintaining uniform standards of weights and measures; and measurement of value and, say, passage of time are isomorphic operations.

Measurement of weight and of value, once coincident, became

disjoint; and the disjuncture carries the seeds of 'public finance, money supply and inflation.' Anciently the metrics for 'price' and 'weight' space were identical – but the mapping ceased to be 1:1.

1.2.2 Money Illusion and Neutrality

A scale can be unique only up to choice of origin and unit distance; an object worth x units on one scale will be measured at $2x$ units on a scale calibrated so that unit distance is half that of the first. The preliminary remark leads into *money illusion* – violating postulates of rational behaviour requiring that demand functions be invariant against universal shifts in nominal measure. Real choices should be invariant against a k-fold change in *all* nominal values (see Patinkin, 1956, 1965).

1.2.3 Seven Sets of Propositions

(1) Long ago, values commonly were expressed in weights of precious metals that could be obtained in exchange for sundry goods and services.

(2) It became desirable to produce authenticated quanta of precious metals. Unit coins were of unit weight on scales calibrated in pounds, marks, etc. Coins were called *money*: their fabrication early became a state prerogative for reasons that no longer seem obvious: Jean Bodin (1576, 1606) shows that the minting perogative was *au fond* a seizure of power by the state, not a necessary contrivance for the public good (see Hayek, 1976, p. 2 ff).

(3) Early metallic standards of value were one-for-one with weight scales: a unit coin measured out at unity on a weight scale that was eponymous with the value scale. And coins, corporeal objects, took on the names of abstract units of measurement of weight such as the mark.

(4) As time passed, coins were lightened (sweated, clipped, abraded, etc.), sometimes retaining their original names, sometimes acquiring new ones. Measures of value became disjoint from measures of weight. Coins came to be accepted by *tale* rather than by weight. A one-mark coin ceased to weigh one mark.

Proposition (4) further develops 'legal tender' (see Section 1.1), while probing the origins of endemic price inflation, that is, persistent deterioration of the purchasing power of a unit coin (measured by *tale*).

Lord Farrer (1898, p. 45) writes: '[A legal-tender act] may enable a debtor to pay and require a creditor to receive something different from that which their contract contemplated. In fact it is a forced and unnatural construction put upon the dealings of men by arbitrary power.' Indeed the gravamen of such American episodes as the post-Civil War Greenback controversy and the abrogation of gold clauses in private contracts by Congress in 1933 lies precisely in whether creditors should be forced to accept less than they have bargained for.

As for the legal tender/fiscal policy/money supply/inflation complex, consider the calculus of a typically impecunious Crown. It may owe x marks to its dunning creditors – and the mark of the value scale may map one-for-one with that of the weight scale. Simply by wrenching the value scale apart from the weight scale, that is, by assigning the value 'one mark' to a coin weighing one-half mark, the precious metal weight of the Crown's debt would be halved. And the money supply, measured in new marks (and so by *tale*) would double.

(5) Consider A's promise to pay y dollars to B. 'Dollar' is an abstract measure dysfunctionally called 'money of account'. Practice will determine what quantities of admissable classes of property can discharge the debt.

'Money of account' (*so* misnamed) has no more to do with things called *money* than a one-inch long object has to do with the abstract measure, *inch*. And the process conferring the power to discharge debt not only naturally operates outside the ambit of state action; it may be more impeded than expedited by the idea of legal tender.

(6) It bears repeating that practice *cum* law led to calibrated scales or rulers on which debt is measured; and to terms of trade between eligible property (some of which may be called *money*) and debt measured in money of account. Eligible property may be assigned the same symbol as money of account so that one dollar of debt is extinguished by tender of one dollar.

(7) *Monetary rulers squirm*. It has been explained that rational behaviour, in real space, is invariant against universal changes in measure – just as in physics laws are invariant against measurement in kilograms rather than grams. But changes in the general level of prices are not simply universal changes in measure: a higher general price level entails deterioration of the real value of 'money fixed' claims. Even 'regular' price inflations lead to changes in relative prices, for example, the price of treasury currency, measured in the

issuer's money of account, is fixed. Transformation of price measurements into statements tenable for correct economic analysis must take into account depreciation or appreciation of the standard of value. A truly general change in prices is like a switch from grams to kilograms. Thus General de Gaulle, in 1958, redefined French money of account so that a new franc equalled 100 old ones – leading to a mere change in measure (see Lucas, 1981a).

To deepen understanding of the squirming rulers, consider the *metre*, defined since 1960 as equal to $1.65(10)^6$ wavelengths of the red-orange light emitted by the krypton-86 isotope *under certain conditions*. And the *kilogram* is defined as the mass of a platinum-iridium cylinder kept at Sèvres. If 'certain conditions' are not properly controlled, physical standards become unstable in the way standards of value are unstable. We thus are led towards *imaginary* standard conditions such as transmission-in-vacua or surrounding temperature. The *operations* concomitant with the specifications are explained by Bridgman (1927, p. 5): 'To find the length of an object, we have to perform certain physical operations . . . In general we mean by any concept nothing more than a set of operations; the concept is synonomous with the corresponding set of operations.'

Einaudi (1952, p. 233) is concerned with imaginary standards of *value*: 'In former times because of the existence of [imaginary] money of account, men every day set a price on the florins, doubloons, etc. which they received and paid out.'

Americans could reckon relative to the Golden Eagle coin. Nor would the coin be revived. The country would not 'return to gold'; but the money of account might become the Eagle so that a debt of z Eagles would be discharged by a tender worth at the time of tender the amount of gold, of the same fineness, contained in the extinct Eagle coin. The Eagle would perform the function of Patinkin's guinea (see Patinkin, 1956, 1965, noting that his gloss is confused). Since the relative worth of gold is not constant, the Eagle standard would squirm. But a hyper-Eagle, based on a vast market basket of commodities, would not squirm (see Friedman, 1951a, 1953, discussed in Chapter 4).

1.2.4 Coda to Section 1.2: Colonial Monetary History (see Chapter 11)

The monetary system of the eighteenth-century British American colonies exhibits Einaudi's imaginary money. It is impossible to confuse means of payment like tobacco with the pounds, shillings and pence in which debt may have been reckoned – although many debts paid in tobacco were reckoned in tobacco (see Klein's *competitive supply of money*).

Colonials easily could protect themselves against inflation, perceived as *depreciation.* Contracts written in British money of account were immune from depreciation of the paper media that sometimes discharged debts created by such contracts *so long as colonial legislatures were thwarted from upsetting the contracts by passing ex-post legal-tender act.* The Westminster Parliament acted as Cerberus.

1.3 MONEY AS PROPERTY AND MONETARY PROPERTIES

1.3.1 Preliminary Remarks

> Although we usually assume that there is a sharp line of distinction between what is money and what is not . . . there is [in fact] a continuum in which objects of various degrees of liquidity shade into each other in the degree to which they function as money . . . It would be more helpful . . . if 'money' were an adjective. (Hayek, 1976, p. 47)

> Money belongs to the class of things performing monetary functions. (Burstein, 1963, p. 1, line 1)

Indeed I suggested the following Venn diagram.

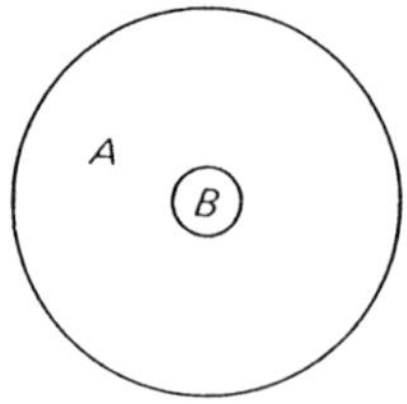

FIGURE 1.1 *A Venn Diagram*

In Figure 1.1 *A* is the class of things performing one or more monetary functions; *B* is a subset of *A* that is called *money*. Indeed there may be a complete monetary theory without money!

According to a traditional trilogy money performs three functions:

means of payment; standard of value; store of value. The trilogy is to be explored – noting that to identify monetary functions is not to identify monetary substances.

1.3.2 Means of Payment

The means-of-payment leg of the triad looks deceivingly robust. Looks are deceiving for the following reasons (further developed in Section 1.4).

The supply of means of payment is apt to fluctuate with demand and may be poorly correlated with 'high powered money' supplied by the authorities. Correlation with prices or nominal income may be spurious: so to speak, prices may drive the supply of narrowly defined money. And demand for narrowly defined money is volatile relative to that for liquid assets for the same reason that demand for pork is volatile relative to that for meat.

Means-of-payment analysis typically is based on crude schemes in which debts are discharged, moments after being incurred, by coins crossing palms. In payments processes, illustrated by the clearing union scheme of Section 1.4 – or sixteenth century Antwerp (see Section 11.1.3.4) – transactors cover deficits by putting up sundry assets as collateral or by putting assets on to a network for sale. Or transactors may have lines of credit, including automatic overdraft facility, so that they need not transfer property to discharge debts – granting that currency will remain in demand for use in small-value transactions for which transactions costs on the gyro would be prohibitive.

It is impossible to identify uniquely-monetary substances. Today, time deposits with a variety of financial institutions and balances with brokers (based on stocks held in street name) are *de facto* means of payment; and, experimentally, equities in houses have been put into street name – thus becoming chequeable.

1.3.3 Standards of Value

Section 1.2 showed that the standard-of-value problem belongs to measure theory. The idea that things called money *ipso facto* are standards of value is a fossil remain, preserved by the State Theory of Money, from a time when 'money' meant 'coins'. Thus a sight claim against the Morgan bank is not a standard of value.

Measure theory aside, the standard-of-value idea is important only as it slides towards the store-of-value idea. The proper problem concerns the stability of the rate of transformation of nominal quantities of financial substances against a numéraire. US treasury currency, a standard of value, transforms perfectly stably into money of account, valued under the American coinage acts. Maturing US government securities are *not* standards of value, but behave virtually as well as treasury currency in this respect – as does General Motors Acceptance Corporation paper. But neither is called *money*: the juice that can be extracted from the standard-of-value idea lacks a monetary flavour.

1.3.4 Intermezzo: The Idea of Money is Amorphous

Two examples further support the thesis that monetary properties, not money, are the proper objects of monetary theory.
(i) Surely the monetary properties of a Treasury obligation to pay \$$x$ in y days are superior to those of a similar obligation of the State Bank of Tupelo. Yet the latter may be counted as money; and the former, never.
(ii) In real-world open economies, agents hold substantial quantities of liquid assets (some called money) issued outside the nation-states in which the agents are domiciled. Nor can j authorities control the global quantity of \$-j-denominated issue.

1.3.5 Intermezzo: The Spectrum of Government Securities and Money

In a notable passage of the *General Theory* (1936, pp. 370–1), Keynes discusses *stamped money*, advocated by Major Douglas and other soldiers in the brave army of heretics. Stamped money's explicitly negative rate of interest entails a tax on hoarding, intended to choke liquidity preference. (This solution violates that of Friedman (1969) et al. for the optimum quantity of money (see Chapter 8).)

If currency, like bearer bonds, bore interest, it would be counted routinely as part of the national debt – so that it would be difficult, if not improper, to distinguish it as *money* pure and simple.

Nor does the fact that currency does not yield interest support a proper distinction: true, the state extracts a seigneurage profit from currency issue – as it does from any security it issues whose convenience yield leads to a premium. Currency circulates at a nil yield because of its convenience, buttressed by legal tender acts: purchasers of currency obtain enough convenience to offset yields of alternative investments; lower yields of Gilts, compared to securities issued by little known names, are explained in the same way.

Closing up the argument that currency can well be treated as a bond, currency resembles *consols* in that the issuer is not committed to redeem at a fixed time.

Section 1.4 develops another reason why government debt *en général* is money-like, especially as innovations unfold. Members of the Clearing Union may have to collateralise their positions. For this purpose, very-long-dated differ from very-short-dated stocks only because of the sensitivity of their prices to interest-rate fluctuations. Margin requirements for long-dated stock of comparable quality are apt to be higher – but the difference is not qualitative.

1.3.6 Stores of Value

'Store of value' intersects the equally amorphous idea of 'liquidity'. And the liquidity idea is incomplete: it does not encompass *real* worth.

An asset is liquid if its market value can promptly be inexpensively realised. A liquid asset typically is fungible and widely traded on well-developed markets. (See Telser, 1981. And note that 'market value' may be less than the purchase price of the principal: US bonds are highly liquid; and their market prices are volatile.)

'Liquidity' entails a money-illusory bias; but repair of this fault stretches 'store of value' so far that it snaps.

Assured nominal worth can be a paltry quality in at least two ways. The agent who has assured the nominal value of a future receipt may be able to buy little with it. Or a successful matching of assets with liabilities may prove chimerical: real values of insurance policies, successfully carried by insurers (see Robinson, 1951), may so erode that beneficiaries are not provided for after all.

It is appealing to take liquidity into the real domain. So *indexing* is introduced. But indexing shatters much of the idea of money: thus, if a time deposit bears a fixed *real* rate of interest, its nominal value is uncertain. And a perfectly indexed economy cannot achieve more than a metastable equilibrium in 'price space': one price motion is indistinguishable from another.

If the idea of liquidity is extended into the real domain, it loses touch with money. Many securities, including shares of common stock, can be liquidated by picking up a telephone. And real values of diversified portfolios may vibrate less erratically than those of conventionally monetary ones – as indeed also may be the case for high quality real estate and inventories of goods.

1.4 MONEY AND FINANCE

1.4.1 Monetary Theory Studies Residues of Financial Actions

Some theorists, recognising that all assets have monetary properties, eschew the idea of money. They might practise hedonics and build a theory of monetary properties – like the theory of quasi-banking of Chapter 11. Others, hoping to rescue money as a special idea, emphasise *clearing*.

1.4.2 A Clearing Union Model

Consider an electronic clearing union. Each transactor on the network will, to a degree depending upon the rules of the game, have a credit balance and/or overdraft facility, so that deficits can be covered. Reckonings may be periodic – or indeed continuous as innovation burgeons. Inability to cover will provoke a penalty (see Leijonhufvud, 1981, pp. 138–9).

An electronic transfer process produces no paper; on a standard clearing bank network, each transaction produces at least one piece of paper. In time, it may be said that the idea of money is a fossil remnant of an extinct clearing system in which transactions were settled one at a time: in the Union's *dénouement*, financial assets (liabilities) available as means of payment comprise an open set. (Note that an excess of a transactor's debits over his credits can be extinguished by sale of his IOU for clearing-union credit.)

Membership in the clearing union need not be exclusive; perhaps any reputable firm whose customer balances exceed some minimum may join. Balances, reckoned in money of account, are generated by deposit of a wide variety of securities, including common shares; in principle, any asset traded on an organised market is eligible to generate credit on the union's books.

The union will contrive an incorporeal heriditament, *bancor* – confirming its structural analogy to the old Keynes – Triffin plan (see

Triffin, 1957, 1961, discussed by Burstein, 1963, pp. 852–61). Bancor will be measured in dollars, the money of account. Or, in an extended version of the scheme, the money of account may be IMF special drawing rights (SDRs); or the ECU, a spontaneous concoction of European financial markets that also is defined on a bundle of currencies (see Chapter 11.6.3).

The union will take over all clearing: clearing will be electronic; cheques will be no more. At the end of each day, members' bancor balances will be debited or credited. Clients' daily statements from members, read on viedeo display, will reflect the day's events. Members might call on clients to deposit more collateral against debit balances. Collateral will be created by sales generating credit union credits; or clients may instruct members to purchase more stocks for them, thus working off undesired credit positions equivalent to call loans to members.

The credit positions of clients resemble money – as do their unused drawing rights, comprising reserves of immediately available purchasing power; as does eligible collateral not so far put up. 'Money' goes off the board: if everything is money, nothing is money.

Say that bancor, although defined in dollars, is inconvertible so that there is no inherent limitation, so far as we have gone, on total issue: 'Yet the Union could not extend unlimited credits to the deficit countries without encouraging total irresponsibility on their part, and without risking stimulation of a boundless spirit of international inflation' (Triffin, 1957, p. 97).

And assume that bancor credits and debits sum to zero: each member's bancor balance is the cumulant of his daily surpluses or deficits from dealings with other members.

The system is closed, or capped, by limits on cumulative deficits. Worried about deflationary bias, Keynes suggested limits on positive positions – a proposal loosely descended from Silvio Gesell and Major Douglas (again see Keynes, 1936, pp. 370–1).

A member, up against her deficit limit, will compel clients to reduce credit taken from her. Or she might offer higher yields to clients for advances. Alternatively she might sell some of her capital. The analogy to international payments systems is perfect.

Changes in caps relax or tighten liquidity constraints on union members and their clients in ways that do not require the idea of *money* – confirming Hawtrey's 'credit without money'.

If uncapped, the clearing union model determines real, but not nominal, prudential limits. It can be capped, or closed, in a number of ways; for example, the aggregate of negative positions, in the zero-sum system, can be controlled so that pressures on members promptly translate into excess supply and demand in credit markets. Or consider the system of the Second Bank of the United States, the most important lender in its market – the controlling logic is supplied in Chapter 2, Section 2.

Coda to Section 1.4.2. Important supplemental references include Alchian (1977), Black (1970), Cipolla (1956), Fama (1980), Girton and Roper (1981), Greenfield and Yeager (1983), White (1984a), White (1984b) and Wicksell (1898, 1936, p. 68ff). White (1984a) is concerned about 'metrical' difficulties following from abolition of currency, taken to be the standard of value. Of course, the *i-th* economy can make the *j-th* currency its standard of value – and use no currency in domestic transactions; see the discussion, in Section 1.2, of colonial currency. In a strictly closed economy analysis, White's concerns can be satisfied at no substantive cost by preserving some rôle for currency as a means of payment and deploying it as the standard of value.

1.4.3 Seigneurage

Seigneurage is quite common. Liquid instruments pay lower rates of interest than illiquid ones; premia paid by lenders for monetary properties of residues of financement are forms of seigneurage. Granted, perhaps the most prominent monetary property that may command seigneurage is the power to activate debt discharge.

Seigneurage works especially simply under a *full-bodied coinage*: the mint maintains a spread between the price it pays for specie and that at which it supplies coins. If the intrinsic worth of the coins is less than their nominal value – as in a *token coinage* – the controlling theory merges with that of *fiat paper money*. (See Robertson, 1948, including his discussion of *limping standards*.)

Seigneurage proceeds from sales of paper money to the public are like tax proceeds and alternative to debt finance. So the *inflation-tax* analysis of Chapter 7 concerns seigneurage profit: there may be a rate of money-growth maximising seigneurage profit.

In modern economies, the equivalent to production of paper money in simpler ones is a pseudo-fiscal process in which securities are sold to the central bank for credit on its books. The government draws cheques on these credits to pay for its purchases. The fiscal process leaves a permanent residue in the form of financial assets (liabilities).

Friedman (1974a, 1974b) extends the analysis in the following way. He argues that effects of monetary residues are permanent; while those of actions not yielding monetary residues are transitory. But why should a maturing government obligation be less money-like than a time deposit lodged with a Tupelo bank? (See Tobin, 1974.) Friedman's argument is accepted, or rejected, along lines defined by the immortal Currency School/Banking School debate (see Chapter 5).

1.4.4 Concluding Remarks: The Perpetual Perplex of Monetary Theory

Should some residues of financement be called *money*? Should the supply of liquidity, including whatever is called money, respond to demand? Should the control process be open- or closed-loop? If many assets activate debt discharge, increases in lending automatically increase the rate at which residues, in the form of stocks of securities able to discharge debt, are being created; closed-loop control is intrinsic to the situation – the relationship between money and nominal income may be weak, if not unstable. And, if the equivalent to idle cash balances is easily mobilised for debt discharge, linkage between money and nominal income again may be loose. Thus, in the clearing union scheme, 'idle balances' are drawn from a cornucopia. (See Chapter 7 for extensions.)

2 Choice of Currency and Other Topics

2.1 COMPETING CURRENCIES

Klein (1974a) and Hayek (1976) argue that, if transactions costs permit, a number of currencies, each with its own metric, will compete so that the transactors will gravitate towards currencies that stretch and squirm least, causing better-behaved to oust worse-behaved ones. They do not stress enough that there is now choice between national currencies (see Burstein, 1978). True, greed for seigneurage causes governments to seek currency monopolies, partly under cover of legal tender acts – a point pounced on by Hayek. Still, in the real world, where information is costly, official currencies, sometimes one or two, may naturally dominate a national market.

Standards and currencies. A unit quantum of the *i-th* currency measures out at unity on the *i-th* ruler. Competition between *standards* is a better locution than competition between currencies: debts measured in the *r-th* metric can be discharged by tenders reckoned in the *s-th* metric. And competition between standards does not require entrepreneurial sponsorship: transactors can spontaneously evolve debt clearing procedures – Einaudi's imaginary monies being a perfect example. Imaginary standards leave open the identity of substances that discharge debt: a debt of x meta-dollars (a meta-dollar measuring out unit distance on a scale measuring real purchasing power) can be discharged by consideration, measured in *some* money of account, able to purchase x meta-dollars.

Because he centres on competing private *currencies*, Hayek overstates welfare losses from obstructions to markets in private currencies; but his strictures against the typical operation of legal tender acts then become the more important.

Finally, there is no general price level in a perfectly Hayekian model. Nor can there be an inflation problem: inflation averters can contract in well-behaved measures.

2.1.1 Coda to Section 2.1: Measurement of Currency Supply Change

Growth of a currency supply can be measured relative to real activity in the currency. The following formula helps measure that part of the growth of the *i-th* currency stock due to increased real demand for the currency – in the sense that, as $m_{i1}/m_{io} \gtreqless 1$, the work accomplished by a unit of the *i-th* currency stock has increased, stayed the same or fallen between periods zero and one.

$$[M_{i1}/p_{io}T_{i1}]/[M_{io}/p_{io}T_{io}] = m_{i1}/m_{io}$$

Transactions activity in the *i-th* currency in period one (in constant dollars) is given by $p_{io}T_{i1}$. If real transactions activity in the *i-th* currency were to increase by 10 per cent, than,

$$M_{i1}/M_{io} = p_{io}T_{i1}/p_{io}T_{io} = 1.0$$

if the *nominal supply* of the currency were to increase by 10 per cent. Real work done by a unit of the *i-th* currency would be unchanged: all of the increase in its quantity could be attributed to increased demand for it.

2.2 CONVERTIBILITY

Convertibility imposes a closure on models otherwise in *neutral equilibrium* – an exceptionally important concept for monetary theory. In a neutral equilibrium, relative prices are determined – but a neutral equilibrium is consistent with any steady, uniform inflation rate. The properties of neutral equilibrium are like those of systems obeying *Galileo's relativity principle*: 'This basic law of nature is called Galileo's relativity principle. The laws of mechanics are equally valid in all inertial reference frames; or, more concisely, all inertial reference frames are equally justified' (Yavorsky and Pinsky, 1975, vol. 1, p. 32). As for inertial reference frames, 'there are frames of reference with respect to which all bodies which do not interact with other bodies move uniformly in a straight line. Reference frames satisfying this condition are called inertial reference frames' (Ibid., p. 31).

2.2.1 Convertibility at Micro and Macro Levels

An agent under convertibility pressures can convert long bond holdings into Treasury currency in time to meet looming demands for legal tender by holders of his paper; indeed demand deposits (current accounts) are unlikely to be refused by creditors entitled to legal tender; and overdraft facility can be arranged. (Long-dated stock can be so much like cash because *bridging finance* against one's right to receive sale proceeds can be obtained.) In general, an agent requiring property that can discharge debt can turn to other entities within the system.

In a closed economy whose collective reserve stock is given, the *system* cannot augment its conversion capacity. And we shall see that, since basal stocks normally are but *fractions* of the obligations of institutions of final recourse, successful régimes of convertibility have set up smooth-running procedures for occasional *suspension* of convertibility.

2.2.2 Reserves, Pyramiding of Reserves and Access to Reserves

We have seen that holdings of government stock (securities) and, for that matter, any asset readily liquidated on an organised market, are feasible reserve assets for an agent whose liabilities are not reserve assets. Now consider an agent whose liabilities *are* reserve assets – implying *pyramiding* of reserves, so that *A*'s reserves are *B*'s liabilities against which *B* holds fractional reserves, including claims against *G* (perhaps the government). His calculations pivot on the terms on which he can avail himself of a mass of manoeuvre (*cf.* the American Federal Funds market) and/or obtain recourse (*cf.* discounting at the central bank). Thus the Federal Funds market, made by traders of claims on the Federal Reserve, more efficiently deploys, but does not increase the total of, systemic reserves; while discounting at the central bank increases this total. We shall see that, under a fiat paper standard, elastic response of supply of central bank liabilities to changes in demand for them may puncture the 'closure' otherwise imposed by a convertibility principle. But, if the supply of central bank liabilities is made highly inelastic, a set of perplexes, analysed by Mints (1945), is created – leading to the '100 per cent (banking) reserve' proposals of an earlier Chicago School.

2.2.3 Panics and Convertibility

Under an inconvertible paper standard, a crisis of confidence or *panic* will not undermine government security markets; and, under specie-conversion régimes, governments have broader avenues of recourse than others. True, non-maturing government stock might be difficult to convert during a panic: prices of long-dated stock might sharply fall. (See the discussion of support operations below.)

Primary and Secondary Panics. In a primary panic of the non-banking sector under a convertible régime, specie and currency would be sought; under a fiat régime, currency and currency equivalents. Surely in a closed fiat system, government stock will be less vulnerable to a primary panic than claims against banks. Indeed, prices of government stock might come under pressure only because banks being dunned for specie and currency offer to sell it.

Secondary panics arise when creditors, including banks, call in loans out of fears about the quality of debtors' balance sheets; but are content to hold liabilities of financial intermediaries.

The logic of the *transfer problem* of Chapter 10 explains why prices of government stock may hold up during secondary panics. Thus *A* may offer to sell a $100 government security in order to raise funds to meet *B*'s call. *B* wants to switch from loans to the non-financial sector to ones to intermediaries or the central government. In effect, *B* becomes the buyer of *A*'s security; *A*'s assets (government stock) and liabilities (debt to *B*) fall by the same amount. Of course, the upshot confers monetary properties on public debt.

Support Operations. Modern convertibility analysis must study support operations. Bagehot's dictum that central banks should lend without stint during internal drains is now obeyed *partout*: central banks are prepared massively to increase their assets (and liabilities) when the public wishes to convert non-monetary into monetary assets; and indeed federal deposit insurance in the United States leads *de facto* to automatic intervention of this sort. (Perhaps the biggest support operation of all time occurred in summer 1984: the rescue of the Continental Illinois Bank.) And modern authorities are prepared to do more than help banks convert their liabilities into currency; they help banks increase their liabilities when the public want to switch from non-financial company securities to bank liabilities.

The policy reasons calling for support operations when the public wishes to convert claims against banks into currency – or claims against non-financial companies into ones against financial intermediaries – require that prices of government securities sometimes be supported. This remark has two corollaries. The first is on a general plane: since government stock has important monetary properties, arguments for support of the liquidity of bank deposits apply to support of the liquidity of government stock. The second corollary is specific: during a crisis of liquidity, the solvency of the banking system will be undermined if the value of its marketable securities plunges: prices of government stock may have to be supported to keep the banks afloat.

2.2.4 System-Wide Restrictions on Convertibility

Peel's Act, the Bank Charter Act of 1844, was to establish a definitive convertibility principle: British money supply was to behave like one based on bullion, and convertible into bullion. Yet it became evident within three years of passage of the Act of 1844 that it would have to be suspended during panics: the banking department of the Bank of England inevitably had to expand its issue, and discounts, when the public craved Bank notes (see Fetter, 1965). Under fractional reserves, suspension of convertibility is coeval with the idea of convertibility.

The American equivalent to suspension of Peel's Act was *restriction of cash payments*, interestingly analysed by Friedman and Schwartz (1963) and Hammond (1957). Under the National Banking System (1863–1914), much of the banking reserves was in liabilities of New York banks whose specie reserves comprised a small fraction of their demand liabilities. From time to time, they temporarily restricted conversion into specie. And *group* restrictions worked out quite well:

> As usual, the immediate effect of stopping specie payments . . . was ease. The banks, relieved of having to pay their own debts, ceased their harsh pressure on their borrowers. The general understanding that specie payments must sooner or later be resumed impelled a continuance of liquidation but of a milder sort. (Hammond, 1957, p. 713)

2.2.5 Corollaries to Convertibility and Reserve Principles; The Federal Funds Market; Discounting at the Central Bank

Consider in more depth reserves of firms whose liabilities are reserves for others – banks, for example. As operators of chequeries, their sight liabilities are immediately available to discharge clearing deficits. Under *laissez faire*, banks would hold prudential reserves, including *im-*

mediately available funds; in the real (regulated) world, banks also are subject to reserve requirements based on official targets for credit flows and asset (liability) levels.

Today, reserve requirements mostly are vestigial remains of historic prudential concerns, well stated by Bagehot, about the ability of banks to convert their liabilities into currency and/or specie. Thus, while the federal funds market and the discount process do supply immediately available funds, so that bank liquidity is supported, movements in the federal funds rate fluctuations mostly are important as indirect evidence of current and projected Federal Reserve monetary aggregate targets.

The Federal Funds Market is made by non-central-bank entities dealing in sight claims against the Federal Reserve. It is insufficiently recognised that non-banks are substantial holders of federal funds: securities' dealers acquire them; and money-market funds use the federal funds market to make immediate funds transfers for their clients (see C. M. Lucas *et al.*, 1977).

Discounting at the Central Bank. In the nineteenth century, nascent central banks typically were the largest lenders in the market – their asset portfolios mostly consisting of discounted, and rediscounted, trade bills. And they typically were large net lenders to other financial houses: so their principal policy instruments were the volumes of their lending and the rates they posted. The underlying control mechanism was direct: if the Bank sent out massive calls, the market would experience severe pressure; speculative bubbles were easily pricked. And being price leaders in their markets, their lending and borrowing rates dominated the markets (see Sayers, 1957, Hammond, 1957 and, focusing on the remarkable 'Bank War', more or less between Andrew Jackson and Nicholas Biddle, Temin, 1968 and Temin, 1969).

Bagehot (1873) points out that the Bank of England was willy-nilly a public institution, obligated to let its discounts expand more or less passively during an internal drain – to 'lend without stint'. And central bank discounting retains traces of this primitive recourse problem.

Today the assets of a central bank mostly consist of government securities and loans to the money market – or, in the United States, directly to member banks. Only trace quantities of rediscounted tade bills remain, and the volume of recourse to the central bank, together with its discount rate, is important, not as a measure of succour, but as an indicator of monetary policy. And open-market operations, not discounts, are the principal device for monetary aggregate control.

Chapter 5 shows that the discounting principle is central for open-loop *v.* closed-loop money-supply control. And the history of the American Federal Reserve System exhibits an interesting rôle-reversal in this connection (see Keynes, 1930, vol. 2, and Friedman and Schwartz, 1963). From about 1914 until at least 1925, the Federal Reserve, following its commercial loan theory of banking (that is, the Real Bills Doctrine), permitted its discounts freely to expand and contract in response to demand for credit; and did not make its discount rate penal. Keynes (1930, vol. 2, p. 236) points out that another reason for permissive discount rates flowed from hopes to develop the New York bill market and to encourage bill broking.

Summing up, the history of central bank discounting is one of many examples of ongoing central bank practices of ancient origin whose *raisons d'être* have utterly changed.

2.3 MONETARY AND OTHER LIQUIDITY BASES AND PRICES AND OTHER NOMINAL VALUES

We are like Moses at Mount Nebo: a complete theory of money and prices may seem near to hand, but Chapter 2 does not reach the promised theory. Still considerable progress is made: after developing models in which an official currency is the standard of value for a universal metric – so that British debts would simply be contracted in pounds and pence, and discharged by direct or indirect tenders of British currency – we inject competitive currency supplies into monetary/fiscal models.

2.3.1 Model One

The system is to be solved for $n-1$ relative prices of n commodities, together with the equilibrium level of *real* monetary balances. The first good is to be numéraire; but it is not assigned monetary properties. And we incorporate by reference a vast supporting literature explaining properties that are necessary for there to be a solution.

Compare vector $\bar{\pi}$: $\bar{\pi} = (\bar{\pi}_2, \bar{\pi}_3, \ldots, \bar{\pi}_n)$

Thus $\pi_3 = \Pi_3/\Pi_1$, all prices being stated in money of account.

The general price level, p, may be the geometric mean of prices – or some other function of prices. And, where the monetary base is x, $M = \phi(x)$. If the equilibrium value of real money balances is $1/k'$, and the liquidity base x^0:

$$d\bar{p} = k' dM = (k')\phi'(x)dx$$

The model builds up from the monetary base to the stock of money, in turn rigidity linked to the equilibrium general price level. The equilibrium value of real monetary balances is invariant against the monetary base; and no specific money-demand function need be specified.

2.3.2 Model Two

The results obtained in Section 2.3.1 flowed from a peculiar stipulation: the nominal quantity of but one asset was policy-determined. It is wondrous that so severe a stipulation has, until quite recently, commanded monetary theory. Relaxing this stringent stipulation, assume that the nominal stock of a second preferred asset is also under the control of the authorities.

There are n commodities with prices $\Pi - (\Pi_1, \ldots, \Pi_n)$. Again the nominal value of the stock of money is determined by fiat. In early trials of the model, money does not yield interest. The second preferred asset, government bonds, yields $100r$ per cent per annum. The market value of the bonds depends on the principal sum, B, and on r.

Transactors are subject to budget constraint in the Walrasian system: if $m - 1$ markets clear, so does the m-*th*. ($m = n + 2$.)

$$
\begin{aligned}
&f^1(\Pi, r; M^0, B^0) = 0 \\
&\cdots\cdots\cdots\cdots \\
&f^n(\quad . \quad) = 0 \\
&f^M(\quad . \quad) = 0 \\
&f^B(\quad . \quad) = 0
\end{aligned}
$$

The left-hand sides of the first n equations define excess demands for 'commodities'. Equations $n+1$ and $n+2$ concern money and bonds. There are at most $n+1$ independent equations in the $n+1$ unknowns (Π, r). Subject to appropriately stringent restrictions, the system can be solved for the equilibrium values $(\bar{\Pi}, \bar{r};\ M^0, B^0)$. Starting from such a solution, assume that M and B are scaled up by λ. Rational behaviour requires that the new solution be $(\bar{\lambda}\Pi, \bar{r}; \lambda M^0; \lambda B^0)$. The 'new' and 'old' solutions are identical in real space.

Now scale up money supply, leaving the principal value of the bonds unchanged. Ponder on $(\lambda\Pi, \bar{r}; \lambda M^0, B^0)$ as a solution. The proposal is improper. It requires a reduction in the real quantity of bonds; but, logically, demand for 'real' bonds should be unchanged.

Deepening comment on the 'improper proposal', if we accept Ricardian equivalence of debt to tax finance, and extend the Modigliani–Miller theorem to public debt, '*B*' is identically equal to zero – so that higher public sector borrowing requirements do not crowd out private expenditure (see Tobin, 1980).

Why not apply the Modigliani–Miller theorem to money too? At this level of generality, privately issued instruments can be perfectly substitutional with publicly issued ones – just as are shareholder and company securities in the M-M model.

Two further probes complete discussion of Model Two. (i) How are changes in '*M*' and '*B*' brought about? (ii) How does the analysis link up with inflation? But first observe that the following remarks by Hahn (1982, p. xi) go far to explain why we have not yet reached the promised theory: '[Keynes's] insights seem to me to make it impossible to take a Walrasian long-run equilibrium or, for that matter, a rational expectations equilibrium, as descriptively satisfactory.' Also see Robinson (1974) and Burstein (1968, chapters 1 and 13).

How Are Changes in 'M' and 'B' Brought About? At date *t*, fiscal actions have generated a mass of liquid claims, including government debt and part of what is to be called the money supply. Still, monetary authorities, dealing in asset markets, can change the quantity of money, however defined, by offering money for 'stock'; or can sell from tap stock in order to reduce the quantity of money. So it becomes fruitful to deepen understanding of open market operations.

Open market operations, entailing exchange of monetary-base components for government stock held outside the official sector, disturb liquidity positions; and so, at their outset, perturbate credit markets.

After an open market purchase by the central bank, banks seeking to increase their non-monetary assets make acquisitions by increasing their monetary liabilities; and the public reduce their non-monetary assets (partly by issuing paper against new loans from banks) while increasing their monetary assets. But, for the most part, agents will not plan permanently to increase their monetary assets with fresh credits from banks, *not at the outset anyhow*. Asset markets will be in disequilibrium; and attempts to restore portfolio balance will disequilibrate credit (flow) markets throughout the adjustment process.

A principal adjustment mechanism restoring stock/flow equilibrium – encompassing increased demand for monetary assets – is change in levels of equilibrium prices. In models in which prices of goods are rigid, or sticky, changes in real yields of securities are of principal importance. In classical models in which prices are perfectly flexible, and in which government stock not called *money* is ignored, goods prices, along with nominal volumes of securities, change proportionately with the monetary base; but securities prices (yields) are, in once-and-for-all market experiments – unchanged.

We do not ignore government stock; nor did Clower and Burstein (1960). What then is the fate of classical monetary neutrality? Tobin (1974, p. 87) consolidates the argument:

> Much monetary theory, modern as well as ancient, has developed from a model in which government debt and the monetary base are one and the same. But, in a model with various kinds of government liabilities, time and demand obligations, it is easy to show that the real equilibrium depends on the proportions in which these liabilities are supplied. Even in the long run the real quantity of money depends on monetary policy, and accordingly monetary policy has real consequences.
>
> The critical issue is whether government interest-bearing debt is of any significance . . . If all kinds of debt matter, then the genesis of new money makes a difference . . . [Is] a 'rain' of Treasury Bills – promises to pay currency in three months or less – of no consequence for the price level, while a 'rain' of currency inflates prices proportionately?

How Does the Analysis Link Up with Inflation? Inflation concerns price velocities, not price levels. And, indeed, so far we have but related price levels to levels of basal stocks – but the properties of steady inflation are implicit in our results. In addition to implying that, if $\bar{\Pi}$ is an equilibrium vector, and *all* 'nominal' parameters are scaled by λ, $\lambda\bar{\Pi}$ is an equilibrium vector, *absence of money illusion* implies that, in a dynamic process in which prices, the monetary base, etc. all grow steadily at rate ρ, and in which money yields competitive rates of interest, the real economy – once contracts properly reflect the state of play – evolves invariantly against the rate of steady uniform inflation. (Chapter 7 shows that acceleration or deceleration of prices may be associated with real disequilibrium. See also Section 4 of this chapter.)

2.3.3 Model Three

Building on Klein (1974a) and Hayek (1976), Model Three injects competitive currency supplies into Model Two. We assume that, although currency writers do not make convertibility commitments, competition limits the growth of currency supplies: the market disdains improperly controlled currencies.

Interpolation. Two corollaries to Model Three require development. One corollary issue is quite general; the other is specific.
(i) Recalling that Einaudi's problem is richer than Hayek's – in frictionless economies, transactors would develop 'imaginary' standards so that 'currency choice' would be a shadow of the proper problem, namely, selection of a metric (money of account).
(ii) Turning to the second corollary issue, if private-sector currencies are convertible into state money, the analysis is controlled by the Banking School/Currency School literature: is control of the supply of state money sufficient for control of supplies of substitutes for state money?

Continuation of Development of Model Three. In Model Three, M_1 may be the stock of state currency and $(M_2, \ldots, M_m)$ stocks of privately issued currencies. Arbitrarily appointing state currency numéraire, the price of a r-dollar is the number of state dollars (or cents) it trades for.

Demands for currencies are influenced by *expectations* about their relative growth rates and the evolution of currency preferences. Thus the cost of holding a r-dollar is greater if the r-dollar depreciates over the holding period.

Model Three adds m equations and unknowns (exchange rates of privately issued currencies) to Model Two – as well as m parameters (i.e. supplies of private currencies).

In Model Two the price of a unit of *the* currency is defined as unity. And, since preferred assets merely are 'M' and 'B', it is proper to scale equilibrium prices by λ in the event of a once-over λ-fold increase in M^0 and B^0. This procedure is inadmissible for Model Three. If currency supplies ($M_2, \ldots, M_m$) and their exchange rates against state currency were invariant against scaling up of government stock and prices (stated in the official metric) by λ, real holdings of private currencies would shrink despite unchanged demand. If all real stock values are to be invariant in equilibrium – so that the point in 'real' space comprising real equilibrium, is invariant against the actions scaling up government stock – currencies ($M_2, \ldots, M_m$) must appreciate relative to state currency so that, if M_2 and M_1 initially traded at par, a unit of M_2 will purchase λ units of M_1 in the new equilibrium. And equilibrium prices stated in a j-metric ($j \neq 1$) – except for the price of M_1 – are invariant against the scale of M_1 (and government stock in general). Indeed, further generalisation is possible.

Remark. Currency School orientation leads to ($M_2, \ldots, M_m$) becoming endogenous so that 'conventional' invariance is preserved (see Clower and Burstein, 1960).

2.4 MONETARY THEORY AND RELATIVITY

The analysis has reached its proper region: *choice of frame of reference.* Assume that M_1 and B grow at 100ρ per cent per annum; and ($M_2, \ldots, M_m$) not at all. And M_1 does not yield interest – while nominal yields of B include a 100ρ per cent per annum premium. A transactor reckoning according to a j-dollar reference frame ($j \neq 1$) observes stationary prices, except for the shrinking price of state money – matching appreciation of ($M_2, \ldots, M_m$) at 100ρ per cent per annum in the M_1-based metric. A transactor reckoning according to a M_1-based frame of reference finds all prices expanding at rate ρ. Measurement in a real frame of reference permanently replicates a single observation. *No one frame is privileged in the pure theory of standards of value. We have hit upon a relativity principle.*

> What is a relativity principle? It is an assertion about the laws of nature as they would be determined by observations made in different frames of reference. The assertion is made in an explicit form, founded on experience, that there are whole classes of reference frames with respect to which the laws of physics have precisely the same form. Observers stationed in these different frames make measurements which may in themselves be different, but which lead to the same conclusions about laws of force, etc. A relativity principle is a

> statement . . . about an essential lack of privilege in nature; it places a whole group of reference frames on a precisely equivalent status. (French, 1968, p. 66)

An invariant of transformation from one unprivileged reference frame to another is *acceleration.*

> It is the purpose of every physical theory to describe in a concise manner a wide variety of phenomena. In many cases this will necessitate, as part of the theory, a prescription for applying the theory to systems in different states of motion.
>
> It is in the nature of transformation laws to change most quantities but to leave some quantities unchanged. These [latter] are called the invariants of the transformation and . . . define its character. A physical statement of what these invariants are is called a principle of relativity. (H. Bondi, 1959, cited by French, 1968, p. 67)

These concepts will be fully deployed in Chapter 7 which considers unprivileged frames of reference identified by different rates of unaccelerated inflation. An invariant of transformation from one such frame to another is any acceleration of prices.

3 Interest on Money

3.1 PRELIMINARY REMARKS

Section 3.2 studies a paradigm in which interest yields of monetary assets are fixed, perhaps at zero; Section 3.3 analyses effects of flexible 'interest on money'; Section 3.4 concerns applications of the theory – including the model of Robertson (1926); and Section 3.5 discusses results obtained by Tobin (1982a).

Perhaps the chapter's pole star is a property of the model of Friedman (1974a), stipulating that key real rates of interest are determined outside the monetary sector and leading to lines of development different from those of the *ISLM* model, which implies that, if the interest elasticity of demand for monetary assets is nil, real income may be determined by the quantity of money. And indeed it it said that the most important consequence of 'interest on money' is that *LM* becomes vertical.

Sections 3.2 and 3.3 negotiate an awkward corner: if real interest rates are to be in line with those ground out by the implicit equilibrium model, interveners must supply arbitrage services, letting their portfolios change shape so that financial markets stay in equilibrium. Tobin (1974, p. 81) writes, perhaps with a touch of asperity: 'Friedman invokes the memory of Keynes, as well as that of Fisher, as inspiration for this construction. The keynesian touch is that speculators keep the actual nominal rate at its proper value. But . . . these are not keynesian 'liquidity preference' speculators between money and bonds. They are fisherian speculators between goods, or equities in goods, and bonds.'

3.2 MONEY DOES NOT YIELD INTEREST

3.2.1 Analysis

3.2.1.1 *The Central Bank Does Not Pay Interest on Its Deposits.* Open-market operations are to increase the volume of central bank credit. The banking sector $[(B_i)]$ is the exclusive holder of central bank credit; and it is subject to binding required reserve/deposit ratios. Gratuitous fresh deposits, leading to revenue expansion without interest cost, are always profitable for B_i (see Tobin, 1963). (But the upshot should be a quasi-rent: in the full equilibrium of a competitive banking industry, long-run effects of open-market purchases on the return to capital should be nil: for example, liquidity/capital ratios should be unique.)

Equilibrium is restored by substitution of (B_i) liabilities for other assets, substitution being induced by lower interest rates.

Effects on total intermediation depend on what happens to the balance sheets of non-banking financial intermediaries (B'_j). If the (B'_j) deposit rate falls, so that the sector's deposits fall, total intermediation will increase by less than the increase in the banking sector's liabilities.

Coda. Keynes (1936, p. 167) accommodated his analysis to 'interest on money': 'For the rate of interest is, in itself, nothing more than the inverse proportion between a sum of money and what can be obtained for parting with control over the money in exchange for a debt (1) for a stated period of time.' The footnote, marked (1), reads: 'Without disturbance to this definition, we can draw the line between "money" and "debts" at whatever point is most convenient for handling a particular problem . . . It is often convenient in practice to include in *money* . . . even such instruments as (*e.g.*) treasury bills. As a rule, I shall assume that money is co-extensive with bank deposits.'

3.2.1.2 *The Central Bank Pays Interest on Its Deposits.* The deposit and lending rates of the central bank are to increase, but its spread, on a ratio scale, is not to change. The opportunity cost of lending for B_i will increase; at initial market rates of interest, B_i will want to maintain a higher reserve/deposit ratio. The resulting contraction of deposit liability will be a by-product of attempts by banks to transmute earning assets into credit at the central bank. (Sales of B_i assets do not lead to an increase in the liabilities of the central bank but do reduce the quantity of the system's monetary assets.) For the public to be induced to reduce the quantity of their monetary assets, interest rates must increase.

In *ISLM* terms, an increase in the borrowing rate of the central bank shifts *LM* leftwards so that equilibrium output falls and *the* equilibrium interest rate increases.

3.2.2 Eschew Monetary Determination of the Real Cost of Capital; The Central Bank Does Not Pay Interest on Its Liabilities

Although (B_i) liabilities do not yield interest, the liabilities of (B_i) and (B'_j) are substitutes. And it is necessary to introduce a (B'_j) deposit rate, implying a spread.

Central bank credit is to expand. 'Speculators', supporting the real cost of capital, will seek (B'_j) paper – not barren (B_i) paper: (B_i) liabilities will be in excess supply. For equilibrium to be restored, the price of (B_i) liabilities must fall relative to that of (B'_j) liabilities. And, since the convertibility of (B_i) liabilities is assured, the nominal price of a unit (B'_j) liability must increase – on a scale with treasury currency as numéraire. The yield of (B'_j) liabilities must fall.

Total intermediation may decrease: a lower deposit-rate will encourage more direct holding of non-financial sector liabilities.

Restoration of Portfolio Norms. Relaxing the rigour of stipulations about the behaviour of 'speculators,' downward pressure on the real cost of capital may trigger higher inflation until the price level is high enough for the real stock of financial-sector issue to conform to the norm again.

The adjustment process can flow in either of two channels. In the first, expansion of the liabilities of the monetary authority above the established trend rate may briefly have stimulatory real effects – so that inflation increases, draining excess liquidity. Once excess liquidity is drained off, real equilibrium will be restored. In the second (Rational Expectations) channel, it is immediately recognised that the adjustment process will converge on the system's rest point. Convergence may be very rapid; or drag, due to embedded contracts, difficulties in determining whether deviations from trend are stochastic or structural, etc. may delay convergence.

3.3 MONEY FLEXIBLY YIELDS INTEREST

3.3.1 Preliminary Comments

Again the analysis may flow in either of two channels. In the first – evoking the historic link between British discount houses and the Bank of England – there is unique liaison between (B_i) and the central bank: (B_i) alone is eligible to borrow from or freely discount at the central bank – so that (B_i) liabilities enjoy a cachet; and reserve pyramiding is encouraged. When the analysis flows in the first channel, one need not be concerned about (B_i) *qua* chequery operator: then (B_i) is distinctive because of the exceptional liquidity of claims against it – due to its peculiar access to the Bank.

In the second channel, (B_i) is distinctive *qua* chequery operator. To opt for it is to take a poisoned pawn. In future, clearing will be accomplished on computerised networks. The special rôle of banks, and concomitant haulage of bales of soiled paper as part of the clearing process, will disappear.

In Section 3.3.2 (B_i), because of its liaison with the central bank, is distinct. In Section 3.3.3, supplying a theory of a *laissez-faire* financial sector, *the* financial intermediary sector is labelled (B_k^*).

3.3.2 A Distinct (B_i) Sector Pays Flexible Interest Rates on Its Monetary Liabilities

At least three interest rates are important: the deposit rates paid by (B_i) and (B'_j) and r, the vector of rates paid by borrowers other than financial intermediaries.

To repeat, the scheme is influenced by Friedman (1974a, p. 40): '[It] seems entirely satisfactory to take the anticipated real interest rate . . . as fixed for the demand for money. There the real interest rate is at best a supporting actor. Inflation and deflation surely are centre stage . . . The situation is altogether different for saving and investment.'

Conventionally, the solution to the problem in comparative statics following a change in the expansion path of the central bank's liabilities is obtained by an exercise in Hicksian temporary-equilibrium analysis. But sequences of temporary equilibria entail the fault of the cobweb model before it was transformed by Muth (1961), that is, before agents were endowed with rational expectations. The following methodological interpolation makes this clear.

Interpolation. In the original cobweb model, suppliers' expectations are incorrect unless the system is at its rest point; and, in temporary-equilibrium sequences, agents typically do not optimise relative to foreseeable events: 'in the non-stochastic world of standard stock-flow theory, rational transactors would achieve an equilibrium at the onset of a process spanning the phase space of the system' (Burstein, 1982, pp. 901–2).

Resumption of the Central Argument. We wish to exploit possibilities opened up by the relative deposit rate r_B/r'. In a conventional temporary-equilibrium sequence, including the ancient 'money as a temporary abode of purchasing power' theme, sellers of securities to the central bank might at first lodge their proceeds with (B_i), planning to diversify their positions later. This would give (B_i) an opportunity to widen its spread – which would narrow later, as diversification increases.

Having touched upon the rich possibilities of a disaggregated analysis of the financial-intermediary sector, we turn to a unified one: after all, the effects of an increase in the real quantity of central bank credit (or a decrease) on r_B and r' should be in the same direction.

3.3.3 A Unified Financial Intermediary Sector (B_k^*)

The thrust of financial innovation is towards unification of the financial intermediary sector. Indeed, if (B_i) and (B'_j) are to become functionally indistinguishable, (B_i), if not deregulated, will disappear. (On this matter, and indeed in general, see Hadjimichalikakis, 1982.)

Formally, unification merely increases the degree of aggregation while leaving intact the principal conclusion that will be extracted: for temporary equilibrium to be restored after an increase (for example) in central bank credit above trend, the unified deposit rate must increase – the real cost of capital being stipulated. The conclusion is to be explained at once.

Define the consolidated financial intermediary sector as $(B_k^*) = (B_i) \bigcup (B'_j)$. The central bank makes an open-market purchase. At impact, deposits lodged with (B_k^*) – that is, its acquisitions of claims against the central bank in exchange for claims against itself – increases its liquidity *and* interest expense.

If expectations are formed rationally on all sides, financial intermediaries will not passively sell claims on themselves, and later wake up to what has happened, and only then thrash about trying to restore profitability. Instead, rates and spreads will be realigned simultaneously with deposit flows: under rational expectations, adjustment processes are notably rapid, or at least forward looking.

Abstracting from commodity price change, in the new equilibrium: (1) the public's holdings of non-intermediary issue will be reduced in favour of increased intermediary-debt holdings; (2) the supply of direct debt and equity will be governed by an unchanged cost of real capital; (3) the stock of government debt, including tap stock, will be reduced by central bank purchases. The increase in mediation must be accompanied by a narrower spread: deposit rates paid by intermediaries must increase. Short-term interest rates *increase* because the monetary base expands above its trendline.

3.4 APPLICATIONS OF THE THEORY OF SECTIONS 3.1–3.3

3.4.1 A Model Suggested by Robertson (1926): *Banking Policy and the Price Level*

(Also see Robertson, 1940, 1966, *op. post.*; and Hicks, 1967.)

If, in a closed economy, monetary disturbance can be ignored, the *natural rate of interest* will be the root of equation (1.1):

$$s(r) = i(r) + (g - \tau) \qquad (1.1) \quad \text{System 1}$$

Variables $i(r)$, $s(r)$, g and τ are proportions of full employment output. The supply of finance $[s(r)]$ is, in equilibrium, exactly absorbed by public-sector borrowing $(g - \tau)$ and investment demand $[i(r)]$ – the proportion of output absorbed by public-sector demand being g; and the tax-rate, τ; while all saving is attributed to households, owners of the industries.

If the demand for money increases, *the* interest rate may be pushed above $\bar{r}$ (the root of equation (1.1)); an increase in the propensity to hoard may, at least temporarily, depress the 'real economy'; while a decrease in the propensity to hoard may lead to $r < \bar{r}$, etc.

If nominal income expands faster than the monetary base, liquidity will be drained off until the 'money market' is equilibrated. And an increase in liquidity preference is deflationary: real liquid assets will increase even if the monetary authorities are passive – but see Tobin (1980, chapter 1) on depressive effects of deteriorating debtor balance sheets on 'real' demand, studied in Chapter 9, Section 2.

Forced Saving and All That. Robertson primarily was interested in trade cycles, as was Keynes until he shifted course in the *General Theory*.

Robertson (1926) studies ways in which dys-synchronisation of monetary and real flows may rupture equilibrium and be followed by cyclical aftershocks. Of course, an optimal banking policy would offset underlying vibrations in liquidity preference and 'animal spirits' to an optimally *feasible* extent: Robertson was sympathetic to closed-loop control (see Chapter 5).

To illustrate Robertson's scheme, assume that banks, elastically supplied with reserves, finance increased absorption of resources by the capital-spending projects of 'excited' companies in a fully employed economy – distorting both the structure of absorption of production and techniques so that the model has 'Austrian' features. Distortion will be amplified if information sets, and forecasts, of entrepreneurs, workers, savers *et al.* differ. For example, if wages lag prices and entrepreneurs make better inflation forecasts than savers (see Makinen's (1977) discussion of Irving Fisher's trade-cycle theory), 'forced saving' will be the greater; and the analysis intersects the trade-cycle theory of the neoclassical macroeconomists (see Barro, 1984). Finally, as workers and savers become better informed and correctly programme their information (to take the Fisherine case), and as bank liquidity drains off, the processes that distorted structures of expenditure and production go into reverse; and a downswing begins.

Closure of Robertson's Model. Closing up the scheme implicit in equation (1.1), a second interest rate, the deposit rate of a unified financial-intermediary sector is introduced – and labelled q. Intermediaries' reserves include holdings of government securities; and it is assumed their holdings are small enough, relative to the totals outstanding, for the supply of intermediation to be perfectly elastic in System 3 – and, in System 2, not constrained by reserve shortages. Finally, weak preferences between government and private-sector securities hint at a Modigliani–Miller theory of public finance.

System 2: Variable Intermediary Spreads

$$\left.\begin{aligned} i(r)+g-\tau &= f(q,r)+h(q,r) && (2.1)\\ \phi(q,r) &= f(q,r) && (2.2)\end{aligned}\right\}\text{System 2}$$

Net saving is mirrored by demand for incremental intermediate liabilities, that is $f(q, r)$ – plus demand for directly issued securities, that is, $h(q, r)$. The incremental supply of intermediation is determined by $\phi(q, r)$.

Figure 3.2 graphs System 2, recall that interest rates (q, r) are real yields calculated relative to correct expectations. Initial equilibrium is at P. Point R results from a surge in 'animal spirits', not shared by portfolio managers: the cost of capital and the deposit rate both increase. Point Q follows from an increase in demand for intermediation: the spread enjoyed by (B_k^*) unambiguously widens. If authorities wish to undo effects of an increase in demand for intermediation, they will reduce the public sector's borrowing requirement (or increase its surplus) – reducing the equilibrium cost of capital and narrowing the (B_k^*) spread.

(Systems 2 and 3 have points in common with Modigliani and Papademos (1981).)

Turning to Figure 3.2, the graph of System 3, the radius vector implies that the supply of intermediation is perfectly elastic – so that the quantity of intermediation is demand determined – on terms described by tan (θ). An increase in demand for intermediation does not affect the cost of capital: intermediaries simply exchange their liabilities for private-sector and government securities at initial prices.

Intermediation supply is perfectly elastic at spread $(r-q)/q$ and conveniently represented by $\tan\theta = q/r$.

System 3 preserves equation 2.1

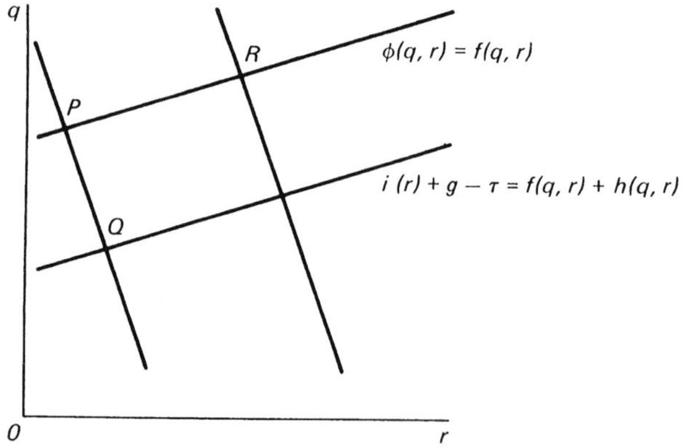

FIGURE 3.1 *Graph of System 2*

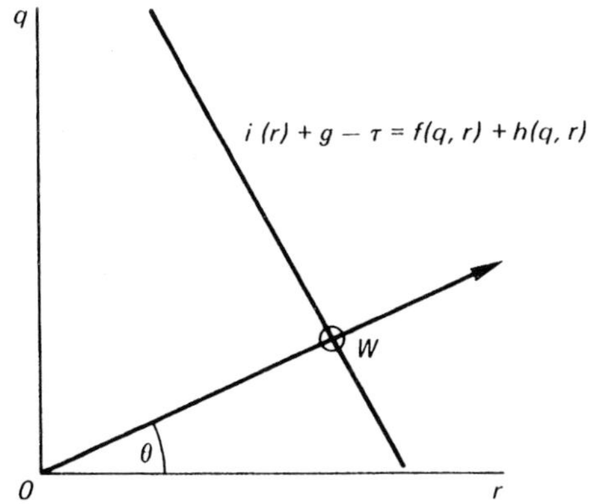

FIGURE 3.2 *Graph of System 3*

3.4.2 A Supply Side Equivalent to the Liquidity Trap

If the long-run supply of intermediation is perfectly elastic relative to a 'required spread', and if the public are prepared to hold additional liquid intermediary liabilities only on a yield basis violating the required spread, the market cannot be induced to absorb additional central bank credit: 'rational' potential buyers of central bank credit (sellers of securities) will know that the counterpart dynamic problem's transversality condition bars them from obtaining demanded yields on deposits purchased with claims on the central bank received from sales to the Bank.

3.4.3 Concluding Remarks: Sections 3.3 and 3.4

Interest on money supplies additional relative prices – and so additional opportunities for portfolio adaptation; it promotes robust damping response to shocks. And 'interest on money' shatters money-supply paradigms calling for money, however defined, simply to be injected into the system: unsolicited deposits create problems, not opportunities, for intermediaries operating at margins determined in pure competition (see Tobin, 1963).

These conclusions do not entirely conform to those reached by Tobin (1982a).

3.5 TOBIN (1982A): 'FINANCIAL STRUCTURES AND MONETARY RULES'

LM becomes steep, if not vertical. And 'proposals to pay interest on bank reserves at a rate indexed to the central bank discount rate, and in turn to index the discount rate to market rates' would weaken correlation between spontaneous changes in open-market interest rates and bank-borrowing from the central bank. Finally, Tobin focuses quite strictly on the (B_i) sub-sector.

3.5.1 Shocks

Tobin considers three sorts of shocks: shocks to real demand (*IS* shocks); financial shocks (*LM* shocks); price shocks (in oil for example – but, since he channels price shocks into the *LM* stream, two categories suffice.

An IS *Shock.* In *ISLM* theory, if *LM* is vertical, *IS* shocks cause wider swings in *the* interest rate and do not affect equilibrium output. This is so blatantly a monetary theory of the real economy that one is impelled to soften its tone, if not its substance.

Under *ISLM*, a leftward shift of *IS* leads to a lower interest rate; but the fall is broken by consequent increased demand for money. If the analysis is conducted in a space of higher dimension – if a vector of interest rates is introduced – effects of *IS* shocks are less clear-cut. Thus, if intermediary liabilities yield competitively determined interest rates – and expectations are formed rationally so that an *IS* shock is recognised as a transitory event – the cost of capital will be sticky, *as in the General Theory*; and deposit rates will adjust so that the 'money market' is equilibrated.

The Hicksian version of Keynesian economics implies effects of *IS* shocks on interest rates and output differ from those extracted from the *General Theory*; and, indeed, the *General Theory* contains the preferred analysis of this chapter.

The preferred analysis centres on the behaviour of the real cost of capital. If it falls sluggishly (or increases!) in the wake of a negative shock to demand, output and employment will fall. As for the deposit rate, if disequilibrium of the 'real' economy does not communicate directly to liquidity preference, decreased demand for monetary balances in the wake of a negative *IS* shock will lead to a narrower intermediary spread.

If balance sheets of non-financial companies deteriorate, demand for intermediation might increase – leading to wider intermediary spreads.

A Worked Example. The example develops Tobin's interesting analysis of effects of central bank deposit rate being passively maintained at a constant 'logarithmic distance' from intermediary deposit rates, while deepening our study of *IS* shocks.

$$\left.\begin{array}{ll} F(r^*, q; \alpha) = H(r^*, q; x, M') & (4.1) \\ (F_q - H_q)dq = -F_\alpha d\alpha & (4.2) \end{array}\right\} \text{System 4}$$

Let

$F(\cdot)$ = demand for intermediary liabilities,

r^* = the (parametric) cost of long-term capital,

q = the deposit rate paid on intermediary liabilities,

α = a shift parameter reflecting effects of *IS* shocks on industrial profitability and non-financial intermediary balance sheets and transmitting these effects to demand for intermediary liabilities,

$H(\cdot)$ = supply of intermediary liabilities,

x = central bank discount rate,

M' = the quantity of central bank credit made available

Differentiating equation (4.2) around a solution-point, and rearranging terms,

$$dq/d\alpha = [(-)(+)]/[(+)-(-)] = (-) \qquad (4.3)$$

Increased demand for intermediary liabilities leads to a wider intermediary spread.

Since the preferred analysis entails at least two interest rates, substitution is active: effects of shocks are *not* importantly redistributed because intermediary liabilities offer competitive yields – so long as r is roughly parametric. But deterioration of non-financial balance sheets and pessimism about profit prospects may force the 'speculators' defending the real cost of capital to cave in, so that ratios of stock prices to current earnings deteriorate, making it unattractive to plan to accumulate real capital. The real economy may cumulatively contract (see Salant, 1983).

An LM *Shock.* In ordinary *ISLM* analysis, if *LM* is vertical, effects of *LM* vibration on income and employment are uncushioned; but, if *LM* is positively sloped, *LM* shocks are cushioned by effects of changed interest rates on demand for liabilities of intermediaries. In the preferred analysis, *LM* shocks are completely absorbed by changes in the intermediary spread.

3.5.2 Further Discussion of Central Bank Deposit Rate

Ordinarily in *ISLM*, a positive *IS* shock leads to higher monetary velocity – responding to *the* higher interest rate. Also to an increase in bank lending – responding to a wider spread between loan rates and the sticky central bank lending rate.

In Tobin's model, when central bank lending and borrowing rates are keyed to market rates of interest, and monetary liabilities flexibly earn interest, velocity is *not* stimulated by a positive *IS* shock: the opportunity cost of holding money does not change.

In our model, a positive *IS* shock may be accompanied by diminished liquidity preference, encouraging a higher deposit rate; and by increased transactions demand for liquid balances, encouraging a lower deposit rate. In general, the upshot will not be neutral for 'velocity', since it is not neutral for the deposit rate.

To the extent that a positive *IS* shock leads to a lower deposit rate, substitution effects generated by the new-model financial structure induce pro-cyclical velocity movements: the short rate paid by intermediaries is an opportunity cost for investors in non-financial sector liabilities. The central bank can counter such a tendency by raising its deposit rate when rates paid by the financial-intermediary sector are falling(!). Our result differs from Tobin's because we deploy more than one interest rate.

3.6 CODA: THE STRUCTURE OF THE MARKETS IN FINANCIAL AND NON-FINANCIAL LIABILITIES IN THE MODEL

Ordinarily, when an elasticity of substitution is 'infinite', preferences between the products are very weak – strictly, nil. But, in our model, the fact that 'speculators' support yield r^* does *not* imply indifference towards portfolio composition.

Defence of r^* has lexiographic priority: capital gain (loss) prospects dominate those for running yield. But a speculator, having allowed his portfolio to absorb 'bond' placements, will want to realign it in the 'second round'; much as sellers of securities to the central bank – in the neo-classical paradigm – hold the proceeds in money, the temporary abode of purchasing power, over the 'first round' and begin to rejigger their portfolios in the second. He is not indifferent between assets; in particular, he is sensitive to deposit rate.

The preferences of sector (B_k^*) are not lexiographically ordered: sector (B_k^*) is not prepared to defend r^*.

In the 'second round', speculators will try to trade securities, valued at yield-basis r^*, for (B_k^*) liabilities. In the 'second round', the financial markets will not clear at initial prices. As deposit rate is cried down, there will be some reflux of publicly-held (B_k^*) liabilities in favour of non-financial securities. A Walrasian-like tâtonnement unfolds. System 4 summarises this process while masking the market structures.

Part II
Operational Studies

4 The Pure Theory of Commodity Money

4.1 PRELIMINARY REMARKS

Properties of systems of zero-order-homogeneous excess-demand functions are explored, and then contrasted with the non-homogeneous functions intrinsic to a commodity-money régime. And stock-flow analysis is studied in some depth.

Corollary objectives are historical and doctrinal. Classical writers lived under commodity-money standards that had prevailed for many centuries.

Friedman (1951a, 1953) spans a larger region of theory than does this chapter. His study encompasses effects of the monetary standard on price stability: if the monetary standard encompassed the entire spectrum of commodities, not only would the general price level be stable, but its motion could be insulated from the factors that determine relative prices. Namely,

> Because current output of the currency commodity is generally a small fraction of the existing stock, deviations from equilibrium can be substantial . . . Considerable movements in the price level can thus take place even in the absence of any changes in technological conditions. The equilibrating forces will clearly be stronger, the higher the short-run elasticity of supply of the currency commodity and the greater the sensitivity of expenditure to changes in the quantity of currency. (Friedman, 1951, 1953, p. 208)

> In principle, the ultimate extension of the idea of symmetalism is to include in the standard every commodity and service produced in the economy roughly in proportion to the amounts produced . . . Since the price of this . . . basket would be the price index, stability of the price index would be immediately and perfectly attained. (Ibid, pp. 213–14)

(A symmetalic currency has a specified weight of silver plus one of gold. Think of a physical combination of the two in a single bar. Under bimetallism either gold or silver may be tendered on terms defined by the coinage act and embodied in the mint ratio.)

Section 4.2 concerns 'homogeneity and commodity-money systems'. Section 4.3 develops implications of Section 4.2 for general macro economic reasoning: we study commodity money in Keynes's *General Theory*; and perform thought experiments relative to a 'common brick' standard. Section 4.4 develops a general stock-flow paradigm, specialised in Section 4.5 to a commodity-money model. Section 4.6 makes some dynamic extensions. And the Coda concerns bimetallism.

4.2 HOMOGENEITY AND COMMODITY-MONEY SYSTEMS

The system of Lange (1944) suits our purposes – but perhaps few others (cf. Friedman's *Review*, reprinted in Friedman, 1953). Lange operates an equation system of the form:

$$x_i = f^i(p_1, p_2, \ldots, p_n) = 0 \qquad i = 1, 2, \ldots, n+1$$

The $(n+1)st$ good is paper money; $p_{n+1} = 1$. Goods $1, 2, \ldots, m$ are commodities; goods $m+1, m+2, \ldots, n$ are fixed-income securities. Functions f determine excess demands x.

Before continuing study of Lange's model, Hicksian *perfect and imperfect stability* should be explained (see Hicks, 1946). Hicksian systems are *partially stable* if displacements from equilibrium prices can be corrected by price changes, if and only if, some prices are rigid. And, as in Lange (1944, p. 93), 'Partial stability of order m is said to be *perfect* when the system shows partial stability of *all* lower orders with respect to *any* prices being held constant. Otherwise the partial stability is said to be imperfect.' Here, when $n-m$ securities prices are rigid, the system does not exhibit partial stability of order m.

Resuming study of Lange's model (1944, p. 102): 'the excess-demand functions of commodities and stocks are homogeneous in zero-degree in the prices of commodities and stocks, interest rates . . . being constant.' It follows that excess demands for goods $1, 2, \ldots, m$ are unaffected by proportionate changes in the prices of *all* commodities (including factors of production): price flexibility does not promote employment.

The subsystem comprising equations $1, 2, \ldots, m$ can be solved for $m-1$ relative commodity prices. The equilibrium point about which the system is to vibrate, or be perturbated, lies on a ray (manifold) defined by $m-1$ relative prices of commodities. The order of stability of the homogeneous system does not exceed $m-1$: stability requires that at least one of the m 'commodity' prices (perhaps the money-wage rate) be rigid.

Continuing our stability analysis, assume that all elasticities of substitution are unity; then, *inter alia*, changes in current prices do not lead to intertemporal substitutions. And the $n-m$ securities prices are rigid. Now, following Lange, a factor of production is to be in excess supply while the other $m-1$ commodity and factor markets are in equilibrium. If the price of this factor falls, it might be substituted for other factors; and there would be substitution in favour of commodities for which it is 'important'; causing excess supply in other factor/commodity markets. Clearance of the other $m-1$ factor/commodity markets requires maintenance of the initial set of price-ratios – in which case excess supply in the initially disequilibrated market persists.

Flexibility of m factor/commodity prices cannot lead to rediscovery of equilibrium so long as we adhere to the Hicks–Lange adjustment path along which equilibrium must continuously be maintained in the other $m-1$ factor/commodity markets – if the order of stability is m.

So price flexibility of an order as high as m is counterproductive. And Lange precludes income effects as well: 'his' money stock consists of debt instruments. (See the real-balance effect and inside/outside money analyses of Chapter 9.) Anticipating Section 4.3, more price-inflexibility becomes welcome. Taking the r-th market to be the labour market, excess supply in that market does not lead to cumulative deflation if the money-wage rate is rigid. In particular, taking $m-1$ factor and commodity prices to be flexible, and the $n-m$ securities prices, along with p_r, to be rigid, the resulting system

$$x_i = f^i(p_1, p_2, \ldots, p_{r-1}, p_{r+1}, \ldots, p_m; p_r, p_{m+1}, \ldots, p_{m+n}) = 0$$

$$(i = 1, 2, \ldots, r-1, r+1, \ldots, m)$$

is *not* homogeneous in its $m-1$ commodity prices. The rank of its stability may be $m-1$.

Introduction of Commodity Money. If a commodity is numéraire, system $f(p) = 0$ cannot be homogeneous. Then a uniform price decline makes the numéraire good cheaper to produce and causes it to command a higher real price; the industry producing the numéraire will absorb resources. And a uniform price rise causes that industry to disgorge resources, up to the point it shuts down.

4.3 COMMODITY MONEY IN KEYNESIAN AND OTHER MACROTHEORY

Keynes understood the link between properties of the monetary standard and the dynamics of employment:

> Thus the characteristic that money cannot be readily produced by labour gives at once some *prima facie* presumption for the view that its own-rate of interest will be relatively reluctant to fall; whereas if money could be grown like a crop or manufactured like a motor car, depressions would be avoided or mitigated because, if the price of other assets was tending to fall in terms of money, more labour would be diverted into the production of money; – as we see would be the case in gold-mining countries, though for the world as a whole the maximum diversion in this way is almost negligible. (Keynes, 1936, ch. 17, pp. 230–31.)

(Also see Rueff, 1947 and 1948; and Tobin, 1948. Rueff shows that an export industry can be like a commodity-money industry.)

Keynes's *prima facie* presumption is shown by Lerner (1952) to be incorrect. Wage/price flexibility can rheostatically generate real monetary balances even if money is incorporeal; or if a commodity money is inelastic in supply. But, in the same chapter ('The Essential Properties of Money and Interest'), Keynes reaches higher ground, pointing out that prices must be sticky if money is to be liquid! 'The usefulness of money depends intimately on a certain degree of stability in its purchasing power.' (Lerner, 1952, p. 384.)

So the spontaneous adjustment processes of a monetary economy in which the primary liquid asset is not elastic in supply are flawed in a way suggested by Lange's homogeneous system.

Properties of a Common Brick Standard

Following Charles O. Hardy, cited by Friedman (1951a, 1953), we shall study a commodity-money system in which the supply of money is perfectly elastic (see also Burstein, 1963, ch. 8). This polar case shows that Keynes's distance from Nassau Senior (1830) and other classical writers is less than Keynes admitted.

Assume that a standard brick can be made by a worker, shaping free raw material, in one hour. Storage and depreciation costs are nil. The level of aggregation is extreme: there is but one non-monetary commodity; and non-monetary financial assets are ignored.

The wage rate cannot fall below one brick per hour. A worker can always make bricks (money!). If the wage rate rises above one brick per hour, money production ceases.

Involuntary unemployment is precluded. Money production can absorb any number of workers at a (shadow or objective) wage rate of one brick per hour. For 'full employment', it does not matter if positive investment demand for money persists regardless of the mass of the real stock of money. Persistence of high convenience yields from money balances is immaterial for the volume of employment: only the duration and intensity of money industry operations are affected. Of course, one regrets resources squandered in operating the money industry.

Section 4.6 casts the problem studied in Section 4.3 into an explicitly dynamical form.

4.4 A GENERAL STOCK-FLOW PARADIGM

The paradigm arises from the Knight–Friedman model of capital accumulation and from Bushaw and Clower (1957), Clower and Burstein (1960), Clower (1968a) and Burstein (1982). Let

$\dot{x}$ = the rate of net accumulation of sources,
p = the price of a unit source. (Markets for used sources, along with quality change, are elided),
π = the periodic rental rate,
x = the stock of sources,
r = the rate of interest, determined outside the model,
$\phi(\pi, p; r)$ = the target level of the stock of sources. Adjustment is lagged in ways explained by Allen (1967). Expectations are not formed 'rationally' (cf. Burstein, 1982),
$s(p)$ = the desired rate of production by source producers as a function of the source price
$\psi(x)$ = the maximum rental rate that can be obtained, at the margin, by source holders,
$f[\phi(\cdot)-x]$ determines $\dot{x}^d$, i.e. the *desired* rate of source accumulation.

Remark. The quantity $x_t - x_{t-1}$ has the dimension of a stock, not a flow.

Discrete-time models sometimes are improperly called stock-flow models.

System 1 A System Determining Temporary Equilibrium

Equation 1.1 determines demand for sources; equation (1.2) supply of sources. System 1 determines $(\bar{\pi}, \dot{x}, \bar{p})$ relative to x_t. *All variables are observed at date t; the subscript 't' is suppressed.*

$$\left.\begin{aligned} \dot{x} &= f[\phi(\cdot)-x] && (1.1)\\ \dot{x} &= s(p) && (1.2)\\ \pi &= \psi(x) && (1.3) \end{aligned}\right\}\text{System 1}$$

System 2 Determining Stock-Flow Equilibrium

In stock-flow equilibrium, the system attains a rest point or absorbing state in which it transists into itself.

$$\left.\begin{aligned} \phi(\pi, p; r) &= x && (2.1)\\ s(p) &= 0 && (2.2)\\ \pi &= \psi(x) && (2.3) \end{aligned}\right\}\text{System 2}$$

System 2 determines $(\bar{x}, \bar{p}, \bar{\pi})$.

System 3 A Linear System by Way of a Worked Example

$$\left.\begin{aligned} \pi &= \alpha - \beta x && && (3.1)\\ p &= \delta + \varepsilon\dot{x} && \text{supply price of sources} && (3.2)\\ \delta + \varepsilon\dot{x} &= (1/r)(\alpha - \beta x); && \text{the demand price for a source is } \pi/r && (3.3) \end{aligned}\right\}\text{System 3}$$

Remarks

(1) Equation (3.3) is based on static expectations.
(2) Depreciation is ignored; the model works only when $x(0) < \bar{x}$.
(3) The adjustment path cannot be efficient: forecasts of rents are correct only when $x = \bar{x}$.

Reduction to the Canonical Form. System 3 is reduced to the canonical form $\dot{x} = f(x)$, simply by treating it as a set of three equations in four unknowns. The system can be reduced to one equation in $(x, \dot{x})$. Namely,

$$\left.\begin{array}{ll} \dot{x} = \varepsilon^{-1}[(1/r)(\alpha - \beta x) - \delta] & (3.4) \\ \delta\dot{x}/\delta x = -\beta/r\varepsilon < 0 \text{ (assuring stability)} & (3.5) \\ \bar{x} = (\alpha/r - \delta)(1/\beta) & (3.6) \end{array}\right\} \text{System 3}$$

The portemanteau equation (3.4) determines the stationary level of stock in long-run equilibrium – if we set $\dot{x} = 0$.

4.5 SPECIALISATION OF THE STOCK-FLOW PARADIGM TO A COMMODITY-MONEY MODEL

Let

M_t = the stock of money going into the $t-th$ period,
m_t = the production of the golden money during the $t-th$ period,
r = the rate of interest,
w_t = the wage rate in the $t-th$ period,
p_t = the price level in the $t-th$ period; $p_t = p_{t-1} + \delta$
δ_t = the change in the price level during the $t-th$ period,
K_t = the real stock of capital taken into the $t-th$ period,
$y_t^* - y_t = x_t$ = the excess of full-employment output over actual output.

The Model

('Temporary equilibrium' is preferable to 'flow equilibrium' in describing certain states of discrete-time models of this sort.) Following common usage, we distinguish *flow* from *stock-flow* equilibrium. Demands equal supplies, expressed as flows, in the flow equilibrium of a counterpart continuous-time formulation; but stocks may be changing. In simple stock-flow equilibria, stocks taken in equal those taken out at the system's rest point. In richer formulations, there can be regular (e.g. log-linear) growth.

Operating the Model

Flow Equilibrium (although $x_t - x_{t-1}$ has the dimension of a stock)

$$\left.\begin{array}{lll} M_t + m(p_t, \delta_t, w_t) = l(p_t, \delta_t, w_t, M_t, K_t) & \delta'(x) < 0; & (4.1) \\ \delta = \delta(x_t) & \delta_t = p_t - p_{t-1}; & \\ & \delta(0) = 0 & (4.2) \\ x_t = x_{t-1} - \phi[m(\cdot)_{t-1}] & & (4.3) \end{array}\right\} \text{System 4}$$

System 4's three equations are in the unknowns (w_t, x_t, δ_t). Or equation (4.3) can be substituted into equation (4.2), leaving two equations in (w_t, δ_t), relative to parameters (p_t, M_t, K_t, r) – in the short-period analysis.

Stock-Flow Equilibrium In stock-flow equilibrium, $m(\cdot) = x = \delta = 0$. System 5's four equations, in the unknowns (p, M, K, w), determine an absorbing state or rest point. In particular, satisfaction of equations (5.3) and (5.4) assures that desired equals actual capital and money production is nil.

$$\left.\begin{aligned} M &= l(p, w, M, K, r) && (5.1)\\ \psi(\cdot) &= 0 && (5.2)\\ g(\cdot) &= K && (5.3)\\ m(p, w) &= 0 && (5.4) \end{aligned}\right\} \text{System 5}$$

Excess demand for goods is determined by $\psi(\cdot)$; the volume of desired capital by $g(\cdot)$.

4.6 EXTENSIONS TO A PROPERLY DYNAMIC ANALYSES OF COMMODITY MONEY

Recall that, in commodity-money systems, excess-demand functions are not homogeneous in prices and wages; and that money supply is endogenous. When prices and wages fall, 'gold' production is encouraged.

A number of factors promote stability in commodity-money systems. Excess supply of goods leads to increased money production – to an extent depending on elasticity of supply and reaction speeds of prices. Rising prices make money growth slow down; real monetary balances shrink as inflation progresses.

(Wage behaviour is not modelled: it can be read from the motion of prices. And the desired money stock is labelled M^*.)

$$\left.\begin{aligned} Dp &= \alpha(M - M^*) && (6.1)\\ M^* &= ap - bDp && (6.1a)\\ DM &= \Lambda - \gamma p && (6.2)\\ \mathrm{D}p &= \alpha M - a\alpha p + \alpha bDp && (6.3)\\ D^2p &= \alpha DM - a\alpha Dp + \alpha bD^2p && (6.4)\\ D^2p(1-\alpha b) + a\alpha Dp + \alpha\gamma p &= \alpha\Lambda \quad \text{(recalling (6.2))} && (6.5) \end{aligned}\right\} \text{System 6}$$

Equation (6.1) establishes the velocity of the price level as a lagged function of the excess of money supply over M^*. Equation (6.1a) determines the desired money stock. Equation (6.2), the model's power house, determines the planned rate of production of money. ($\Delta(DM)/\Delta p < 0$.) The real purchasing power of money falls as prices increase; and the cost of production of money increases.

Equations (6.3) and (6.4) manipulate the body of the model, leading to equation (6.5), a second-order differential equation. A particular solution of equation (6.5) is:

$$D^2p = Dp = 0;\ \bar{p} = \Lambda|\gamma;\ \bar{M} = \alpha\Lambda|\gamma \tag{6.6}$$

The equilibrium quantity of money is determined endogenously.

The solution's remainder part is obtained from the characteristic equation

$$\lambda^2 + \{a\alpha|1 - \alpha b\}\lambda + \alpha\gamma|1 - \alpha b = 0 \tag{6.7}$$

The roots of the characteristic equation are

$$\lambda_1, \lambda_2 = (1/2)[-\{\ \} \pm \sqrt{\{\ \{\ \}^2 - 4(\gamma\alpha|1 - \alpha b\}}] \tag{6.8}$$

Try $\alpha = 1$, $b = 1/2$, $a = 2$ and $\gamma = 3$. The solution, where A and ε are arbitrary constants determined by initial conditions, is

$$p_t = \Lambda|\gamma A e^{-2t} \cos(1.415t - \varepsilon) \tag{6.9}$$

Damping is strong. Prices and 'gold' production oscillate about stationary norms (that for 'gold' being nil). The amplitudes of the oscillations asymptotically approach zero.

A Second Dynamic Model

Consider an economy with points in common with that of South Africa. It has a gold-mining industry; and it produces gold indirectly by exporting. Nor is it perfectly open: neither demand for its exports nor supply of imports to it is perfectly elastic. Finally, the economy operates under fixed exchange rates.

Methodological Interpretation (see Arrowsmith and Place, 1982). The underlying system is of higher rank than the subsystem whose phase portraits are sketched. Linear systems of this sort can be reduced to differential equations of the form $D^n x_i = f^i(x_i)$ where the rank of matrix

A in $\dot{x} = Ax$ is 'n'. But the procedure, although mathematically proper, elides the rule governing Hicksian perfect and imperfect stability.

$$\left.\begin{aligned} \dot{M} &= f(M, p) \qquad (7.1) \\ \dot{p} &= g(M, p) \qquad (7.2) \end{aligned}\right\} \text{System 7}$$

Denoting the system's rest point $(\overline{M}, \overline{p})$, and transforming the variables so that $(\overline{M}, \overline{p})$ becomes (0, 0), the transformed variables (M', p') – that is, the deviations from the system's equilibrium values – are found to oscillate in opposing phases.

Finally: any open economy exhibits the principal macroeconomic properties of a commodity-money system – confirming the thrust of Rueff (1947) and, for that matter, the *General Theory*. (See Chapter 10.)

4.7 CODA TO CHAPTER 4: A SKETCH OF A THEORY OF BIMETALLISM (cf. Burstein, 1963, chapter 2)

A bimetallic régime monetises two metals (for example, gold and silver). The Coinage Act *permits* a gold coin weighing x grains or a silver coin of y grains to be tendered at par to discharge a one-dollar debt – where the money of account is the dollar.

In an equally pure form of bimetallism, never practised, the mint stands ready to supply the tenderer of x grains of gold or y grains of silver with a paper dollar; or to supply the tenderer of a paper dollar with x grains of gold or y grains of silver (see Kemmerer, 1937). The reason that this form has not been practised is that, unless the authorities possess large-enough stocks of the metals, they cannot impose their 'view' on the market: if the authorities do not have enough of it, convertibility of the 'undervalued' metal must be abandoned.

Either procedure establishes a *mint ratio* between gold and silver. Thus, in 1834, when the gold and silver dollars contained 23.22 grains of pure gold and 371.25 grains of pure silver, the mint ratio was 16:1.

Assume that a closed system initially is in equilibrium at a market ratio of 17:1; and that a mint ratio of 16:1 is imposed so that silver is overvalued, and gold undervalued, at the mint. So long as the 371.25 grain silver dollar can be tendered at par with the 23.33 grain gold dollar, it would be irrational to hold gold coins: by swapping 23.22 grains of gold for 394.74 grains of silver in the open market, the holder of a gold dollar could acquire about 17/16 silver dollars. So long as the dollars circulate at par, the undervalued metal will be withdrawn from monetary circulation. If, after all coined gold were melted down and used as a commodity, there still were excess demand for gold at a 16 : 1 ratio, the mint and market ratios could permanently differ. But keep in mind Robertson's (1948, pp. 46–7) caveat: 'And let me tell you this too . . . If they ['haughty' gold coins] all got the sack at once, goodness knows where they'd be: for this dentistry yarn has worn a bit thin – there aren't that many rickety teeth in this world.' As Robertson also says, 'the chief reason men run after them now is because they're *money*'.

Now open up the economy and assume that foreign mint and market ratios are 16 : 1: the undervalued metal will disappear from monetary circulation – as happened during American bimetallic experiments, causing many to conclude that *bi*metallism is a misnomer; that the exclusive monetary metal will be *either* gold *or* silver.

Continuing to assume that monetary gold and silver circulate at par, is there a way out of the quandary? Mint ratios could continuously be adjusted to conform to market conditions. Not only would transactions, and information diffusion costs be prohibitive; the nominal value of tomorrow's money stock would be uncertain.

Invariable Circulation at Par is Economically Irrational

Why should traders feel compelled to obey the mint ratio? Should there not be price quotations in the form: '\$1(*Au*) or \$1.06(*Ag*)'? Disparate mint and market ratios should not cause the undervalued metal to disappear from the coinage; instead it should trigger an agio. Sir Ralph Hawtrey both deepened the analysis and anticipated 'choice in currency' (see Chapter 2).

> If a debtor hold some coins which are, and others which are not, worth more as metal than as money/at official rates/, his creditors cannot compel him to pay the former. The debtor may stipulate that the more-valuable coins be accepted . . . above their nominal value. Usually the inconvenience of making payments in a medium the money value of which varies with the market prevents this, but that is not invariably the case . . .
>
> A legal tender law can do no more than prescribe the means of discharging a debt expressed in the existing unit of account. People who choose to make bargains in terms of another medium can thereby evolve a new unit of account. (Hawtrey, 1950, pp. 48–9)

Recall from Chapter 2 that, in régimes of competing, or co-existing, monetary metrics, nominal-value properties are relativistic: fluctuations in the gold value of a silver coin are isomorphic with those of the silver value of a gold coin. There is no meaningful sense in which the nominal value of a unit of money is certain if there are *alternative* metrics. This point proves vital for understanding open economies–in which, typically, *n* monetary metrics coexist. (See Chapter 11.)

The Fin de Siècle Free-Silver Controversy: Politics, Inflation and Bimetallism

(See especially Friedman and Schwartz, 1963, and Kemmerer, 1937.) Gold appreciated relative to other commodities o'er the world between 1873 and 1896. (Cf. The Crime of 1973 when silver effectively was demonetised in the United States.) American prices fell correspondingly: otherwise the United States could not have 'stayed on gold'. And the value of silver in terms of gold fell by about 50 per cent from 1873 to 1896. *Inter alia*, production of silver rapidly increased in the latter part of the nineteenth century while that of gold failed to keep pace with real growth of output in general.

The Free Silverites, including William Jennings Bryan, proposed almost to double the coinage price of silver so that the mint ratio would massively overvalue silver. The resulting increase in American prices (as the purchasing power of silver adapted to its real cost of production) would have reduced the real burden of mortgages for farmers and others. (See the discussion of real-balance effects *à la* Fisher and Pigou of Chapter 9. And note that the gold standard enjoyed salad days from 1900 to 1914, importantly because of discoveries in Alaska and South Africa.)

Concluding Remarks: Bimetallism and Price Theory

The common proposition that bimetallism leads to faster monetary growth than monometallism because the faster growing metallic stock comes to dominate the money stock – tacitly accepting the faulty stipulation that the undervalued metal does not command a premium in monetary use – should be qualified. Infusions of the overvalued metal into the money stock would be offset by outflow of the undervalued metal from the money stock. Thus, if the initial non-monetary stock of gold were large relative to the stock of monetary gold, and gold became undervalued at the mint, monetary gold might become absorbed into the stock of non-monetary gold at an almost unchanged price, quoted in a silver metric. Significant enhancement of monetary growth could not occur until the outflow of monetary gold ceased (perhaps because there was none left!); and monetary gold had been wholly replaced by monetary silver.

5 Open-Loop *v.* Closed-Loop Money Supply Control Systems

5.1 INTRODUCTION

Should money supply (or liquid-asset supply) adhere to an expansion path that is unresponsive to events in the economy? Or should the money-supply process include a feedback channel? We must choose between *open-loop* and *closed-loop* control systems (see Allen, 1967, pp. 97–9). Figure 5.1 illustrates this schematically:

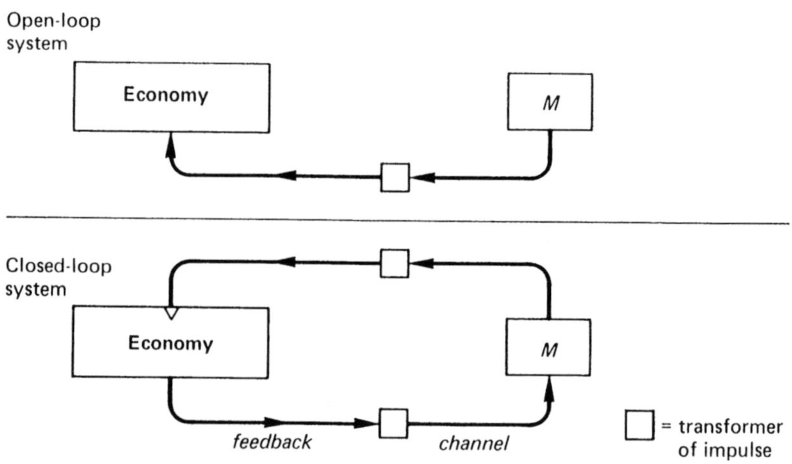

FIGURE 5.1 *Open-loop and Closed-loop control systems*

Four problems are selected for study. The first (Section 5.2) concerns the Banking School's Principle of Reflux. Its study reminds us that *money* should not be confused with *credit*.

The second problem (Section 5.3) concerns monetary aggregate *v.*

interest-rate targeting. An influential paradigm, based on Poole (1970), is studied, and then criticised. The critique leads to a quandary: surely in the plane of theory, the secular growth rate of the central bank's assets (liabilities) should not determine the real cost of capital. The critique also shows that 'real' disequilibrium may induce monetary disequilibrium that can be corrected on a feedback channel. Even if *LM* is stationary, monetary disequilibrium can be caused by *IS* vibration. And the more 'unstable' *IS* is, the more desirable closed-loop monetary control may be, a proposition starkly contradicting Poole (1978).

Section 5.4 glosses the formal analysis of stabilisation by Friedman (1953).

The fourth problem (Section 5.5) concerns effects of supply shocks and owes much to Modigliani (1977). It turns out that Modigliani's analysis is co-extensive with that controlling money-supply adaptation to a proposed drastic tax increase for the Cambodian economy in 1974–5.

5.2 ON THE PRINCIPLE OF REFLUX

5.2.1 Introductory Remarks

Under a Principle of Reflux, money growth is a function of demand for credit. A surge in credit demand leads to one in money growth; but the resulting bulge in the money stock may be expunged by debt repayment, i.e. *Reflux*.

Friedman and Schwartz (1963) and Sargent and Wallace (1981) point out that, under a gold standard, money supply in the long run is capped by the convertibility constraint; but, transitorily, under a Principle of Reflux, money supply may behave badly.

5.2.2 Origins of Invalid Forms of the Principle of Reflux (Commercial Loan Theory of Banking, Real Bills Doctrine)

Merchants holding stocks are carried by bankers or commercial factors (in turn typically carried by banks). A merchant's vantage point encourages belief that loans financing stocks that periodically turn over are self-liquidating. It is a short step to believe that, so long as the banking system confines itself to properly commercial lending, over-issue of bank money, perverse fluctuations in the stock of money and manic speculation are all precluded. And indeed the Federal Reserve System took that step.

It is easy to support the condemnations of the Principle by Mints (1945) and others in closed economies. But, if bank liabilities are *convertible* into specie or foreign currency, excessive bank issue puts pressure on bank liquidity that forces contraction in bank lending (see Friedman and Schwartz, 1963; and Sargent and Wallace, 1981). Still, depending on properties of lag structures studied in this section, major crises can occur in open economies governed by the Principle.

Why will not restriction of bank lending to real bills, or their modern equivalents, automatically desirably limit the quantity of bank liabilities?

A reform of the banking system might abolish reserve requirements *and* prohibit bankers from changing the scale of their loans and investments, except passively in response to demands for trade finance. Lending on real bills would be immune from liquidity constraint: real bills could be freely discounted at the central bank.

Perhaps supplies of goods demanded by merchants are price inelastic; and the economy is overheated. Merchants will fail to obtain new stocks; instead prices will be bid up. Additional bank money will seep through the economy as merchants pay suppliers. A cumulative inflation process will have begun.

Attempts to reduce inventories, causing prices to fall, may lead to cumulative contraction of money supply and prices under the reform. Then needs of trade can be financed by a lower nominal volume of credit: the value of bills tendered to banks for discounting will decline even if physical inventories are stationary. Resulting deterioration of collateral values will compel liquidation of loans; and real cash balances – 'cash' being a residue, in the form of bank liability, of credits extended by banks – will contract, not expand, as a result of deflation. Cumulative contraction will intensify the *reflux* of credit taken from the central bank: bills presented for redemption by the central bank will exceed fresh bills offered for discount as the contraction continues.

In the more formal analysis (below), ill-behaved outcomes are not ineluctable even in a closed system – because of richer lag relationships than have up to now been explored.

5.2.3 Prologue to a Formal Analysis of the Principle of Reflux

Under a Principle of Reflux, credit creation leaves a monetary residue; and debt repayment (reflux) reduces the stock of liabilities of the banking system 1 : 1. And, if holdings of bank liabilities exceed desired levels, excess liquidity can be drained by repaying debt to banks: there is a channel, hitherto neglected, running from 'money' to 'credit'.

Entrenched criticism of the Principle of Reflux boils down to a breeder-reactor theory of inflation along the following lines: demand to take credit intensifies: under the Principle, 'proper' demands will be met: inflation will accelerate, triggering an acceleration of nominal credit taken: proceeds of fresh loans will be tendered in goods markets. An unstable cumulative process may seem inevitable; but it is not!

What if the demand for money (or, better, financial assets) were very slow to respond to price change. In a polar case,

$$M^d = k.$$

Then an increase in (flow) demand for credit generates excess supply of money: the stock of money, but not the demand for it, grows. More generally, growth of the stock of financial assets exceeds demand growth. Excess holdings of financial assets are diverted into debt repayment. (Another channel concerns acquisition of equities: the real cost of capital may fall at the process's outset.)

Cumulative credit expansion may induce cumulative debt repayment. Debt repayment, caused by stock disequilibrium, may move counter to the flow of credit – reflecting the public's unwillingness to hold additional liabilities the banks want to create.

Yet another lag-structure may dampen expansion of free banking systems. If the rate of credit expansion lags behind that of price inflation, liquidity will dry up; the inflation process may be self-braking. Under rational expectations, damping is the more plausible: lenders equipped with the model will insist *ab initio* on inflation premia. ('Interest on Money' complicates the story.)

Coda to Section 5.2.3 (see Wicksell, 1898, 1936, especially p. 148). Wicksell's cumulative process, incident to disparity of market from natural rates of interest, largely neglects the fact that the bank liabilities generated by bank credit expansion must somehow be *held*. Wicksell recognises the difficulty, but treats it too lightly – I should think with fatal consequences. A corrected analysis would treat banks merely as 'currency writers'; and would not confuse their lending rates with the real cost of capital. That said, Wicksell's analysis must command our admiration.

5.2.4 The Principle of Reflux in an Open Model

Important concepts include *net foreign assets* (x) and z, $\dot{z}$ being *domestic credit expansion*—equal to the rate of increase in the domestic assets of the banks whose liabilities are money (see Chapter 11, Section 5). The mass of domestic assets of 'banks whose liabilities are money' is a cumulant, z.

The behavioural relations described by equations (1.1) and (1.2) nest in the following context. There is an equilibrium relationship linking the volume of 'our' issue, z, and global issue, $ce^{\rho t}$ so that $\bar{z}_t = kce^{\rho t}$—the value of global issue being c at date zero. The path of global issue *forces* the system.

Each portfolio manager chooses from a menu including issue everywhere. In principle, transactions everywhere are defined in monies of account, or weighted combinations of monies of account, according to specific circumstances and transactor preferences. The nation-state is a foreign substance in the continuous field of neo-classical theory.

The domestic liquidity norm is: $z = \delta x$. And, defining the logarithm of δ as δ', the norm's log $= log\,(x) + \delta'$, while $log\,(k) = k'$ and $log\,(c) = c'$.

$$\left.\begin{aligned} Dlog\,(x) &= \lambda[log\,(z) - c' - \rho t - k'] \quad &(1.1)\\ Dlog\,(z) &= \Lambda[log\,(z) - log\,(x) - \delta'] \quad &(1.2)\end{aligned}\right\}\text{System 1}$$

Equations (1.3) and (1.4) are obtained by manipulating equations (1.1) and (1.2). Since domestic credit expansion is a time derivative (that is, $\dot{z}$) a third-order differential equation is obtained.

$$\left.\begin{aligned} D^2log\,(z) &= \Lambda[Dlog\,(z) - log\,(x)] \quad &(1.3)\\ D^2log\,(z) &= \Lambda[Dlog\,(z) - \lambda(log\,(z) - c' - \rho t - k')] \quad &(1.4)\\ D^3log\,(z) &= \Lambda[D^2log\,(z) - \lambda Dlog\,(z) + \lambda\rho] \quad &(1.5)\end{aligned}\right\}\text{System 1}$$

A particular solution is

$$\Lambda\lambda Dlog\,(z) = \Lambda\lambda\rho; \quad Dlog\,(z) = \rho(!) \tag{1.6}$$

Credit grows at the global rate, ρ, starting from the base-level $kc(0)$.

The remainder part of the general solution is obtained by solving the characteristic equation

$$\mu^3 - \Lambda\mu^2 + \Lambda\lambda\mu = 0; \quad \mu^2 - \Lambda\mu + \Lambda\lambda = 0 \tag{1.7}$$

So far as we have gone, the system is unstable. But, under regulation, 'free' stability properties are not critically important: a loss function, defined on states of the system is minimised by the optimal path.

The Lags. The lag in equation (1.4) may reflect buffering of national reserve losses by the IMF or large banks. The lag in equation (1.2), reflecting the loose engagement of the gears controlling *laissez-faire* credit systems, is less well articulated. It is broadly true that credit expansion is slowed by deteriorating lender liquidity, but it is difficult to say how the restraint operates. During booms, prudence may be put aside; during crises of confidence, credit-worthiness criteria become stiffer – along lines explained in Section 5.3's study of communication of effects of deteriorating non-financial sector balance sheets to the 'money markets'.

5.2.5 The Principle of Reflux in Closed Models

The difficulties of this subsection are of sterner stuff than those just overcome. Cumulative inflation is plausible: liquidity cannot drain out of sealed systems as credit expansion and inflation accelerate. If the system is to be stable, it must be 'self-drying'; it must soak up its own liquidity.

Call the cumulant (stock) of credit taken *money*: nominal lending will equal new credits less a reflux based on the excess of supply over demand for money. (Tacitly, money yields a market-determined rate of interest.)

Exposition is in two stages: the first is quite general; the second, technical.

General Exposition. We do *not* show that closed banking systems operating under the Principle of Reflux (real-bills doctrine) are inherently stable. Indeed, frictions must be introduced to block instability.

We *do* show that when the engine of liquid-asset evolution, credit expansion, is subject to enough inertia, a closed banking system operating under the Principle can be stable.

The controlling mechanism is the following. Price acceleration cannot persist unless *real* liquidity is preserved. But, since real liquidity will decay if the velocity of credit expansion lags behind that of prices, a rule restricting credit growth to x per cent per annum suffices to abort price acceleration (see Modigliani and Papademos, 1981). The rule protracts the period of adjustment of liquid asset stocks to target levels, *i.e.* it requires a small value for λ in

$$\dot{l} = \lambda(l^* - l)$$

where l and l^* are actual and target values for the quantity of liquid assets.

If prices accelerate more rapidly than lending, price acceleration will choke itself: real liquidity will drain away, since nominal income will expand more rapidly than nominal liquidity.

Mathematical Exposition. Define real liquidity as $l/p = \hat{l}$. Hence

$$log\,(\hat{l}) = log\,(l) - log\,(p) \tag{2.1}$$

The system's natural, or embedded, rate of inflation is π^*. And, ignoring secular real growth, we assume that the equilibrium value of $\hat{l}$ is k'; $log\,(k') = k$.

The acceleration of prices is a function of excess liquidity:

$$D\,log\,p = \pi^* + \alpha[log\,(l) - log\,(p) - k] \tag{2.2}$$

i.e.,

$$D\,log\,(p) = (\pi^* - \alpha k) + \alpha\,log\,(l) - \alpha\,log\,(p) \tag{2.3}$$

Differentiating equation (2.3),

$$D^2\,log\,(p) = \alpha D\,log\,(l) - \alpha D\,log\,(p) \tag{2.4}$$

Writing $D\,log\,(p)$ as π,

$$\dot{\pi} = \alpha D log\,(l) - \alpha\pi \tag{2.5}$$

True to the Principle, lending is a function of price behaviour; causality runs from 'prices to money'.

Next assume that

$$D log\,(l) = \beta\pi \tag{2.6}$$

Substituting into equation (2.5),

$$\dot{\pi} = (\beta - 1)\alpha\pi \tag{2.7}$$

Integrating equation (2.7),

$$\pi_t = (c)\,exp\,(\beta - 1)\alpha t \tag{2.8}$$

Stability is assured if $\beta < 1$.

Possibilities for Instability. Specify that acceleration of credit growth is a function of the shortfall of actual from desired stocks of liquid assets; and write $D log\,(l)$ as ξ. Cf. System 3.

$$\left.\begin{aligned} \dot{\pi} &= -\alpha\pi + \alpha\xi & (3.1)\\ \dot{\xi} &= \beta\pi - \beta\xi & (3.2) \end{aligned}\right\} \text{System 3}$$

System 3 is of the form $\dot{x} = Ax$. And, since $|A| = \alpha\beta - \alpha\beta = 0$, *the system is non-simple*. Its *trace*, i.e. the sum of its diagonal elements, is $\alpha + \beta$. The eigenvalues of A are the roots of

$$\lambda^2 - (\alpha + \beta)\lambda = 0 \tag{3.3}$$

i.e., $(\lambda_1, \lambda_2) = [(\alpha + \beta), 0]$. The rank of the system is 1.

A linear system $\dot{x} = Ax$ is non-simple if A is singular (i.e. $det(A) = 0$) and at least one of the eigenvalues of A is zero). It follows that there are non-trivial solutions to $Ax = 0$ and the system has fixed points other than $x = 0$. For linear systems in the plane, there are only two possibilities: either the rank of A is one or A is *null*. In the first case, there is a *line* of fixed points passing through the origin; in the second, every point in the plane is a fixed point (Arrowsmith and Place, 1982, p. 52).

The rest points of System 3 are obtained by solving equations (3.4) and (3.5):

$$\left.\begin{aligned} \alpha\xi - \alpha\pi &= 0 & (3.4)\\ -\beta\xi + \beta\pi &= 0 & (3.5)\\ \text{i.e.,}\quad \xi &= \pi & (3.6) \end{aligned}\right\} \text{System 3}$$

Graphically, we see this in Figure 5.2:

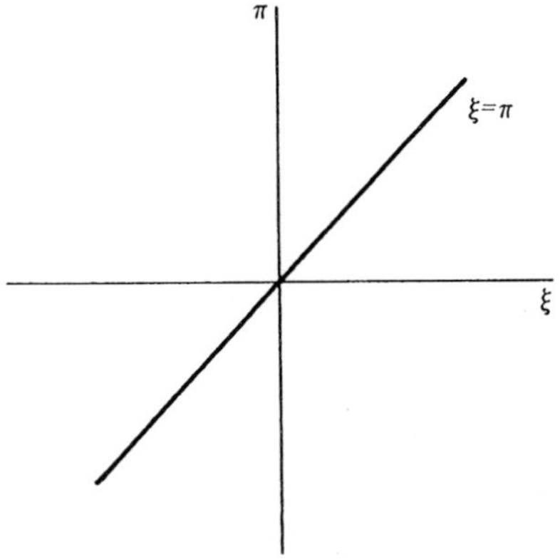

FIGURE 5.2 *The rest points of the system*

The unstable system is indifferent to its steady rate of inflation; any unaccelerated rate of inflation can belong to a rest point.

Interestingly, a system like 3, defined on nominal magnitudes (i.e. π and l), must be *non-simple* to conform to postulates of economic rationality precluding money *illusion*. In particular, since no unaccelerated price path is privileged, any value of 'π' is eligible to belong to a rest vector. The set of rest points of an n-dimensional linear system of this sort typically comprises a $n-1$ dimensional manifold.

5.3 MONETARY-AGGREGATE *v.* INTEREST-RATE TARGETING

5.3.1 Introductory Remarks

In Burstein (1968), I pointed out that, in a non-stochastic universe of discourse, the LM tail of $ISLM$ analysis best would be docked; cf. *a suggestion for simplifying the theory of Professor Hicks* (see Gordon, 1984, p. 466). Authorities choosing y^* as a target, can be completely successful by defending r^* relative to an IS relation,

$$\phi(y, r; \zeta) = 0, \tag{1}$$

ζ being a vector of parameters that can be neglected here. The pair (y^*, r^*) solves the equation. Monetary equilibrium will require extraction of the root, M^*, of equation (2):

$$\psi(y^*, r^*, M; \gamma) = 0 \qquad (LM) \tag{2}$$

An open-market operator, defending r^*, *automatically* will supply M^*.

Stochastic Factors. Raising the analysis to a higher pitch, we assume that $\psi(\cdot)$ is subject to stochastic disturbance, but $\phi(\cdot)$ is not. Then Pelion is piled upon Ossa. Not only may y^* have been erroneously selected: stochastic vibration of LM (and perhaps specification error too) make the upshot uncertain. The procedure may generate $M' \neq M^*$, which may not map into r^* in any case.

Poole (1970), glossed by Poole (1978), took the next short step, showing that, if $\psi(\cdot)$ were non-stochastic, and $\phi(\cdot)$ stochastic, monetary-aggregate targeting is preferable.

5.3.2 Poole's Analysis

Figure 5.3 lays a foundation for a précis of Poole's work. It concerns a case in which *IS*, but not *LM*, vibrates. Controls are set so that the expected outcome is at *Q*. Since *ISLM* holds for this nanosecond only, the diagram merely concerns possibilities revealed by the next pulse of the stroboscope: curves χ and Ω define a confidence interval. Under interest-rate targeting the range of outcomes for *y* is *ef*; if monetary-aggregate controls are locked into their initial setting, the range for *y* is *bc*.

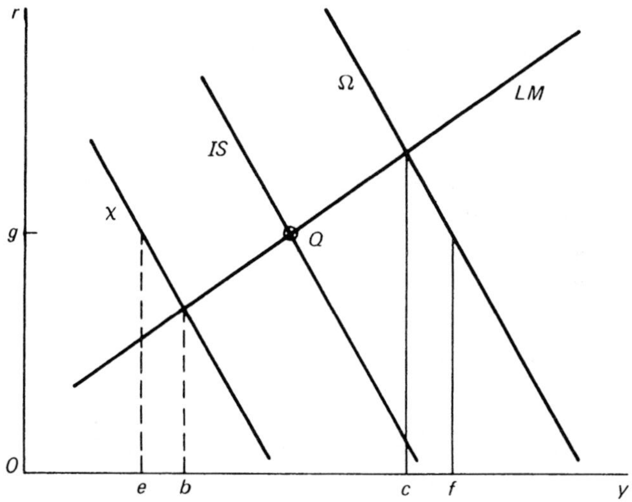

FIGURE 5.3 *A stochastic ISLM system*

For any *IS* shift, monetary-aggregate targeting leads to a smaller effect on equilibrium output: if the interest rate is locked into the *Og* position, an *IS* shift induces a money-supply shift that exacerbates intrinsic effects of the *IS* shift. If *IS* shifts positively, the money-supply valve must be opened up to prevent interest rates from rising. If *IS* shifts leftward, the valve must be tightened up to prevent interest rates from falling. Otherwise, higher interest rates will restrain expansion in the first instance; and lower interest rates will damp contraction in the second. Interest-rate targeting, *as defined by Poole*, is dysfunctional.

If both *IS* and *LM* vibrate, a *mixed strategy* – entailing interest-rate *ranges* – is called for. In a mixed strategy, pre-set controls let interest rates float between upper and lower bounds. The operator may be programmed not to resist upward interest rate movements if indicators point towards $y > y^*$; and not to resist downward movements if indicators point towards $y < y^*$.

A mixed strategy is often described in the following way. Interest-rate targets are raised when money supply growth exceeds a targeted rate; and lowered when money growth is below it. This variant is effective only when *IS* vibration substantially exceeds *LM* vibration.

Why not programme the operator *actively* to push down interest rates so long as indicators point to $y < y^*$?; and *vice versa* in the '$y > y^*$ case. Friedman's 'formal analysis' (see Section 5.4) shows that, in the real stochastic world, attempts to achieve complete correction can be counterproductive: the target may be wrongly chosen; the model may be misspecified; the data may be inaccurate, and always are stale to some extent; official response to data change inevitably is delayed, as is that of the economy to official actions. Think of the problem of controlling events on a distant star; or recall the bismuth/castor oil problem in Keynes (1930).

5.3.3 Some Poolian Algebra

(In System 4, $E(\alpha) = E(\beta) = 0$ – where α and β are deviations from norms.)

$$\left.\begin{array}{lll} (y, r, \alpha) = 0 & IS & (4.1) \\ (y, r, \beta, M) = 0 & LM & (4.2) \end{array}\right\} \text{System 4}$$

Vectors α and β include deviations from norms of *IS* parameters, intensities of liquidity preference, etc. The control is to be M. The optimal feasible solution, (y^*, r^*), is obtained relative to $(M^*; \alpha = \beta = 0)$.

After transformations, so that the origin is at (y^*, r^*, M^*), new variables are defined as follows: $\hat{y} = y - y^*$; $\hat{r} = r - r^*$; $\hat{M} = M - M^*$. Differentiating around the solution-point of System 4:

$$\left.\begin{array}{ll} \Phi_y\hat{y} + \Phi_r\hat{r} = -\Phi_\alpha\alpha & (4.3) \\ \psi_y\hat{y} + \psi_r\hat{r} = -\psi_M\hat{M} - \psi_\beta\beta & (4.4) \end{array}\right\} \text{System 4}$$

Polar Case One: $\alpha = \hat{r} = \hat{y} = 0$. Substitution into equation (4.3) confirms that, if *IS* is stationary, interest-rate targeting works perfectly.

Substitution into equation (4.4) leads to the following relation between money-supply change and vibration of LM:

$$\hat{M}/\beta = -(\psi_\beta/\psi_M) = -[(+)/(-)] = (+)$$

Polar Case Two: $\beta = 0$. Even if LM is stationary, monetary-aggregate targeting cannot completely stabilise output: IS shifts lead to changes in equilibrium interest rates if money supply is fixed – supporting the proposition that a channel, based on IS vibration, runs from the 'real economy' to monetary policy:

$$\begin{aligned}\hat{y} &= [-\phi_\alpha \alpha \psi_r + \psi_M \hat{M} \phi_r]/[\phi_y \psi_r - \psi_y \phi_r] \\ &= [-(+)(-) + (-)(-)\hat{M}]/[(-)(-) - (+)(-)] \\ &= [(+) + (+)\hat{M}]/(+) = (+)\end{aligned}$$

The variance of output is minimised by setting $\hat{M}$ at zero.

The General Case: Both Relations Vibrate Stochastically. The analysis is based on a probability density function: $\int\int f(\alpha, \beta) d\alpha d\beta = 1$. A loss function is defined on replacement sets α and β relative to $\hat{y}$ in Pooles problem – and relative to $(\hat{y}, \hat{r})$ in richer ones. Each set of policy rules leads to a particular relation between $\hat{y}$ and points (α, β). The problem's solution consists of a set of feasible policy rules yielding $g^*(r, y, \alpha, \beta)$ where $g^*(\cdot)$ determines the particular loss function $\chi^*(\alpha, \beta)$ minimising expected loss as determined by $\int\int [f(\alpha, \beta)\chi(\alpha, \beta)] d\alpha d\beta$.

5.3.3.1 *Some More Poolian Algebra: The Model of Poole* (1978).

System 5:

$$(1-c)y + er = a + u_1 \qquad (5.1)$$

$$by - gr = M + u_2 \qquad (5.2)$$

Under interest-rate targeting,

$$\sigma_y^2 = (1-c)^{-2}\sigma_{u_1}^2 \qquad (5.3)$$

For $\sigma_u^2 > 0$ and $\sigma_{u_2}^2 = 0$, the variance of output exceeds zero: LM's disturbance term (u_2) is shut off by interest-rate targeting; but IS's disturbance term (u_1) cannot be shut off by monetary-aggregate targeting.

Prove that, if LM is stationary, and IS stochastic, the variance of output is less under monetary-aggregate than under interest-rate targeting. Under monetary-aggregate targeting:

$$\sigma_y^2 = [(1-c)+((eb)/g)]^{-2}\sigma_{u_1}^2\text{: } (1-c)+(eb/g) \text{ exceeds } (1-c)!$$

QED.

The general case is messy. If neither variance is zero, the variance of output depends on gradients as well as on variances of disturbances: parameter values matter. For example, if $g = 0$, disturbances of money supply have maximum effect on the equilibrium level of the interest rate (as per Tobin, 1982a); as $g \to \infty$, the régimes become indistinguishable.

5.3.4 The State of Play under a Non-Monetary Theory of the Equilibrium Real Rate of Interest

There are many formidable lines of attack against monetary theories of the real rate of interest – such as Poole's – but the following remarks suffice.

The inflation premia in long-term yields should adapt to secular money growth so that equilibrium paths of real long-term interest rates are invariant against secular rates of monetary growth. Nor should blips in money growth or money-market interest-rate targets of central banks affect long-term yields determining costs of capital to companies and consumer-durable purchasers: central banks do not supply real resources to borrowers – and established theory along this line is buttressed by Rational Expectations. *Fiscal policy* – at best a non-rheostatic instrument – is left as the public policy device for real interest-rate management.

The Proper Rôle of Monetary Policy. There is a line of communication from the real to the monetary sector complementing that from monetary disturbances to the real sector (*à la* Friedman and Schwartz, 1963). Thus a massive *IS* shock, leading to deterioration of private sector balance sheets, will make lenders reluctant to extend or renew credit to private agents. If such situations can be identified in time, central banks should vigorously expand their assets, defending against internal drains *à la* Bagehot. This seems to have been the proper *raison d'être* for expansion of Federal Reserve assets during the Penn Central and Chrysler crises and the more general crisis of liquidity feared in 1982–3: it seems proper for the central bank to augment supplies of riskless debt, in the aftermath of certain interactive *IS/LM* shocks, rather than wait for any deflationary effects of 'commodity market' disequilibrium to do the job.

Distilling the principal conclusion from the analysis, assume that liquidity-preference parameters do not vibrate intrinsically, that the supply of a well-defined *money* can be firmly controlled and that *IS* vibrations are substantial and erratic. It does *not* follow that open-loop is preferable to closed-loop control: if the properties of an *IS* shock can be ascertained in time, closed-loop control may be mandated: one reason is that, as we have seen, strict adherence to a money-growth rule cannot shut off real effects of *IS* vibration.

5.3.5 Multiple Interest Rates in Poole's Model

At least in the short run, changes in liquidity preference, basal monetary stocks, financial-intermediary supply functions, etc. may be expected to change real interest rates; but effects on long-term rates may be slight, albeit easily exaggerated by analysts who over-aggregate, let alone confine themselves to *a* rate of interest (sometimes a *nominal* rate!). Thus we saw in Chapter 3 that, even if liquidity-preference parameters vibrate substantially and erratically, induced motion of short-term rates of interest can maintain monetary equilibrium without disturbing the cost of capital. It would be imprudent to conclude from an over-aggregated model, like Poole's, that characteristically erratic vibration of *LM* vitiates monetary-aggregate targeting and calls for interest-rate targeting (*what rate*(s)?). *Par contra cf.* Evans (1984).

5.3.6 Coda to Section 5.3: More Sophisticated Approaches to Interest-Rate Targeting

We have seen that interest-rate *range* targeting is more effective than *point* targeting in Poole's model. And interest-rate targeting can be enhanced in other ways – so that indeed it is not true that 'there is no interest rate rule that is associated with a determinate price level' (Sargent, 1979, p. 362).

Equation (6.1) shows how targeting can be enhanced by *error-learning* (see Allen, 1967, pp. 88–9, and note that $\pi = \dot{p}/p$ while Bank Rate $= q$).

$$\pi(t) = \int_0^\infty \omega(\tau) f[q(t-\tau)]\, d\tau \qquad (6.1)$$

Equation (6.2) defines the expectation of inflation for $\omega(t) = \lambda e^{-\lambda t}$

$$E(\pi_t) = \lambda \int_0^\infty e^{-\lambda\tau}\pi(t-\tau)d\tau \tag{6.2}$$

Equation (6.2) entails adaptive, not 'rational' expectations: it merely suggests a plausible way in which experience may influence the functional, $E\pi\{t\}$. See the classic exposition of Cagan (1956).

Course-correction procedures are easily built into the model.

$$\left.\begin{array}{lll} \text{Procedure One:} & \dot{q}/q \gtreqless \pi \text{ as } \dot{\pi} \gtreqless 0 & (6.3) \\ \text{Procedure Two:} & \dot{q}/q \gtreqless \pi \text{ as } \pi \gtreqless \pi^* & (6.4) \end{array}\right\} \text{System 6}$$

If inflation is accelerating or, better, has been accelerating, the rule of equation (6.3) assures that Bank Rate increases faster than prices—so that real Bank Rate increases so long as inflation is accelerating. And the Appendix to Chapter 5 confirms that, as real Bank Rate increases, banks will contract their assets so that money growth slows.

Procedure Two (equation (6.4)) enters play in the following way. Upon real equilibrium being restored, the unaccelerated rate of inflation that gets locked into place may seem too high: real Bank Rate will be pushed up, and up, until the cumulative effect of price deceleration establishes the desired inflation rate. True, real-world procedures are apt to overshoot their marks: a high price may be paid for the elusive, if not illusory, objective of the 'right' rate of unaccelerated inflation. (Friedman, 1969, supplies an interesting analysis of overshooting.)

Characterisation of the Traverse by the Calculus of Variations. Procedure Two entails *fixed end* points. A point mass, travelling at velocity π_0 at t_0, is to attain velocity π^* at t_1; its motion over the traverse is to minimise a loss function. The problem is quite comparable to Bernoulli's; see Allen (1956, pp. 523–4) for a discussion that remains remarkably clear. And, if the terminal condition is relaxed, a better result can be obtained (see Kamien and Schwartz, 1981, pp. 135–56).

Another Characterisation of the Problem. (See Arrowsmith and Place, 1982, pp. 50–1.)

(1) $\dot{\pi}' = \overset{(+)}{\beta}\, q'$

(2) $\dot{q}' = \overset{(+)}{\gamma}\, \pi'$

where $q' = q^* - q$ and $\pi' = \pi - \pi^*$ – and money is supplied perfectly elastically. The eigenvalues are $0 \pm i\sqrt{\alpha\beta}$. So the phase portrait displays a *centre*: Bank Rate and inflation ceaselessly orbit the target (in this purely-heuristic example) until the computer is reprogrammed.

Authorities May Become Tempted to Exploit Confidence They May Have Earned. Inflation may have been constant at a low level for some time. If the Bank Rate is cried down, banks and other institutions, forming expectations adaptively, will want to increase their lending at going rates: excess supply of credit will push down market rates of interest. The economy may be kept on a high for some time before Bank Rate is restored to its natural level – after the election? But agents will react differently if the trick is tried again. They will better forecast the sequel to an easy-money episode; indeed, the only path consistent with Rational Expectations entails immediate price acceleration.

5.4 FRIEDMAN'S FORMAL ANALYSIS: 'THE EFFECTS OF A FULL EMPLOYMENT POLICY ON ECONOMIC STABILITY: A FORMAL ANALYSIS' (IN FRIEDMAN, 1953)

5.4.1 Preliminary Comments

Committed Keynesians can endorse Friedman's conclusions: lack of information, processing limitations, etc. may make stabilisation infeasible within a Keynesian framework. Metzler (1948) exerts the same thrust. His three lags concern the length of time before an event is noticed, the delay in reaction to perception of the event and the lag in the effect of a policy action on the economy. And recall the bismuth/castor-oil cycle of Keynes (1930) – as well as the problem of influencing events on a distant star. Tobin (1980, p. 22) points out that arguments for open-loop control obtained in this way are part of 'Monetarism Mark One', and contrast with the 'new-classical macroeconomics': 'The new school denies disequilibrium and denies that policies can help or speed the natural processes of stabilization . . . [i]t is not farfetched to say that both earlier monetarist macroeconomics and Keynesian macroeconomics are under attack'.

5.4.2 A Gloss of Friedman's Formal Analysis

Friedman's fundamental relation is

$$z_t = x_t + y_t \quad (7.1)$$

x_t, y_t and z_t are: income in the absence of policy; the effect of policy; income, allowing for stabilisation-policy effects.

$$\sigma_x^2 + \sigma_y^2 + 2\rho\sigma_x\sigma_y = \text{the variance of 'stabilised' income} \quad (7.2)$$

We first establish that an attempt to stabilise output can be destabilising even when the correlation coefficient is negative. Assume that the variances are equal. Then the variance of income is: $2\sigma_x^2 + 2\rho\sigma_x^2$. If the correlation coefficient is -1, stabilisation will work perfectly. But, if it is algebraically greater than (absolutely less than) -0.5, the variance of income will be greater, not less, than before.

Next establish the optimum value of σ_y as a function of the value of the correlation coefficient (see equation (7.2)). Set the partial derivative of the variance of 'stabilised' income with respect to σ_y equal to zero:

$$2\sigma_y + 2\rho\sigma = 0; \; \sigma_y = -\rho\sigma_x; \; \sigma_y/\sigma_x = |\rho| \quad (7.3)$$

Of course, equation (7.3) is relevant only after a screening process has determined that *some* stabilisation should be attempted.

For a correlation coefficient of -0.6, it is optimal to try to remove only 60 per cent of the intrinsic fluctuation of income. The optimised outcome finds the variance of income reduced by 36 per cent; so to speak, 64 per cent of the intrinsic variance persists.

5.5 SUPPLY SHOCKS AND RÉGIMES OF MONEY SUPPLY CONTROL

The analysis is rooted in the study by Burstein (1976) of financial aspects of the Cambodian economy *circa* 1974. The model of Modigliani (1977), discussed in Section 5.5.1, is cut from the same cloth.

The following excerpts from Modigliani (1977) and Barro (1976) offer starkly different interpretations of the same events. And they lead to polar diagnoses: Barro's calls for open-loop control; Modigliani's for a closed loop.

> There is ample evidence that [nine per cent unemployment during 1974] was largely the result of the astronomic rise in interest rates

around the middle of the year. That rise in turn was the unavoidable result of the Federal Reserve's stubborn refusal to accommodate, to an adequate extent, the exogenous inflationary shock due to oil, by letting money supply growth exceed the six per cent rate announced at the beginning of the year. (Modigliani, 1977, p. 14)

In the case of supply shocks there is no macro policy which can both maintain a stable price level and keep employment at its natural rate. (Ibid., p. 15)

The United States economy in 1974 was affected by two important real shocks: the oil cartel and the shortfall of harvests . . . [E]ither of these shocks can be represented by a downward movement in aggregate supply . . . and a lesser downward movement in aggregate real demand . . . It follows that output (in a 'typical' market which experiences zero relative shifts) would fall while prices would rise. What is the rôle for monetary policy in this situation? . . . [T]here is a substantive rôle only to the extent that the monetary authority has better information than the public . . . Hence . . . there is no rôle for monetary policy in offsetting these real shifts . . . Added monetary noise would only complicate and lengthen the process of adjustment. (Barro, 1976, p. 26)

Barro qualifies his conclusions in a way that makes the contrast with Modigliani's result starker still: 'further, to the extent that there is any rôle, it would be a contraction of [money growth] in response to the positive value of $v_t = v_t^d - v_t^s$'. Random shock is measured by v. And since the absolute value of the supply shock exceeds that of the demand shock, and both are negative, $v_t^d - v_t^s > 0$.'

Barro's result follows from what Tobin (1980, chapter 2) calls 'continuous market clearing'. Then the best thing for the authorities to do is to minimise variance of money supply; that is, minimise the volume of smoke blowing into the eyes of agents who form their expectations rationally relative to the best available information; and induce continuous clearing of flex-price markets (in Hicks's phrase).

5.5.1 A Framework for a Closed-Loop Control Response to a Supply Shock

The unit cost of production in the oil-importing country is $wa_1 + p^*a_2$ where: w = domestic-input cost (including wages), a_1 = the quantum of domestic resources necessary for the production of one unit of output, p^* = the cost of imported oil (and we assume that all oil is imported), a_2 = the quantum of imported oil necessary for the production of one unit of output. Enterpreneurs work to a profit margin so that, where p is the price of the final product, $p = \bar{k}(a_1 w + a_2 p^*)$.

As for terms of trade between oil and the oil-importing-country's goods – denoting terms of trade by λ: $p^* = \lambda p$. Therefore:

$$p = \bar{k}(a_1 w + a_2 \lambda p)$$

Differentiating with respect to p, w and λ:

$$dp(1 - \bar{k}a_2\lambda) = \bar{k}a_1 dw + a_2\bar{k}p d\lambda$$

Rearranging terms,

$$dp/p = \bar{k}[(a_1/p)dw + a_2 d\lambda)]/(1 - \bar{k}a_2\lambda)$$

It makes political–economic sense, and simplifies the algebra, to stipulate that $dw = 0$, so that

$$dp/p = \bar{k}a_2 d\lambda/(1 - \bar{k}a_2\lambda)$$

Adding the monetary relation, $dp = vdm$ (where $y = 1$; $dv = 0$), the pieces are in place.

If the real price of oil is to increase ($\lambda > 0$), and if the rate of profit is to rest intact, real wages must fall. Adopting Modigliani's political–economic conjecture that it would be socially suicidal to rely on money-wage cuts to cut real wages, stipulate that:

$$\bar{k} = 1.1$$
$$a_2 = 0.4$$
$$\lambda = 1.0$$
$$d\lambda = 0.75$$

The required value for $dp/p \simeq 0.6$: prices must increase by almost 60 per cent if the real price of oil is to increase by 75 per cent; nominal wages the same. A massive *once-over* increase in the price level is required; and the continuing effects of the *oil-tax* increase are *deflationary*. Unless a once-over bulge in money supply is permitted, there will be a liquidity crisis. Supply shocks *do* call for deviation from money-growth rules.

The 1979 *Oil Shock*. Eisner and Pieper (1984) point out that Barro's prescription was tried in 1979: United States fiscal policy was contractive; and a credit squeeze was imposed as well. A severe business contraction followed.

APPENDIX TO CHAPTER 5: MONEY SUPPLY THEORY SKETCHES

A5.1 Preliminary Remarks

The money stock, for the most part, is a residue of credit flows; and credit flows are sensitive to yields or, better, spreads, that can be earned. Section A5.2 sketches one implication of this point; Section A5.3 shows how dynamic models of bank expansion or contraction can be built and operated.

A5.2 A Rudimentary Money Supply Mechanism

(See Branson, 1979, pp. 276–80.)

Write LM as

$$L(y, r) = \psi(r, x)$$

Desired money supply is determined by $\psi(r, x)$: r = the rate of interest; x = the monetary base

$$dy/dr_{dM=0} = (\psi_r - L_r)/L_y$$

Even if the interest elasticity of demand for money (L_r) is nil, LM's slope is positive. This result is important for an unimportant controversy: in a simple *ISLM* model, fiscal policy is impotent if LM is vertical; if LM must be positive, fiscal policy cannot be impotent.

A5.3 Simple Dynamic Models of Bank Expansion and Contraction

Money as a Residue of Credit Consider a once-over change in the supply of reserves – or, better, their core expansion rate – to the banking system. At impact bank balance sheets are disequilibrated: banks want to make more loans. And the resulting increase in lending triggers a deposit expansion.

During the adjustment interval, i.e. along the *traverse*, excess supply of credit exerts downward pressure on interest rates. But the process must grind to a halt if deposit expansion does not trigger further reserve expansion: erosion of bank liquidity blocks continuing expansion even by unregulated banks. So, under an open-loop régime of supply of 'high powered money', continuing stimulus from an isolated expansionary episode depends on effects of the resulting expansion in the stock of money.

The First Dynamic Model The level of bank deposits is represented by ξ; the equilibrium level is $\bar{\xi}$.

$$\left.\begin{aligned} \dot{\xi} &= \mu(\bar{\xi} - \xi) && \text{(A1.1)} \\ \dot{r} &= \lambda(\xi - \bar{\xi}) && \text{(A1.2)} \end{aligned}\right\} \text{System A1}$$

Equation (A1.1) has a stable rest point, $\xi = \bar{\xi}$. And, where the initial deposit level is ξ_0, the evolution of the interest rate can be obtained simply by plugging the general solution of equation (A1.1),

$$\xi_t = \bar{\xi} + (\bar{\xi} - \xi_0)\,exp\,(-\mu t),$$

into equation (A1.2).

The Second Dynamic Model Incentives for banks to expand loans depend on spreads they can obtain, as well as on excess reserves and costs of borrowing reserves (cf. Chapter 3).

$$\left.\begin{aligned} \dot{\xi} &= a(\bar{\xi} - \xi) + b(r - \bar{r}) && \text{(A2.1)} \\ \dot{r} &= c(\xi - \bar{\xi}) && \text{(A2.2)} \end{aligned}\right\} \text{System A2}$$

Differentiate equation (A2.1) with respect to time; and substitute from equation (A2.2):

$$\left.\begin{aligned} D^2\xi &= -a\dot{\xi} + b\dot{r} && \text{A2.3)} \\ D^2\xi + a\dot{\xi} + bc\xi &= bc\bar{\xi} && \text{(A2.4)} \end{aligned}\right\} \text{System A2}$$

A particular solution is

$$\xi = \bar{\xi} \qquad \text{(A2.5)}$$

The general solution is

$$\xi = \bar{\xi} + B_1 exp\,(\rho_1 t) + B_2 exp\,(\rho_2 t) \qquad \text{(A2.6)}$$

B_1 and B_2 are arbitrary constants determined by initial conditions. Roots of the conjugate quadratic characteristic equation are ρ_1 and ρ_2. Or the solution can be written

$$\xi - \bar{\xi} = Be^{\alpha t} cos\,(\omega t - \varepsilon) \qquad \text{(A2.7)}$$

(See Allen, 1967, pp. 325–33.)

A5.4 Kydland and Prescott (1977)

An exceptionally important theorem in closed *v.* open-loop money-supply control is attributable to Kydland and Prescott (1977). It is succinctly summarised by Buiter (1980):

> [They show that] feedback rules derived by dynamic programming, which they call 'consistent' policies, are sub-optimal in models with optimizing agents endowed with rational expectations . . . because . . . consistent policies fail to allow for the effect of anticipated future instrument values on current (and past) states. The optimal policy in such . . . models, they argue, is an open-loop control. (Buiter, 1980, p. 8)

Also see Sheffrin (1983).

6 Speculation, Rational Expectations and the Pure Theory of the Macroeconomy

6.1 PRELIMINARY REMARKS

(See Buiter, 1980; Kydland and Prescott, 1977; and Sheffrin, 1983.)

After publication of the *General Theory*, economists centred on the existence of full-employment equilibrium without reflecting on the principal problem: can the players in the macroeconomic game reach the set of imputations comprising its core?; are they intrinsically incapable of achieving a *strong equilibrium*, i.e. the solution of the problem in welfare economics conjugate to the macroequilibrium problem?; if not, why not?

The agents of the closed economy of the *General Theory* – unlike those of 'new classical macroeconomic' models, when prices are flexible and information cheap – do not reach a strong equilibrium. Is the difference explained by Rational Expectations?

Tobin (1980) argues that Rational Expectations are consistent with equilibrium in the weak sense of the *General Theory*. Lucas (1981a) rejects Tobin's argument. In a weak equilibrium, expectations are fulfilled, except for stochastic disturbance; agents are neither disappointed nor surprised. *Why* cannot the agents achieve strong equilibrium? (Since a weak equilibrium is suboptimal, there is an infinity of motions, including disequilibrium ones, superior to a given weak equilibrium motion.)

The shape of a proper theory of policy emerges. If agents can at best achieve weak equilibria, there is room for the government to help them do better. If agents ineluctably achieve strong equilibria, promptly recognise reasons for transitory disequilibria, do not lock themselves into long-term contracts impeding price flexibility, etc., the government should abstain from intervention – except perhaps to promote some sense of distributive justice.

Rational Expectations

It is improper to stipulate the agents cannot *learn* the properties of models driving them. The Rational (Model-Consistent) Expectations literature starts out correctly. But it is at best unconvincing to stipulate that *identical* agents innately *know* these properties so that differences of opinion and difficulties in learning (global and differential) are neglected (see Tobin, 1980, chapter 2). And it is naive to ignore what Keynes and Knight taught us about fads, manias, herd instincts, hysterias, etc., involving *interactions*, intrinsic to social groups and generating autonomous (i.e. self-feeding) processes not all of whose properties (perhaps none) can be forecast *ab initio*.

Fads, manias, etc., are troublesome for model-consistent expectations as a guarantor of strong equilibrium in at least two ways. These *human* phenomena are self-feeding; they encourage *speculation*. Even if speculators/agents make efficient use of all available information and operate the best available models, evolutions of prices subject to speculation are open ended – as are those of output and employment. These points are made by Keynes, Samuelson, Burmeister, Townsend *et al.* And the *Wicksell Connection* of Leijonhufvud (1981) is based on a related line of argument (see Chapter 10).

Fads, manias, etc., are troublesome in another way: they engender wide dispersions of expectations, and disparate strengths of conviction about forecasts, so that convergence on well-specified endpoints cannot be assured. True, if the system's terminal state is *stipulated* in advance, rational expectations converge; rational agents will correctly operate a *common* model: 'All of the known 'solutions' to the instability problem – including cases where transversality conditions are invoked to justify convergence – *exclude the possibility of speculative booms rather than provide an economic explanation for them*' (Burmeister, 1980, p. 285).

Results like those just obtained are the stuff of moral philosophy. The chilling possibilities of strategic interplay between operators of nuclear-weapons systems, all skilled in probability calculus, supply another example: nuclear catastrophe is consistent with the rational expectations of inevitably neurasthenic humans! More prosaically, severe monetary/financial disequilibrium is consistent with rational expectations. (See the studies of convertibility crises in Chapters 2 and 5.)

The Plan of Chapter 6

The remaining sections of Chapter 6 consolidate the philosophical bridgehead carved out by the preliminary remarks. Section 6.2 demonstrates the futility of the 'existence of full employment equilibrium' debate. The titles of Sections 6.3 and 6.4 explain themselves: 6.3, *A Problem in Macroeconomic Theory Involving Speculation;* 6.4 *Persistence of Shocks, Rational Expectations and Policy Effectiveness.* Section 6.5, *Leijonhufvud's Corridor*, is suggested by Leijonhufvud (1981). At one level, Leijonhufvud merely touches on implications of well-known distinction of global from local stability. But his construction leads to fruitful analogies to physics and differential equations applications to medical research.

6.2 EMPLOYMENT IN THE LONG RUN

Break down a macroeconomy into six sectors: industrial; pure services; inactives; welfare; subsistence; public. Stress terms of trade, that is, relative prices. Even if attention is confined to the industrial and pure services sectors – with passing reference to the subsistence sector – the ghost of secular unemployment is exorcised (see Burstein, 1978, and Bailey, 1971).

If the propensity of industrial sector entrepreneurs to invest should falter, the industrial sector will shrink, or experience a growth recession. It will release labour, or fail to absorb growth of the labour force: the pure service and subsistence sectors must then absorb more labour. Granted the subsistence sector (the Bush) may be a residual claimant: workers may prefer the market economy.

As the industrial sector releases labour, its demand for pure services falls *at initial prices*: industrial sector income has fallen. The pure services sector, facing a cold wind, must absorb labour. How?

Prices of pure services are captured by a portmanteau variable, p, measuring their purchasing power over 'manufactures'. The value of p must fall; and, since pure services simply are labour, wages must fall everywhere.

To take up a simple instance, if demand for pure services in the industrial sector is unit elastic, so that industrial sector expenditure on pure services is constant, additional services readily can be absorbed *at worse terms of trade*. Indeed members of the pure services sector will be worse off, except as buyers of pure services; but, as the wage rate falls, the industrial sector can absorb an indefinitely large amount of pure service sector labour.

In the regressive scenario, an upthrusting capitalist economy staggers into a sort of nineteenth-century decrepitude. The product mix changes drastically: capitalists slip into late nineteenth-century elegance *comme* the Touchetts and their *éminence grise*, Lord Warburton, in James's *Portrait of a Lady*. Workers' standards of living fall as women again operate manual switchboards and perform domestic service; while many men manicure lawns and polish antique silver. But there will not be mass involuntary unemployment.

Remark. See Baumol (1967), discussed by Frisch (1983). Baumol's 'progressive' and 'static' sectors are analagous to our industrial and pure services ones. The models are easily transposed into each other: a slump in our industrial sector promotes Baumol's arts.

Reflection on the Model. The argument can have a clearly Keynesian tonal centre: what assurance is there that savings will be absorbed by real expenditures? Response develops from a number of directions.

The model implies a real balance effect: the purchasing power of a unit of manufactures increases without limit as the price of pure services falls. The substitution effect in favour of services is augmented by a positive wealth effect on the demand for services as wages fall.

Now consider investment in consumer durables. Labour and capital become *complements* so that lower real wages stimulate investment in durable goods like châteaux whose operation is highly labour intensive. Or consider public places. Upon their maintenance cost falling, it becomes attractive to restructure the capital stock so that its services are produced in more labour intensive ways.

In Xanadu did Kubla Khan
A stately pleasure dome decree;
Where Alph, the sacred river, ran
Through caverns measureless to man
Down to a sunless sea
S. T. Coleridge: *Kubla Khan*

The last paragraph (but not *Kubla Khan*) conforms to rigid Keynesian orthodoxy. Accept what Friedman (1974a, b) calls 'absolute liquidity preference'. Grant that convenience yields decrease at the margin as stocks increase. But *net* yields from durables can be increased by wage cuts – promoting lower costs of maintenance and extraction of convenience yields, interest rates the same.

Finally, a frontal assault is feasible. If interest rates are permanently stuck at 'high' levels, and if wages are low enough, the capital stock can be made 'undurable' enough for sufficient labour to be absorbed in maintenance and replacement of a stationary industrial sector capital stock for there to be full employment. And savings are absorbed by creation of consumer durables as well as productive capital. In the worst keynesian case, *when the theory of price is properly deployed*, a labour force sunk in penury will build the equivalent of medieval cathedrals for gorgeously garbed owners of stagnant industries.

6.3 A PROBLEM IN MACROECONOMIC THEORY INVOLVING SPECULATION

6.3.1 Foundations

Keynes (1936, p. 149), echoing Keynes (1921), writes: 'The outstanding fact is the extreme precariousness of the basis of knowledge on which our estimates of prospective yield have to be made. Our knowledge of the factors which will govern the yield of an investment some years hence is usually very slight and often negligible.'

Chapter 12 of the *General Theory* ('The State of Long Term Expectation') also contains the parable of the newspaper contest, analagous to the stock market. The winners are those who come closest to average rankings; not those who somehow picked the prettiest faces.

Townsend (1978, p. 482) writes: 'The activity of forecasting the choice of others is called *speculation* while [that] of forecasting the yield of assets over their whole life is called *enterprise*.'

Anticipating Leijonhufvud's 'corridor' (see Section 6.5), Samuelson writes: '[We] do not need the recent Harrod–Domar models to raise in our minds the question whether social progress and secular growth themselves are not self-fulfilling acts of faith which, once interrupted by a serious enough breakdown in the economic and political fabric, may not give way to self perpetuating trends of disorganization' (cited by Burmeister, 1980, pp. 265–6).

And the following remark by Samuelson is central to the work of Section 6.3: 'in at least one economic model there exists an *infinity* of self-fulfilling motions that are *permanently* explosive. I refer to the *tulip mania* phenomenon. If people think tulips will appreciate at 10 per cent per month, they can be motivated to act so that this will happen.'

Burmeister (1980, p. 267) concludes that: 'in principle this "tulip mania phenomenon" arises in *all* dynamic macroeconomic models, and the only reason it has not received wider recognition is that, typically, expected capital gains are either ignored or treated in a naive fashion (e.g. static expectations.)'

6.3.2 Some Exemplary Modelling

The models, based on Burmeister (1980, chapter 7) evolve from a simple relation quite suitable to a 'tulip' market. Expectations are rational, but 'all available information' may amount to little.

Model One

The controlling relation is:

$$\pi = b + az + c\dot{\pi} \tag{1.1}$$

The share price (π) is a function of animal spirits (z) and elastic expectations of its evolution based on its current time rate of change. It follows that:

$$\dot{\pi} = -(b/c) - (a/c)z + (1/c)\pi \tag{1.2}$$

System 1 has a rest point at

$$\pi = b + az \tag{1.3}$$

$$d\dot{\pi}/d\pi = 1/c > 0 \tag{1.4}$$

The system is unstable.

Model Two

The second, and more interesting, model retains equation (1.1) as equation (2.1), and adds equation (2.2):

$$\dot{z} = \beta(\pi - \xi) \tag{2.2}$$

The velocity of 'animal spirits' is an increasing function of the difference between the share price and a norm based on historic price-earnings ratios or yields; expectations are elastic.

System 2 has a rest point:

$$\bar{\pi} = (\xi/\beta) \tag{2.3a}$$

$$\bar{z} = [(\xi/\beta) - b]a \tag{2.3b}$$

Analysis of the stability of the *affine* System 2 is based on Arrowsmith and Place (1982, pp. 61–6).

Displaying the system in canonical form:

$$\dot{\pi} = (1/c)\pi - (a/c)z - (b/c) \tag{2.4}$$

$$\dot{z} = \beta\pi - \beta\xi = \beta(\pi - \xi) \tag{2.5}$$

We seek a change in variable allowing the affine system $\dot{x} = Ax + h$ to be written as the autonomous linear system $\dot{y} = Ay$. The change of variable is of the form:

$$x = y - x_0 \tag{2.6}$$

where x_0 is the solution of

$$Ax_0 = h \tag{2.7}$$

So

$$x_{01} = \xi \tag{2.8a}$$

$$x_{02} = b/c \tag{2.8b}$$

Stability depends on the eigenvalues of A in the usual way.

There is no privileged evolution sequence for π and z – nor is there one in a game based on Keynes's parable of the contest to choose the prettiest faces.

Rational Expectations. In Systems 1 and 2, if expectations are formed rationally, the change in π over an interval will be that which was expected to occur. And it follows from expectations formulae already supplied that ${}_tE(\pi_{t+\theta})$ is obtained by 'integrating the model'. Expectations strictly imitate the model's behaviour.

Convergent Expectations. The 'simple two-asset model' of Burmeister (1980, pp. 82–96) perfectly illustrates *rational expectations and convergence.* (The second asset is 'money.') Characteristically, the equilibrium is a saddlepoint: if the initial point does not belong to the stable arm, 'asymptotic chaos' will ensue: *in the limit*, some yields will go to zero or infinity (see Hahn, 1966). So, if equilibrium is to be discovered by 'rational' agents with *infinite horizons*, they must generate a price system that converges on the equilibrium point. But, 'is there any reason to suspect . . . that an economy always starts on the . . . stable arm?' (Ibid., p. 92.) Not unless there are futures markets into the indefinite future – up to the time at which the sun will burn out. And we might append the following observation. Following Marshall, one wishes to study 'the economic system as an organism evolving in historical time' (see Blaug, 1978, p. 442). It thus becomes absurd to specify that structures of models are not ephemeral: asymptotic convergence is not proper to economics as a social science.

If we simply *assume* that expectations converge on a given value, 'tulip manias' – implicitly important in the *General Theory* and explicitly developed by Samuelson and Burmeister – cannot roil the waters. Burmeister (1980, pp. 275–6) elaborates on implications of the fact that the assumption of convergent expectations has not been rigorously justified on suitable *economic* grounds. And he goes on to show (pp. 276–82) that the assumption of convergent expectations leads to logical inconsistency if the expected price is not at a rest point.

6.3.3 The Underlying Problem in Economic Philosophy

The weak equilibrium result buried in Keynesian economics is a version of the *Prisoner's Dilemma*. If, while others hold back, a firm expands its capacity, it may regret its choice; if capital expenditure is co-ordinated, all will be pleased. Minimax calculus in games calling for co-operation may lead to stagnation.

Model-consistent, i.e. rational, expectations do not preclude the Keynesian result. At date t, positive economics may accurately forecast the macro data that will be generated over the *t-th* interval by entrepreneurs holding expectations (E_{it}) relative to information sets (I_{it}). But it can only lay out consequences for interval $t+1$ of the infinity of conjecturally interdependent expectations (E_{it+1}) that may flow from (I_{it+1}), reflecting not only differing states of digestion of the new data, but differing expectations of the expectations of others (see Townsend, 1983). Outcomes are similarly open in all fields of human action – including the music that will be composed; styles in building and clothing; attitudes towards the freedom of the press; revival of the Dada movement in literature; etc.

The result just obtained contrasts with the celebrated solution of the cobweb problem by Muth (1961). (For a solution violating rational expectations, see Allen, 1967, pp. 81–3.) If expectations are formed rationally, $p_t = {}_{t-1}E(p_t) + u_t$. That is, if demand and supply are determined by $f(p)$ and $\phi[E(p)]$, and random shock is neglected: $f(p_t) = \phi[{}_{t-1}E(p_t)]$; ${}_{t-1}E(p_t) = p_t$! The system's only admissible solution at any moment is its rest point – excluding storage; with storage, shock-effects persist so that the temporary equilibrium price need not be $\bar{p}$. This result contrasts with ours in the following way. Muth's model is agitated only by exterior disturbance. Our model is autonomous; its motion is self-starting and self-sustaining.

Compare the following remarks by Tobin (1980) – sternly rebuked by Lucas (1981a).

> If the market-clearing assumption is dropped, there can be rational expectations paths along which monetary and/or fiscal policies correct a situation of under-employment . . .
>
> If the economy is not always in market-clearing equilibrium, rational expectations will not necessarily keep it [there] without the help of macro policy. Perfect foresight of price paths is generally not stabilizing, because expectations can be fulfilled along a variety of paths besides the one that returns to equilibrium. [But see Obstfeld and Rogoff (1983).] That singular path will prevail only if agents know the equilibrium and believe the system will return to it. Without belief that government policy will aim for equilibrium, agents have little reason for acting on the assumption that the equilibrium is stable. (Tobin, 1980, pp. 45–6)

The structure of Tobin's implicit model is neo-classical: a set of markets made by price-takers fails to clear; the *crieur* cannot cope; but macro-policy can guide the agents into a better harbour.

Tobin's remarks can be transposed into a more Keynesian key. Perceive agents to be price quoters instead of price takers. Then Tobin's disequilibrium is at most a departure from weak equilibrium: realised outcomes differ from expected ones to an extent inconsistent with mere stochastic shock. The Keynesian agents grope about in a fog. (In tâtonnement, the *crieur* gropes.) Interactive expectations somehow bar the agents from obtaining the optimal feasible results available to them (see Townsend, 1983). They cannot discover the core of the *n*-person game they play. (In a different game, played in Townsend (1978), the agents do discover its core.)

The upshot of the transposition of Tobin's remarks is not a *co-ordination failure* (*pace* Leijonhufvud, 1981); the events are not spasmodic or catastrophic as in Section 6.5). Keynesian economics is not *au fond* about intermittent failures of *laissez-faire* systems; rather it concerns inherent difficulties of unguided macrosystems in attaining optimal feasible paths.

6.3.4 Concluding Comments, Section 6.3

Keynes's Elusive Core. Why is not the core of Keynes's game discovered? A promising line of attack may be *large v. small numbers:* it is hard to see how 'Japan, Inc.' could fail to solve its macroeconomic problem because of inability to 'co-ordinate' expectations. In the upshot, there appears to be a case for indicative planning, although resulting 'guidance' differs from the fiscal policy format Tobin and Baily may have in mind.

More on Convergence. Tobin (1980) and Burmeister (1980) stress how messy solutions (if any) of rational expectations models become if there is not consensus about what the future holds. Ideas may become better fixed if we think about *chess.*

Comrades Karpov and Kasparov, playing for the world championship in autumn 1984, fulfil rational expectations prerequisites as competently as the lusty traders on the Chicago Mercantile Exchange. Yet it is impossible to forecast long sequences that will occur in their games; let alone the *results.* Or, looking back at the Kasparov–Smyslov contest, concluded in April 1984, 'rational expectations' could do little more than supply 'confidence intervals' for the first eight or ten moves of the games, almost certain to entail queen's side openings.

6.4 PERSISTENCE OF SHOCKS, RATIONAL EXPECTATIONS AND POLICY EFFECTIVENESS

6.4.1 Preliminary Comments

The *pièce de résistance* of Section 6.4 is Sargent and Wallace (1976). Already a classic, this article both illustrates how 'rational expectations' can imply *policy ineffectiveness* and the expectionally strong assumptions needed for such a result. See Section 6.4.3. (Throughout, Section 6.4 deals with fluctuations around a norm; not with norms.)

Section 6.4.2 makes two principal points. The first distinguishes response to, say, displacement of the unemployment rate from its 'natural' level; the second concerns displacement of relative prices from *their* natural values. Traders have clear incentives to take positions against the market in the latter case; but proper channels of response are much less clear in the former. The *j-th* firm may see that the economy has slipped back 'too much'. But this would be an insufficient basis for expanding its output: a perceived shortfall of aggregate output from its norm tells little about prospects for resurgance of demand for products produced by the *j-th* firm.

Section 6.4.2 explores the answer to the following question. Is a decline in demand for one's product due to particular or general causes? Insight will be enhanced by study of a problem in Chapter 7: the solution depends on the extent to which an agent believes that changes in the prices of his inputs and outputs are due to particular or general causes (see especially Barro, 1984, chapter 18).

And it is difficult at a macroeconomic level to determine whether a change in data is due to more or less-permanent parameter shifts or to stochastic shocks. Factors studied in Section 6.2 make it more likely that effects of shocks will persist; and that recovery from shocks requires co-ordinated action.

6.4.2 After-Shocks and Inertia

Assume that an economy on a benchmark path experiences a series of random shocks, each triggering a series of after-shocks. To some extent the after-shocks are predictable: the oil-price shocks of 1973–4 and 1979 must have been expected to be adverse for oil-importing economies. The importance of after-shocks depends on the degree to which agents collectively are able to solve the welfare problem conjugate to a strong equilibrium. In an inertia-free system, profit-seeking agents can easily reshuffle their plans without help from the authorities.

Reflect on the enormity of the assumption that shocks, once registered, promptly are well understood by all in the same way; and that after-shocks are promptly tracked by a powerful consensus. Granted, it is bad science to condemn a theory because of its shocking implications, but Okun (1981) and others persuasively have challenged the empirical implications of inertia-free, continuously self-healing models.

Next consider implications of fogged up crystal balls and wide spectra of beliefs about what seeming shocks really mean. Divergence of actual from expected values (outside acceptable confidence intervals) might reflect a random shudder or twitch of an intact structure – or a structural change. Measured consumption, as a proportion of income, may exceed forecast values: has the propensity to consume increased? Opinions will differ. An uninhibited economy might thrash about confusedly before a new consensus (perhaps a weak one) emerges. And each agent must ponder on the states of mind of others.

We have *not* made a case for stabilising intervention. The officials may be as confused as the private agents; and they are constrained by Metzler's lags and Friedman's 'formal analysis' (cf. Chapter 5). Finally, even if the officials can fit together the pieces of the puzzle better than the private agents, they perhaps would best publish their results, relying on the private sector to make optimal use of the information.

6.4.3 'Rational Expectations and the Theory of Economic Policy' (Sargent and Wallace, 1976)

Equation (1) – the equations being labelled as in Sargent and Wallace (1976) – describes y_t, the unemployment rate, or a deviation of real *GNP* from a target level, etc.

$$y_t = \alpha + \lambda y_{t-1} + \beta m_t + u_t \tag{1}$$

In the reduced-form relation (1), 'u_t is a serially independent, identically distributed random variable with variance σ_u^2 and mean zero; m_t is the rate of growth of the money supply; and α, λ and β are parameters'.

We choose g_0 and g_1 in the feedback rule,

$$m_t = g_0 + g_1 y_{t-1} \tag{2}$$

to minimise the variance of y; and indeed that variance can thus be reduced to the level of unavoidable noise from outside the system.

The result just obtained assumes that private agents do not form expectations about policy actions and then react optimally to these rationally formed expectations; the argument by Lucas (1976), in a now classic paper, is violated. The following model *does* conform to rational-expectations logic.

$$y_t = \xi_0 + \xi_1(m_t - E_{t-1} m_t) + \xi_2 y_{t-1} + u_t \tag{7}$$

$$m_t = g_0 + g_1 y_{t-1} + \varepsilon_t \tag{8}$$

$$E_{t-1} m_t = g_0 + g_1 y_{t-1} \tag{9}$$

> ξ_0, ξ_1 and ξ_2 are fixed parameters; ε is a serially independent random term with mean zero. We assume that it is statistically independent of u_t. Equation (8) governed the money supply during the estimation period. The variable $E_{t-1} m_t$ is the public's estimation of m_t as of time $t-1$. According to (9), 'the public knows . . . the feedback rule and takes this into account in forming its expectations. According to (7), unanticipated movements in the money supply cause movements in y but anticipated movements do not'. (Sargent and Wallace, 1976)

Equation (10), the system's reduced form, is obtained by rearranging equations (7)–(9):

$$y_t = (\xi_0 - \xi_1 g_0) + (\xi_2 - \xi_1 g_1) y_{t-1} + \xi_1 m_t + u_t \tag{10}$$

Equation (10) looks like equation (1): $\alpha = (\xi_0 - \xi_1 g_0)$; $\lambda = (\xi_2 - \xi_1 g_1)$; $\beta = \xi_1$. But there is a crucial difference: *the coefficients of* (10) *are functions of control parameters* (g) – as becomes clear from equation (11), obtained by substituting the rationally formed expectation of m_t for m_t in equation (10):

$$y_t = \xi_0 + \xi_2 y_{t-1} + u_t + \xi_1 \varepsilon_t \tag{11}$$

In this model, when expectations are formed rationally, the evolution of y is independent of any monetary feedback rule. Monetary policy becomes entirely ineffective as a stabilising procedure.

Reflection on Sargent and Wallace (1976). Replace the non-autonomous dynamics of Sargent and Wallace with a scheme in which the vibration of y_t is caused by 'animal spirits' (fear and greed), 'internally' amplified as in Section 6.3. The public's knowledge of a feedback rule calling for expansionary policies if fear exceeds certain bounds will establish a lower bound for y; the resulting safety net will block otherwise open-ended possibilities of panic in speculative, i.e. interactive, markets (see Tobin, 1980, pp. 46–8, and Baily, 1978). Or let the vibration of y be driven by that of the demand for financial intermediation. A public, forming their expectations rationally, knows that increased demand for intermediation will be met by faster growth of the monetary base. But this knowledge will *not* neutralize stabilisation policy: instead it will instil confidence in the ability of non-financial firms to float paper indirectly, through intermediaries, if demand for intermediation increases. Reflection on the term

$$m_t = E_{t-1} m_t$$

in equation (7) helps explain why this should be so. Rewrite it as

$$\zeta_t - E_{t-1} \zeta_t,$$

where ζ measures the proportion of major New York financial institutions declared insolvent. Are we to stipulate that, if $E_{t-1}(\zeta_t) = \zeta_t$, the value of ζ_t will not affect real performance?

Finally, note again that, in the Sargent–Wallace model, (ξ) is a vector of fixed parameters; and the variance of $(y_t - y_{t-1})$ is strictly a function of the variability of exogenous disturbance terms: agent interaction is, *by assumption*, irrelevant to the evolution of macroeconomic data. Tobin (1980, p. 46) writes: 'The view that the market system possesses . . . strong self-adjusting mechanisms that assure stability of its full-employment equilibrium is supported neither by theory nor by capitalism's long history of economic fluctuations.'

Hahn (1982, pp. 51–2) makes a related point: 'Even if agents know what the full Walrasian equilibrium prices are, it may not be in the interest of anyone to declare his willingness to trade at the appropriate equilibrium price at the first step. In fact [they] will be participating in a sequential game which is not cooperative.' And Arrow (1978, pp. 278, 283) writes:

> The very concept of the market [is] based on the idea that it greatly simplifies the informational problems of economic agents [who] have limited powers of information acquisition . . . But in the rational expectations hypothesis, economic agents are required to be superior statisticians, capable of analysing the future general equilibria of the economy.

> It is the essence of the decentralized economy that individuals have different information. Each individual is specialized in certain activities and has in general specialized knowledge about [them]. There is no reason therefore, why his forecasts should be based only on the rather general kind of information which the econometrician . . . can use.

6.5 LEIJONHUFVUD'S CORRIDOR

> The system is likely to behave differently for large than for moderate displacements from the 'full coordination' time-path. Within some range from the path (called the *corridor*), the system's homeostatic mechanisms work well . . . Outside that range these tendencies become weaker. (Leijonhufvud, 1981, p. 109)

(See also Howitt, 1974).

If a system cannot achieve strong equilibrium (i.e. Leijonhufvud's 'full co-ordination time-path'), and if model-consistent expectations are preserved, its structure must be autonomous. The convertibility problem of Chapter 2 supplies a good example.

If demand for liquidity increases, small increases in spreads enjoyed by intermediaries may restore equilibrium. But, if non-financial-sector balance sheets have badly deteriorated, confidence in intermediaries may collapse: a public eager to increase its liquidity, and leery of financial institutions whose important customers are sinking, may wish to convert private-sector holdings into currency and other obligations of the government. And if the feedback channel is blocked in favour of a strictly open-loop control principle, homeostatic possibilities may evaporate, along with liquidity; the system may plunge beyond the field in which its equilibrium state exerts attractive force.

An Example from Medical Research

The analysis by Arrowsmith and Place (1982, pp. 216–26), of tumour growth, culminates in a rigorous model of the 'corridor' problem. They are concerned with 'the size of the domain of stability of the fixed point'. Also with influencing the size of that domain by appropriate choice of parameter values. The analysis is based on qualitative studies of non-linear differential equations.

Examples Based on Physics

Consider the following diagram (Figure 6.1).

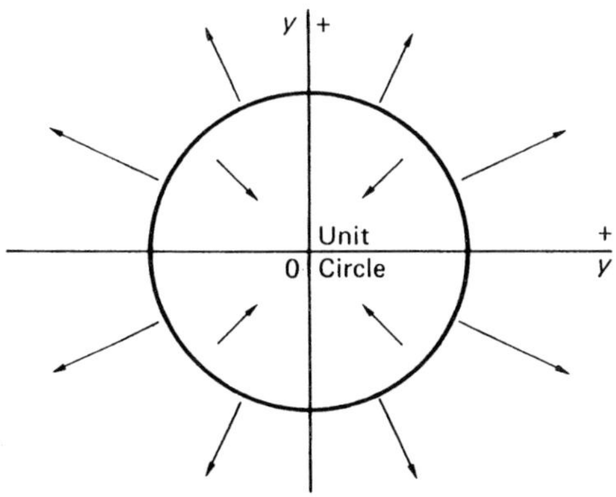

FIGURE 6.1 *Vector Field of D^2 y defined relative to deviations from the rest point y*

Remarks

(1) The unit circle corresponds to Leijonhufvud's corridor.
(2) The length of a vector shows the magnitude of acceleration at the corresponding point in the field.
(3) The co-ordinates of each point in the field are $(y, \dot{y})$.
(4) The upshot is suggested by a differential equation of the form $D^2y = a\dot{y} - b(1/y)$.

Further Examples. Before studying French (1968), note that, up to now, the 'corridor' has, so to speak, been too well defined: a field concerns a continuous distribution of a property; and the model depicted by Figure 6.1 is discontinuous. A more fruitful attack along the lines described by the diagram might be based on a stochastic difference equation. It would concern probabilities of return to the rest point. The relevant probability may approach unity in some regions; and zero in others.

Loosely imitating French (1968, pp. 232–4), the gravitational pull exerted by the rest point competes with a kinetic force. The farther the system is from the rest point, the less powerful is the gravitational pull the rest point exerts; and the more powerful is the destabilising kinetic force of the system's velocity. As for French's illuminating discussion,

A charged particle at a given point may experience a force that depends on its velocity. Such a force arises if there is at the position of the charge what we call a magnetic field. The field has a well-defined direction . . . and the magnetic force on the moving charge is:

$$F_{mag} = (constant)\,(q_2 u \cdot B)$$

where u is the velocity of the charged particle (the charge being q_2) and B characterizes the strength and direction of the magnetic field.

The total electromagnetic force on a charge at a given point can then be written as the sum of the electric force it would experience if stationary, plus [a] magnetic force

$$F = q_2\,(\varepsilon + u \cdot B) \qquad (8.4)$$

a relation known as the Lorentz Force Law. We can regard Eq. (8.4) as a means of defining the electric field ε and the magnetic field B in terms of the forces found to be exerted on charges in various states of motion (including rest) at a given point.

7 Inflation

7.1 THE METRIC OF INFLATION

Correlation between money growth and inflation is one thing – and causality another.

Assume that a competitively determined interest rate on money is perfectly indexed, so that money's nominal yield compensates for real value depreciation. (Only the convenience yield of non-interest-bearing money compensates for inflation attrition – a point leading to the 'shoe leather' theory of optimal monetary growth of Chapter 8, Section 3.) In a closed system, the sum of *the* real rate of interest and the uniform inflation-rate will equal the growth-rate of the stock of money; and the equilibrium rate of inflation is indeterminate – see Chapter 7, Section 2.

The bundle of rights enduing to the owner of a unit of interest-bearing money includes the right to be reimbursed for attrition of real value caused by inflation; money is exempt from the inflation tax of Chapter 7, Section 2.

The purchasing power of a unit of money that does not yield interest is not guaranteed. True, a holder correctly perceives that he can offset depreciation of his zero-yield money stock with part of the imputed proceeds of its convenience yield. But such an offset is collectively impossible unless the mass of money increases at the inflation rate: if money growth were below the inflation rate, the real stock of money would decay until it became extinct. So monetary equilibrium must encompass some sort of quantity theory of money or, better, prices. But the 'quantity theory' so far projected is the beginning, not the end, of a scheme of analysis: it is as consistent with prices driving money as with money driving prices. (For a related discussion, see the analysis by Hahn of 'the fashionable model of overlapping generations first used to brilliant effect by Samuelson, 1958'. (Hahn, 1982, pp. 7–19).

Neutrality of Money. (See Patinkin, 1956, 1965 and Chapter 2, Section 3.) If the nominal masses of two or more stocks are determined arbitrarily, a change in one stock cannot be neutral for the real economy.

Say that the nominal masses of assets i, j and k are determined by the authorities: *cf.* 'high powered money' and two other securities of a consolidated public sector. Provisionally stipulate that the inflation rate equals the expansion rate of the monetary base in a stationary real economy. Assume that the three nominal growth rates differ so that real stocks of the other two assets and ratios x_i/x_j, x_i/x_k and x_j/x_k must change over time: ratios formed with the fastest-growing stock as denominator go to zero as $t \rightarrow \infty$. So 'balanced inflation' is inconsistent with monetary neutrality as well as the idea of equilibrium.

7.2 EXCESS DEMAND AND INFLATION

Leijonhufvud (1981) points out that excess demands should associate with relative, not absolute, prices. And acceleration (deceleration) of prices may be caused by excess demand (supply). *And* general equilibrium, defined in real space, is invariant against the secular velocity of prices; no inflation rate is privileged.

7.2.1 *How to Pay for the War* and its Aftermath

The idea of the *inflationary gap* (see Keynes, 1940) contains a snare: 'With \$70 trying to buy goods and \$50 worth of goods available, at the assumed price level, it may seem that a 40 per cent price rise would close the gap by making the aggregate value of the goods equal to \$70. But, if this were to happen, aggregate income [would increase correspondingly]' (Friedman, 1942, 1953, p. 252).

In fact Keynes (1940) eludes the snare: in his model, higher inflation redistributes income towards groups with higher propensities to save; and so cures excess demand. (See Frisch, 1983, pp. 227–9, and Phelps, 1973.)

Friedman (1942, 1953), having explained the *petito principii* to be avoided, goes on to develop the idea of the *inflation tax*. He assumes that money does not yield interest; and that bonds are indexed, so that bond holders are immune from any 'inflation tax'. The government is to increase its offtake of real resources to \$50 from \$30, monetising the resulting deficit. A seigneurage is to be extracted from the economy: nominal balances are to be sold to the public – annual sales being worth twenty constant dollars. Real cash balances, continuously melted by inflation, are replenished by money purchases; demand for goods falls

1:1 with real balance replenishment (see Keynes, 1923, for a similar analysis).

First assume that the public maintain their real balances intact, come what may. Then the equilibrium rate of inflation, x, will be determined by

$$x = \tau/\alpha \tag{7.1}$$

$$\alpha = (M/p)/y \tag{7.2}$$

The desired ratio of real balances to real output is represented by α; and the tax rate, τ, is the proportion borne by incremental offtake (20) to real output (100).

For $\alpha = 2$ and $\tau = 0.2$, the equilibrium rate of inflation is 10 per cent per annum; seigneurage revenues flow in a rate of twenty constant dollars per annum.

Now assume that α is a decreasing function of the rate of 'taxation':

$$\alpha = \lambda - f(x); f'(x) > 0; f(0) = 0 \tag{7.3}$$

Then,

$$x = \tau/[\lambda - f(x)] \tag{7.4}$$

If demand for real balances is elastic relative to the inflation rate, an 'inflationary gap' will not be closed by inflation taxation; and some inflation tax rate will maximise real revenue yield (*cf.* the Laffer curve): '[t] here is some rate of tax that will give the maximum yield . . . In this case the product taxed is real cash balances, and the supply is, or can be perfectly elastic at essentially zero cost, so that the maximum yield is at a point on the demand curve of unitary elasticity.' (Friedman, 1953, pp. 256–7)

In a perfectly indexed economy, prices and nominal interest rates track money growth, so that inflation has no real consequences. Bomberger and Makinen (1980, p. 550) explain that a reform, forcing the nationalised Hungarian banks to pay indexed interest on demand deposits, 'reduced substantially the tax base against which [the inflation tax] determined by the issue of government currency could be applied'. Of course, an attempt to collect inflation tax revenues at pre-reform levels led to hyperinflation.

Deeper Study of Bonds

If bonds are not indexed, a higher inflation rate causes real values of bond stocks to melt faster – so that bond demand by a public, intent on sustaining real values of bond holdings, would be stimulated like demand for nominal cash balances in Friedman (1942, 1953). The controlling discriminant in Friedman's model is indexation/non-indexation. The 'fiscal' theory of inflation is perfectly symmetrical with Friedman's monetary one.

Developing the counterpart inflation model in more detail: highly liquid government bonds are generated by public sector borrowing requirements; money, however defined, offers an indexed yield; and the initial moving equilibrium contains the set of real interest rates ($\bar{r}_i$).

Upon a higher value for the inflation rate (a state variable) being chosen, the economy is perturbed. Resulting disequilibrium accelerates prices. When equilibrium is restored (e.g. when public spending targets return to normal), the system will indefinitely maintain a new equilibrium trajectory – including a higher rate of steady inflation. If bonds are not indexed and foresight is imperfect, so that yields do not embed correct inflation expectations, an inflation tax, measured by the volume of bond purchases necessary to offset inflation-caused capital loss, will be extracted.

The concept of monetary/fiscal – instead of monetary *and* fiscal – policy is expanded in Section 7.4; where it is also explained why the political economy of inflation is based on pressures against closed positions of valves in the feedback channel of the money supply process.

7.3 INFLATION AND UNEMPLOYMENT: THE PHILLIPS CURVE, ETC.

Our tangential collision with the immense literature on the Phillips Curve (see Frisch, 1983) supports Friedman (1968a) and Phelps (1968a): unaccelerated inflation is not an excess demand phenomenon (see also Friedman, 1977, and Gordon, 1976).

The stasis of economic equilibrium relates to Newton's first law of motion: in the absence of force, a body continues to move uniformly in a straight line. And economic disequilibrium relates to Newton's second law of motion: a force produces an acceleration, etc.

The upshot conforms to the theory of value – a theory of *relative* prices whose results are invariant against uniform unaccelerated price motions – so that, within its domain, hyperinflation is but a highly coloured adjectival phrase.

Friedman–Phelps theory is as 'expectational' as it is 'accelerationist':

the disequilibria that provoke accelerations in this chapter typically are the result of unfulfilled expectations.

Figure 7.1 leads to the following points. Unemployment is lower at *R* than at *Q*: at *R* the inflation rate is higher than was expected; at *Q* it is lower than was expected. At points *P* and *S* inflation is as expected: 'accelerationists' require that, when actual equals expected inflation, unemployment will be at its natural level, *Oc*. Samples collected over intervals on which expected inflation is the same will be fitted by downward-sloping Phillips curves. Pooled samples, covering intervals on which inflation expectations vary, may not imply significant correlation between inflation and unemployment. Finally, if the curves containing points *P* and *S* are generated over different time intervals, it may incorrectly be inferred that the 'true' relationship between inflation and unemployment has shifted, that the terms of a trade-off between inflation and unemployment have deteriorated. (See Frisch, 1983, for a quite complete discussion of Phillips curve theory, including expectations augmentation.)

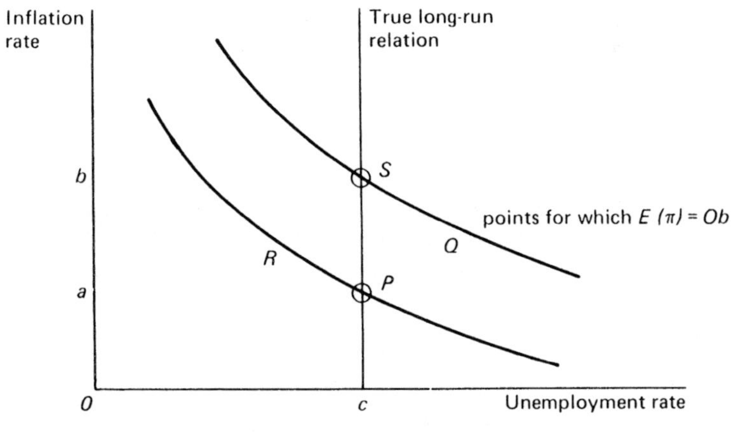

FIGURE 7.1 *A Graph of the theory*

Actual and Expected Inflation

It is absurd that everyone should hold the same expectation about anything. A number of more plausible scenarios have been drafted to supply a foundation for the relation, $U = \overline{U} + f[E(\pi) - \pi]$. Some scripts revolve around the assumption that sluggish worker reactions cause wages to lag behind prices. Others stipulate that labour contracts are typically based on misestimates of inflation that can be exploited by employers – until real wages catch up. Or the typical transactor is to be more aware of prices in his market than of prices in other markets. Prior expectations (priors) may persist despite local price increases, especially if covariances between 'local' prices are weakly positive or negative – so that it will frequently be assumed that higher local prices imply higher *relative* prices; thus stimulating production, capital accumulation, etc. (see Barro, 1984).

These scripts are mostly gratuitous concoctions replacing rather than supplying scientific explanation. Commenting on the model of Lucas (1972), in which much business cycle behaviour is 'explained' by the assumption that sellers work to better price data than buyers – and citing B. Friedman (1978) – Tobin (1980, p. 42) writes:

> It is this specification that allows the model to 'explain the observed correlation of nominal prices and real quantities. Suppose we reversed the positions of buyers and sellers, so that buyers know precisely what they are paying but sellers must offer supplies on the basis of predictions of the price they will get. Then the model will imply that prices and quantities are negatively correlated.

(Milton Friedman 1977 argues that, if higher inflation is associated with weaker price covariance – so that the underlying distribution is heteroscadastistic – resulting uncertainties may stifle economic activity so that the 'true' Phillips curve may be *positively* sloped. Whatever its empirical merit, this argument is invulnerable against the criticisms just voiced.)

7.4 INFLATION AS A FEEDBACK PHENOMENON: OPEN- AND CLOSED-LOOP CONTROLS REDUX

> The substance of the debate is about prime cause, and, plainly, causality can go either way: the authorities can pursue defensive or dynamic policies and thus be passive or active in supplying cash. If they are willing to supply enough of it, or absorb enough, they can always override the effect of a shift in private sector demand. (Chick, 1977, p. 90.)

Keynes's *Tract* (1923) opened up this subject – as it did forward exchange and the interest parity. If a government covers part of a persistent shortfall of its revenue from its expenditure by monetisation, the rate of monetary expansion easily becomes an effect, not a cause, of inflation. The German example, studied in the *Tract* and still green in collective memory, supplies a perfect example: the authorities sought to maintain the *real* money stock: the rate of money growth became a function of the inflation rate. The following scheme explains the upshot.

$$\left.\begin{aligned} m_t &= \alpha\pi_{t-1} && (1.1)\\ \pi_{t-1} &= \beta m_{t-2} && (1.2)\\ m_t &= \alpha\beta m_{t-2};\quad m_{t-2}-(1/\alpha\beta)m_t = 0 && (1.3)\end{aligned}\right\}\text{System 1}$$

The quadratic characteristic equation has equal positive real roots: $\bar{\lambda} = (\alpha\beta)^{-1}$

Strictly, System 1 describes the deviation in money growth, m, from a criterion. (The deviation of the inflation rate from the level associated with m^* is denoted π.) *The system is dynamically unstable.*

The *Treatise* discusses money growth as a function of money wage thrust, as does Hicks (1955). Kaldor (1970) insists that the inflation process exhibits 'reverse thrust', while more eclectic support for incomes policy, wage/price guideposts, etc. is supplied by Eckstein (1981) and Okun (1981). Results similar to those of this section are obtained by Wallace (1984) – from the standpoint of Samuelson's overlapping generations model. Also see Sargent and Wallace (1981), challenged by McCallum (1984).

(Further references for the discussion of Section 7.4 on this point include Frisch (1983) and his copious citations, including Allais (1966) and Laidler and Parkin (1975). See also Friedman (1968b) and his article on the quantity theory of money in the *Encyclopaedia of the Social Sciences*. Cagan (1956) is a classic source. And Lerner (1956) describes how inflation in the South abated – until new printing presses could be set up – after Confederate money printing plants were seized by United States forces.)

7.5 MONETARY/FISCAL POLICY AND INFLATION IN CLOSED ECONOMIES

Some recapitulation of material from Chapters 1 and 5 is necessary to establish a basis. The thrust of ongoing changes in financial intermediation, including banking and the mechanism of debt discharge, is towards erasure of discriminants so that the 'space' becomes amorphous. Thus it can no longer be assumed that means of payment are limited to clearing bank current accounts (commercial bank demand deposits) and currency; many accounts accomplish this work. Nor need means of payment have fixed nominal value; money-market funds are an example.

Chapter 1 showed how a network of varied chequeries, some not resembling clearing banks, may comprise a clearing union. Some, or all, members of the union may not be subject to legal-reserve requirements. In practice, members may choose to hold part of their reserves as short claims against others; there will be reserve pyramiding. And, at *some* point, the network must run up against prudential, if not legal, constraints enforced by the quantity of central bank credit: potential reserves will become fully mobilised to support chequeable accounts. The system will enter Phase Two.

Phases One and Two

We study spontaneous fluctuation of the nominal assets and credit flows of the financial intermediary sector, relative to fixed quantities of central bank credit.

In Phase One, the constraint imposed by a predetermined quantity of central bank credit is slack: we are free to choose a drive mechanism to govern inflation – and opt for the *stock of government debt*.

Anticipating Chapter 9, Section 9.4 and recalling Chapter 3, assume that yields of chequeable accounts are flexibly competitive. And the monetary base may plausibly comprise *all* public sector credit, i.e central bank credit and government stock.

A system in Phase Two is in a Fisherine domain. The nominal volume of clearing activity is rigidly bounded from above by the central bank credit constraint: possibilities for velocity increase are exhausted; nor can fiscal policy influence the inflation rate.

Phase One

Fiscal policy, transmogrified into monetary/fiscal policy, determines the inflation rate.

In Phase One, the expansion rate of the liquidity base is a function of that of the nominal public sector borrowing requirement. Excess monetarist baggage being shed, the 'nominal' economy sails along in empty space at *some* uniform velocity. Price inflation moves *pari passu* with the liquidity base in a sustainable moving equilibrium.

Collecting the Properties of Phase One. The liquidity base is an amorphous mass whose volume is determined by the combined masses of the currency base, central bank credit and government securities. The volume of chequeable accounts is determined by *demand*; and is below its potential level. Reserve-eligible credits – in a regulatory context – are incompletely mobilised to support chequeable accounts; a mass of manoeuvre is in reserve.

The controlling theory concerns *finance*; 'Radcliffe' and Gurley and Shaw (1960) are supported to this extent. The liquidity base is determined by monetary/fiscal policy.

In Phase One, the system behaves quasi-classically. Price behaviour is a function of an aggregate far more extensive than monetarists can accept, but is isomorphic with that called for by 'quantity theories'. And, in the limit, financial assets are perfect substitutes – so that real equilibrium is invariant against the level and expansion rate of the monetary base. In particular, the real cost of capital is invariant against financial policy.

Transition to Phase Two

The liquidity base as a whole, but not central bank credit, is to accelerate while the system is in Phase One. In due course, the federal funds rate will increase, intermediaries' spreads will widen, etc. These developments extrapolate into the binding constraints of Phase Two. In Phase Two, more or less technological constraints dominate cash management.

Phase Two

A trichromism is imposed on the system's assets. See Feldstein (1980): the trichromism leads back to Ricardo's minimum rate of profit necessary to induce physical capital accumulation. (Since, in Phase Two, 'money' balances become determined mechanically, the operational preference frontier separates non-monetary financial assets from shares *cum* real assets.) So, instead of the dichotomy, *financial assets/real assets*, we have *chequeable balances (money)/other financial assets/real assets.*

Price behaviour will be determined by the path of central bank credit. A simpliste quantity theory of money is resurrected.

Once the path of central bank credit is established, changes in the supply of government securities lead to changes in the *real* values of these stocks. A simpliste Keynesianism is also established. And monetary/fiscal policy is replaced by monetary *and* fiscal policies.

A 'fiscal' theory of the real cost of capital – accompanying a monetarist theory of prices (!) – is extracted from Phase Two in the following way. Once impact effects of increased public spending, financed by borrowing, dissipate, continuing effects on real capital accumulation are negative: if relatively more wealth is to be held as public debt, its yield must increase – causing demand, in the schedule sense, for shares and real capital to fall. (See Tobin, 1961, 1965, 1982b and Chapter 8. In Chapter 7 public debt is treated as net wealth; Chapter 8 is more subtle.)

Nominal income becomes rigidly linked to the monetary base in the following way. Since the monetary subsystem generates demand for chequeable accounts as a strict function of nominal income, and real income is determined in the fiscal subsystem, the quantity of central bank credit strictly determines prices.

Conclusion to Section 7.4

The structure of Phase Two leads to stationary velocity of monetary circulation so that

$$m - \rho = \pi$$

The inflation rate (π) equals the rate of money growth (m) less that of real growth (ρ). Higher public sector borrowing requirements, increasing the stock of public debt and the cost of capital, depress real growth – so that the secular inflation rate is higher for a given level of money growth. And reduction of the stock of public debt – perhaps through open-market operations, pulling the analysis into the orbit of Metzler (1951) – stimulates real growth and reduces the secular rate of inflation relative to money growth.

8 Public Debt and Monetary Theory

8.1 PRELIMINARY REMARKS

Section 8.2 develops some stock-adjustment problems, encompassing the *crowding-out* debate.

Section 8.3 concerns *money and economic growth*. Paraphrasing Tobin (1965, p. 671), if government debt is an alternative to physical capital in portfolios, savings can be channelled between portfolio alternatives such as real capital and government debt so that optimal capital intensity is achieved. The analysis owes much to Phelps (1961); and neglects Barro (1974). Section 8.4 seeks to remedy this defect.

As for Section 8.4, just as the real balance effect is shown in Chapter 9 to be inconsistent with economic logic, the stock of public debt in a closed economy cannot comprise net social wealth: public debt, as a social institution, may be welfare productive; but an increase in its nominal mass contributes nothing to social welfare. Still the invariance, or not, of the equilibrium of the real economy against the mass and structure of public debt is an issue separate from its being, or not being, net wealth (see Carmichael, 1982).

Going back to Buchanan (1958), Section 8.4 offers examples clarifying the distinction of the 'invariance' from the 'net wealth' issue. The upshot points up the sensitivity of policy choice to model choice; and therefore the sensitivity of policy choice to the outcome of debate on the plane of pure theory. The discussion provoked by Feldstein (1974), and summarised by Barro (1984), is a good example.

8.2 STOCK-ADJUSTMENT PROBLEMS: CROWDING OUT

8.2.1 An Elementary Differential Equation

Define x^* as the level of wealth at which aggregate demand equals full employment output. And assume that, in a closed system, public debt is reckoned as wealth:

$$z = f(x), \tag{1.1}$$

z being aggregate demand. Next, where z^* is the full employment level of aggregate demand, define $\zeta = z - z^*$. And

$$z^* = f(x^*) \tag{1.2}$$

Defining $\bar{\chi} = x - x^*$,

$$\zeta = \phi(\chi); \quad 0 = \phi(0). \tag{1.3}$$

It remains to supply a dynamic law to the system. Along lines developed by Friedman (1948, 1953), public expenditure and tax policies are to be put into place so that the public sector runs a deficit when output is below its full employment level; and a surplus when the output of an overheated economy exceeds 'z^*'. Thus

$$\dot{\chi} = \psi(\zeta) \tag{1.4}$$

And, since, due to equation (1.3), ζ is a function of χ,

$$\dot{\chi} = \Psi(\chi) \tag{1.5}$$

And,

$$0 = \Psi(0); \tag{1.6}$$

$$0 > \Psi'(\chi) \tag{1.7}$$

The system's rest point is at full employment; and the system is dynamically stable.

8.2.1.1 *Crowding Out: Friedman's Intertemporal Analysis.* Do public-sector deficits crowd out private expenditures, especially on capital formation? Does the finance mode matter? Milton Friedman argues that the proper issue concerns the expenditure of the public sector, not its borrowing requirement (see Friedman, 1984b). Tacit in his argument is a proposition like ours on the 'burden of the money supply', (Chapter 9) – related to one by Buchanan (1958). Even if holders of indexed bonds were paid by printing money, non-holders would be subject to holders' enhanced command over available goods. Non-holders of government debt could preserve wealth only by saving more. *Ergo*, effects on saving in closed economies of tax-financed public spending are the same as those of bond-financed public spending: there is but a cosmetic distinction between compulsory transfers in the form of tax-payments and collective abstinence that does not increase collective productive capital. (This point is made less explicitly by Tobin, 1980, chapter 3.)

We move on to a condensed two-part analysis that is both less subtle on intergenerational aspects and more conventional than Friedman (1984b) or Section 8.4.

8.2.1.2 *Crowding Out: Flow Analysis.* Equation (2.1) describes what Keynes (1936) calls a *classical* system. Its homogeneity properties make it possible to deal with *proportions* of national income saved and invested – that is, s and i – or with the proportion borne by public expenditure (g) or tax-revenues (τ) to national income. (The real rate of interest is denoted r.)

$$(g - \tau) + i(r, \tau) = s(r, \tau) \qquad (2.1)$$

Upon specifying the crude technology – $K/y = v$ – the equilibrium growth rate is seen to be i/v; the warranted rate of growth (assumed to satisfy the natural rate of growth as well) is i/v. (See Allen, 1967, chapter 11 – based on Harrod, 1939 and 1948, as well as Harrod's *Trade Cycle*.)

Turning to fiscal-policy analysis,

$$(s_r - i_r)d\bar{r} + (s_\tau - i_\tau)d\tau = dg - d\tau \qquad (2.2)$$

$$d\bar{r}/dg_{d\tau = 0} = 1\,(s_r - i_r) = 1/[(+) - (-)] = (+) \qquad (2.3)$$

In the classical case, an increase in public spending, *ceteris paribus*, leads to a higher real rate of interest and a lower secular growth rate.

$$d\bar{r}/d\tau_{dg = 0} = (1 + s_\tau - i_\tau)/[(-)(s_r - i_r)] = (+)/(-) = (-) \qquad (2.4)$$

It is possible that $di/d\tau < 0$:

$$di = i_\tau d\tau + i_r dr \qquad (2.5)$$

So:

$$di/d\tau < 0 \quad \textit{if} \quad |i_\tau| > |i_r| \times |[(1 + s_\tau - i_\tau)/(-)(s_r - i_r)]| \qquad (2.6)$$

Tax-cuts stimulate investment if the values of 'i_τ' and 's_τ' are large relative to those of 'i_r' and 's_r' – noting that 'i_r' can be reduced by appropriate tax credit schemes. A critique of the *a priori* case for 'supply side economics' is easily organised around our structure – once we note that revenue collection is stimulated by lower tax rates to the extent that tax evasion or tax avoidance then becomes less attractive. And a dynamic 'Laffer principle' is easily extracted from the analysis: if tax cuts stimulate faster growth, in time tax receipts will increase relative to their previous profile.

8.2.1.3 *A keynesian Case.* In a k (keynesian state), public sector deficits are self-financing – that is what the multiplier is all about! Far from crowding out private sector capital formation, expansionary fiscal policy make full employment possible. And the combined effect of a large public sector and aggressive stabilisation policy may create a safety net that stimulates private sector capital formation in the long run. (See Tobin, 1980, pp. 46–8, and Baily, 1978.)

When the economy is in a k state, the comparative statics of fiscal policy are easily stated – at the cost of swallowing objections to monetary theories of real rates of interest, so common in orthodox Keynesian work.

$$I(y,r) + G = S(y,r) \tag{3.1}$$

$$L(y,r) = M(r,\alpha) \tag{3.2}$$

Taxation is neglected; money supply is a function of the quantity of reserves supplied by the central bank (cf. α) and the positive response of the banking system to the rate of interest (cf. Chapter 5). Differentiating in the neighbourhood of an equilibrium point:

$$(S_y \overset{+}{-} I_y)dy + (S_y \overset{+}{-} I_r)dr = dG \tag{3.3}$$

$$L_y^{(+)}dy + (L_r \overset{(-)}{-} M_r)dr = d\alpha \tag{3.4}$$

If $S_y > I_y$, then, surely, $\Delta < 0$. Setting $d\alpha = 0$,

$$d\bar{r}/dG = (-)/(-) = (+) = -L_y/\Delta \tag{3.5}$$

$$d\bar{y}/dG = (-)/(-) = (+) = (L_r - M_r)/\Delta \tag{3.6}$$

The necessary condition for $d\bar{I}/dG > 0$ is

$$|L_r| + M_r > |(I_r/I_y)L_y \tag{3.7}$$

If interest elasticites of demand and/or supply of money are large enough, an increase in government spending stimulates investment.

Introduce tax policy and consider the effect of a tax cut, ignoring whatever are the wealth properties of public debt. Ignoring 'L_τ',

$$(1 - C_y \overset{(+)}{-} I_y)dy - (C_r + I_r^{(-)})dr = (C_\tau \overset{(-)}{+} (I_\tau^{(-)})d\tau + dA \tag{4.1}$$

$$\Delta = (-)$$

$$L_y^{(+)}dy + L_r^{(-)}dr = \qquad dM \tag{4.2}$$

$$d\bar{y}/d\tau_{dA=dM=0} = L_r^{(-)}(C_\tau^{(-)} + I_\tau^{(-)})/\Delta = (+)/(-) = (-) \quad (4.3)$$

Indeed, a tax increase (decrease) is contractionary (expansionary) in the short run. Effects on investment depend on those on interest rates, together with various parameter values.

$$d\bar{r}/d\tau = [-L_y(C_\tau + I_\tau)]/\Delta = (+)/(-) = (-) \quad (4.4)$$
$$d\bar{I}/d\tau = I_y(d\bar{y}/d\tau) + I_r(d\bar{r}/d\tau) \quad (4.5)$$

Obviously, if consumption were little stimulated by higher disposable income, while investment were strongly stimulated by a higher after tax rate of profit, there would be a Keynesian case for 'supply side economics'.

8.2.1.4 *Crowding Out: Stock-Flow* (n-th *round*) *Analysis.* We have already studied ways in which the stock of government debt may stimulate aggregate demand for consumer goods through wealth effects. Portfolio-balance effects remain to be studied.

The Proportion of Public Debt to Real Output and Capital in the Long Run. Branson (1979, pp. 454–5) relates the deficit/income ratio to the debt/income ratio in the following way. Defining the deficit at date t as x,

$$x_t = \delta y_0 e^{\rho t} \quad (5.1)$$

where: δ = the proportion borne by the deficit to income; ρ = the long-run real growth rate; y_o = an initial condition on output.

The cumulant of public debt issue, X_t, is to be evaluated at $t = T$:

$$X_T = \delta y_0 \left| [e^{\rho t}]/\rho \right|_0^T = [\delta y_o/\rho][e^{\rho T} - 1] \quad (5.2)$$

$$X_T/y_T = (\delta/\rho)[1 - (1/e^{\rho T})] \rightarrow \delta/\rho \text{ as } T \rightarrow \infty \quad (5.3)$$

Each value of δ maps into a limiting X/y value; the controlling function monotonically increases. The agents of the economy must be willing to hold portfolios that, in the aggregate, obey this result.

Finally the analysis relates the structure of interest rates to the *technique of production* rather than to the system's secular growth rate.

8.2.1.5 *Effects on Portfolios of Public Finance Policies.* If government securities and equities are perfect substitutes in portfolios, agents will want to hold more capital of both sorts only at a higher interest rate. So an increase in δ leads to lower capital intensity of production; and secularly higher deficits discourage accumulation of real capital.

As for perfect complementarity between public debt and real capital – absorption of additional real public debt into portfolios is contingent upon creation of additional real capital.

The most-interesting case concerns imperfect substitution between public debt and real capital. Then, if portfolio managers are to hold relatively more public debt, the yield of public debt must increase relative to that of real capital.

Neo-classical economists typically evoke the *marginal productivity of capital* at this point – naturally leading to Knight's *all-inclusive capital* concept, enabling the analysis both to be deepened and simplified. So an interpolation, explaining the proper discriminant of 'classical' from 'Keynesian' analysis, becomes imperative.

Interpolation. Keynes's *marginal efficiency of capital* is as subjective as 'classical' marginal productivity is objective. And surely there is a more robust analogy for modern theory in the tulip manias of Chapter 6 than in von Thünen's crop experiments.

The interpolation helps explain why a mess has been made of the theory of interest. At most, Keynes's work makes it possible to trace out today's yield curve. The Keynesian theory of interest is a *bootstrap* theory, keyed to current notions of what is 'normal'. (See Johnson, 1961 – and recall how, in Chapter 3, following Friedman, 1974, we exploited this property of Keynesian interest rate theory to obtain invariance of the real cost of capital against liquid asset base policy.)

The Principal Argument Resumed. For us, the principal property of Knight's theory is its implication of a unique long-run equilibrium own-rate of real capital (see Friedman, 1962). The equilibrium own-rate of real capital – that is, its yield in terms of itself (see Keynes, 1936, chapter 17) – can define unit distance on a scale measuring yields. The public are induced to hold the equilibrium mix of assets by the appropriate set of relative yields – scaled on the 'Knightian invariant'.

Crowding Out in the Knightian World. The Knightian structure is completed by specification of homogeneity of utility functions so that time preference is determined by *ratios* of dated consumptions; and by the *marginal efficiency of investment* (see Lerner, 1952, 1953). As more of the system's resources are devoted to investment, the rate of return over cost declines – this being Knight's proper application of the law of variable proportions. The rest point of Knight's 'expanding universe' is defined in (ρ, r, i) space; and the rate of growth of the real stock of public debt is floated up (down) to the equilibrium real growth rate by a deflation (inflation) process.

8.2.2 Coda to Section 8.2

Harris (1981, p. 438) points out that crowding out for modern monetary theorists is not restricted to 'full employment equilibria'. (see also Carlson and Spencer, 1975; and David and Scadding, 1974). And Harris recognises how simplistic is the often intricately contrived literature: 'The theoretical models of crowding out are . . . simple models whose conclusions follow simply from particular, restrictive assumptions' (Harris, 1981, pp. 339–40).

The crowding-out literature is bogged down in a sticky problem: how should *interest on public debt* be categorised? It is improper to treat resource-absorbing expenditures (e.g. national defence) and transfers as isomorphic, let alone the same thing. The problem is best solved in an admittedly ugly way: set up a supplementary circuit on which a special tax extracts funds used 1 : 1 to pay interest on the debt: transfers are isolated from real expenditures. If the government chooses not to fund transfers fully from dedicated revenues, the effect is to hand out liquid assets just as in the helicopter drops or money rains of the standard literature.

8.3 THE OPTIMAL SUPPLY OF MONEY AND EXTENSIONS

8.3.1 Saving Shoeleather

Two excerpts from Samuelson (1969) display the monetary statics under study; and two remarks by Friedman (1969) capsulate the policy implications of a correct analysis of *the optimal supply of money*. '[T] here is a fallacy of composition in thinking that what seems to cost [more to individuals] costs more to . . . society. Each man is spared the need to do as much after-hours cobbling because now he has lowered the wear on his shoe leather by virtue of less trips when [the real supply of money] increases' (Samuelson, 1969).

So, when the supply of money is optimally large, marginal convenience yields from money balances approach zero. 'With the inflation rate negative . . . we have splashed him with welfare in the form of more leisure from the task of cobbling shoes to replace shoe leather' (Samuelson, 1969).

The total yield on non-interest-bearing money is equated to the marginal productivity of capital; the convenience yield is equated to the marginal cost of production of money; the gap between that (very low) yield and the marginal productivity of capital is filled by the deflation rate.

> A policy fairly close to the optimum would probably be to hold the absolute amount of money constant . . . Given a growth in output at the rate of about 3 to 4 per cent a year, that policy would produce a decline of prices of about 4 to 5 per cent a year . . . This policy [may] correspond to a full optimum in the capital-labour ratio as well as in the quantity of money. (Friedman, 1969, p. 46)

(Hahn, 1982, attacks Friedman's conclusion because Friedman's model is implicit. The attack has merit; and it may cover all policy prescriptions ever offered by economists.)

After recommending that interest be paid on bank deposits, Friedman writes: 'The analysis supports also the desirability of minimizing restriction of entry into banking. Free entry would promote competition and thereby bring the rate of interest paid on deposits closer to the nominal yield on physical capital' (Friedman, 1969, p. 47).

If interest is paid on bank deposits under pure competition, and if non-interest-bearing money (cf. currency) can be neglected, the market automatically will assure that the real quantity of money is optimal.

8.3.2 Extensions: Optimal Monetary/Fiscal Policy

8.3.2.1 *Tobin*, 1965. After mastering the analysis of Tobin (1965), we shall project a number of generalisations.

The analysis is organised around three models. In Model One, properties of the 'real' economy are studied, but no monetary asset is introduced. The following are among the underlying relations:

$$K = v(r)y \qquad (5.1)$$

$$dK = I = v(r)\,dy + y\,dv \qquad (5.2)$$

$$I/y = v(r)[dy/y] + d[v(r)] \qquad (5.3) \quad \text{System 5}$$

$$I/y = i = v(r)x + d[v(r)]; \quad x = dy/y \qquad (5.4)$$

(In Model One, entrepreneurs make a collective decision on $dy/y = x$ along the lines of Harrod's model.)

Model One

$$s(r) = i(r, x) = [v(r)]x + d[v(r)] \tag{5.5}$$

so that, upon recasting equation (5.5),

$$x = [s(r) - d[v(r)]/v(r) \tag{5.6}$$

Differentiating the right-hand side of equation (5.6) with respect to r, the following sign pattern is obtained:

$$[(+) - (-)]/(-) = (-)\text{:}\ \ dx/dr = (-) \tag{5.7}$$

Model Two introduces 'money' and portfolio choice and leads to a theory of optimum liquid asset growth.

Model Two

Preliminary Notes. The yield, q, of the stock of government bonds, B, is a control.

Define the stock of bonds per unit of output (B/y) as b, noting that b may be negative: B_t may be a cumulant of surpluses in the public sector budget so that the government holds *IOUs* from the economy.

Prices are stipulated, until they are 'released' in Model Three.

In full equilibrium, $d[v(r, q)] = 0$.

Operating Model Two

Try: $x = n^*$; $dv(\cdot) = 0$.

$$\left.\begin{aligned} x = n^* &= s(r, q)/v(r, q) && (6.1) \\ b &= b(r, q) && (6.2) \end{aligned}\right\} \text{System 6}$$

Equation (6.2) requires that the actual value of bonds per unit of output be equal to the desired value, determined as by the r.h. side of equation (6.2).

Equation (6.1) can be reduced to a locus of points (r, q) consistent with growth rate n^*. And equation (6.2) reduces to another such locus, one consistent with portfolio balance. The intersection of the loci is an equilibrium point relative to $x = n^*$.

For a given value of b,

$$dB = bdy;\ dB/y = b[dy/y] = bx \tag{6.3}$$

Equation (6.3) describes the proportion borne by the public sector deficit to national output.

Some Theory of Policy

Recalling that r is the rate of return on physical capital and q that on bonds, v^* may be chosen for v; v^* describes the structure of production (capital intensity) required by the Golden Rule, *de rigueur* in the 1960s. And the scheme is readily transformed into an exposition of the theory of policy *à la* Tinbergen. Compare the underdetermined System 7:

$$x = s(r, q)/v(r, q) \quad (7.1)$$

$$b = b(r, q) \quad (7.2)$$

(7.1)–(7.2): System 7

Potentially, the system's unknowns are (x, r, b, q): there are two extra degrees of freedom. If, along the lines of studies in Chapters 10 and 11, values for r and x are mandated by global capital markets and current-account (of the Balance of Payments) considerations, (r, q) is determined. Or, in a closed system, admissible values of r and q may be restricted to combinations for which $v(r, q)$ takes acceptable values – again see the Golden Rule. Or, along Knightian lines, r may be required to conform to a 'classical' mandate that $r = r^*$; in turn mandating the optimal value for q, q^*. Then (b, x) becomes determined.

If x and r are to be determined by the intrinsic rate of population *cum* productivity growth, and if monetary/fiscal policy is to have something to do, we must proceed to System 8.

$$x^* = s(r^*, q, b)/v(r^*, q) \quad (8.1)$$

$$b = b(r^*, q, \alpha) \quad (8.2)$$

(8.1)–(8.2): System 8

First extract q^*, the root of $v(r^*, q) = v^*$. Substitute this value into equation (8.1) and extract the resulting root, b^*. The control, α, must be set at α^* to satisfy equation (8.2); and, since equation (8.2) describes an

LM type relation, α parameterises liquidity properties of public debt; e.g. the maturity structure.

Model Three: Rudiments of a Stability Analysis (see Figure 8.1)

Tobin deploys *Pigou and Wicksell Effects* rather as he does *Fisher and Pigou Effects* in Tobin (1980, chapter 1), glossed in Chapter 9 below.

A deflationary process, increasing real values of *B* and *b*, makes the paper asset more attractive to hold. Tobin (1965) shows that a Pigou process is stabilising: for example, if the ratio of the value of the paper asset to real capital is too low, the Pigou process – engendering persisting capital gain from paper asset holding – enhances its value. The Wicksell effect resists the work done by the Pigou process: 'The Wicksell effect is destabilizing. An accelerated decline in prices . . . encourages a further shift in portfolio demand in the same direction as the original shock' (Tobin, 1965, p. 683).

Annotation of Figure 8.1 (1) Demonstrating operation of the Wicksell process when Pigou effects are neutralised, say by compensating variations in the stock of paper assets.

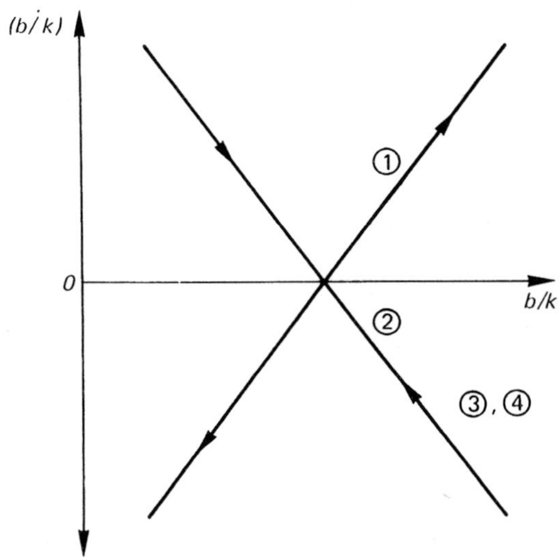

FIGURE 8.1 *Pigou and Wicksell effects*

(2) Demonstrating operation of the Pigou process when the Wicksell process is neutralised.
(3) In the Tobin (1965) model, the stock of paper assets used for debt clearing is demand determined.
(4) The ratio of financial to physical wealth is suggested by $b/v = w$: $(B/y)\,(y/K) = B/K$. B/y = public debt per unit of output; $y/K = 1/v$.

8.3.2.2 *Tobin*, 1980, *Chapter* 3. A pervasive ambiguity leads to Tobin's (1980, p.72) central point: 'In conclusion I express the view that answers to the most important questions . . . are not to be found in appeals to first principles that allegedly support sweeping theorems of equivalence and neutrality.'

We modify Tobin's scheme by eschewing his burnt offering to monetarism in the form of a dedicated money-stuff. The systemic determinant's sign is ambiguous: indeed sweeping theorems are precluded.

Glossary (remaining quite faithful to Tobin's notation)

e = public sector expenditure as a proportion of national income

τ = net transfers to the public sector (so that tax revenue is positive)

ρ = the embedded real growth rate

k = the proportion borne by physical capital to national income

δ, d = the proportions borne by the public sector deficit and public debt to national income

r_k = the before tax real rate of return on physical capital

$f(k)$ = the production function

r_d = the before tax real rate of return on the paper asset (government debt)

The Model

$$(e - t)/(\rho - r_d) = d(r_k, r_d, \tau) \qquad (9.1)$$

$$k = k(r_k, r_d, \tau) \qquad (9.2)$$

$$f'(k) = r_k \qquad (9.3)$$

(9.1)–(9.3): System 9

There are three equations in the unknowns (r_k, r_d, k). Parameters are (e, τ). 'ρ' is like a physical constant.

Equation (9.1) both incorporates public sector budget constraint and requires that supply equal demand for public debt (see Christ, 1968). Equation (9.1) is obtained in the following way. Moving equilibrium requires that δ/d, the growth rate of public debt, equal the embedded real growth rate; i.e. $\delta = \rho d$. Next incorporate budget constraint:

$$e - \tau + r_d d = \rho d:$$

$$(e - \tau) = (\rho - r_d)d:$$

$$(e - \tau)/(\rho - r_d) = d = d(r_k, r_d, \tau)$$

(where $d(\cdot)$ determines demand for public sector debt)

Equation (9.2) requires that demand for physical capital be equal to its supply.

Equation (9.3) requires that the rate of return on real capital equal the marginal productivity of capital.

Differentiating the system around a putative solution point, the determinant of the resulting Jacobian takes the following form:

$$\begin{vmatrix} (-) & (+) & (-) \\ 0 & (-) & (+) \\ (-) & (-) & 0 \end{vmatrix} = (-)(+) + [(+) - (+)] = (?)$$

8.4 THE INVARIANCE, OR NOT, OF REAL EQUILIBRIUM TO THE QUANTITY AND STRUCTURE OF PUBLIC DEBT

First incorporate the discussion of Ricardian Equivalence by Tobin (1980, pp. 49–66); together with that of Barro (1974 and 1984, ch. 15). Next, two remarks: (1) it is unsatisfactory to treat public debt in a closed model as net wealth – see above and Chapter 9, Section 9.2; (2) real equilibria of closed systems generally are *not* invariant against public debt properties. Sections 8.3.1 and 8.3.2 intensify the second remark.

8.4.1 Invariance of Real Equilibrium Against Public Debt Properties: General Discussion

The result of Chapter 2, Section 2.3 – that, if the nominal quantity of more than one asset is arbitrarily determined, real equilibrium cannot be invariant against that choice – was deepened in Chapter 7, Section 7.1: extended monetary analysis establishes that real equilibrium is not invariant against the mass and structure of public debt. Clower and Burstein (1960), as modified by Burstein (1963, p. 781), establish a basis for this conclusion: 'The Clower–Burstein conclusions must be modified for a model in which the total nominal stock of bonds also is fixed in advance. It can be shown that the ratio between the aggregate stock of bonds and the aggregate stock of money appears as an explicit parameter in reduced-form equations.'

In the class of models studied by C–B (1960), if the bond stock is *endogenous*, so that it is geared to the money stock *via* a market-adjustment mechanism, changes in the stock of bonds become directly proportional to changes in money stock; the structure of the analysis indeed is established by the Currency School/Banking School debate – 'Radcliffe' and Gurley and Shaw (1960) being latter day Banking School advocates. (See Patinkin, 1961, and Burstein, 1963, ch. 14.)

8.4.2 Three Examples (see Carmichael, 1982)

Three problems are probed (or nudged). The first, based on Buchanan (1958), concerns 'ants *v.* grasshoppers'. The second studies indirect consumer loans at public sector borrowing costs. The third emanates from Feldstein (1974); and the analysis is applied to a problem dredged up from study of effects of repressed inflation on incentives in the Soviet economy. Carmichael is supported throughout: the *invariance* and *net wealth* issues do not intersect.

1. Ants v. Grasshoppers

Say that a war is financed by bond sales. Wartime ants reduce their consumption expenditures and buy bonds; their heirs' taxes for defrayal of debt service will be financed by their bond income. Wartime grasshoppers sustain their consumption expenditures and do not buy bonds; their children will reap the whirlwind (cf. Hosea 8:7). The capitalised burden of following generation grasshoppers will be equal, and opposite in sign, to the capitalised value of the following generation ant inheritance.

The script can be extended: following generation grasshoppers – for material, if not genetically based, reasons – may support policies reckoned to melt their debt burden.

2. Indirect consumer Loans at Public Sector Borrowing Costs

The *j-th* agent has a mediocre credit rating and wants to finance purchase of a consumer-durable good. The government is borrowing heavily; and, like other fiat issuers in closed economies, *is* creditworthy. Ricardo – Barro logic impels an agent seeking to maintain *status quo ante* to buy securities, thus financing incremental tax obligations for defrayal of debt service. The *j-th* agent will abandon *status quo ante:* she will buy the durable instead of a bond; her subsequent tax burden will be precisely equivalent to the cost of financing at the government's borrowing rate (see Barro, 1984, ch. 15; also Tobin, 1952; and Bailey, 1971).

3(a) 'Social Security, Induced Retirement and Aggregate Capital Accumulation' – cf. Feldstein (1974)

In order to fix ideas, assume that social security entitlements are treated as net wealth. Thus, 'Social insurance . . . is one form of public debt . . . [d]uring working life, citizens build up an immense . . . total of claims on government. Some critics . . . have estimated and deplored the displacement of productive capital investment which they allege this vast accumulation of claims represents' (Tobin, 1980, pp.53–54).

The resulting argument is displayed by equation (10.1) and Figure 8.2. Glossing the structure,

x = private assets
$\dot{x}$ = the rate of increase in net private assets
v = social security entitlement (a parameter)

$$\dot{x} = \phi(x + v) \qquad \partial\phi/\partial v < 0 \qquad (10.1)$$

Direct and indirect strategies can attack the model just displayed. The direct attack is against social security entitlement as net wealth. Stipulate a demographic stationary state: relative sizes of age groups are constant. Then a newborn child who forms his expectations rationally (!) will see that the present value of the cost to him of supporting retirees during his working life is equal to that of his benefits from the system: 'v' becomes irrelevant for socially perceived net wealth.

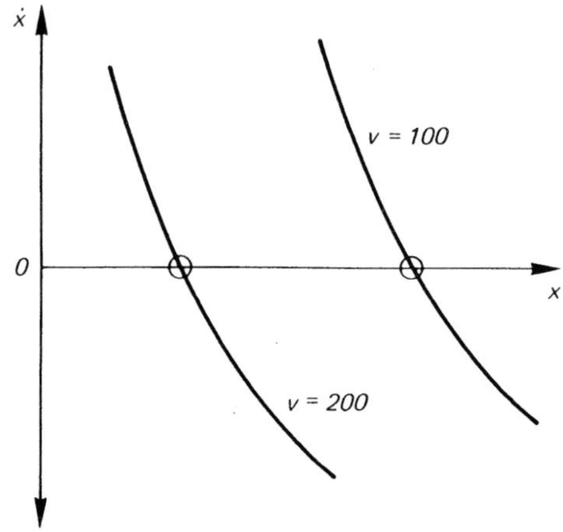

FIGURE 8.2 *Phase diagram for equation (10.1)*

The direct strategy does not assure invariance of real equilibrium against the structure of the old age pension system. Discussion of the second, indirect, strategy will make this clear.

The Indirect Strategy. If the *i-th* agent meekly accepted the intertemporal consumption path implicit in a lavish nationally funded old age pension plan, his consumption expenditures would become 'backloaded'. Life would end, not with a whimper, but a bang.

An agent preferring a more 'frontloaded' consumption path will try to borrow against future entitlements. Then, in a ideally fractionless market economy, retirees repay accumulated debt by diverting part of their pensions to active workers *via* financial intermediaries. Total consumer debt in a stationary economy would be constant.

If the representative agent, upon reaching retirement age, has prespent half the present value of his pension rights, he will devote roughly half his pension receipts over the rest of his life to debt repayment. The repayments will be lent to active workers by the intermediaries, operating a revolving fund.

Assuming that all loans are collateralised by assignment of old age pension rights, the total of loans outstanding in the dynamic system's rest state will be equal to a multiple of the disparity of state suggested post-retirement consumption from the representative desired level of such consumption.

A social contrivance – evoking Samuelson, 1958 – obtaining the above results is the following. At birth (identical) agents assign θ per cent of their old age pension rights to the Institution – thus making up its deposits. The Institution's outlays in the form of consumption loans are always balanced by fresh assignments of pension rights – just as loan repayments coincide with decay of present values of pension rights. From a 'financial' perspective, the old finance the young. The model displays all the principal properties of financial intermediation while lying outside the domain of money.

The Indirect Strategy Continued: Intrusion of Real-World Elements. Results so far obtained are robust only in an ideally frictionless market economy. The following are examples of 'frictions' blocking attainment of the ideal outcome – examples drawn from what Friedman has aptly called 'the infinite world of negation'.

Pension rights cannot in fact easily be assigned: partly because of effects of lenient bankruptcy laws; partly because public policy opposes devices making possible self-destitution that must, in conscience, be offset by the public purse; partly because of uncertainties about the value of the *i-th* bundle – compare actuarial uncertainties about lengths of lives. And 'I today am not I tomorrow': one cannot know what will be one's preferences in future – an argument undermining the logic of intertemporal utility. And the costs of assessing disruptive possibilities, including dishonesty, may bulk so large that required spreads are too wide for 'thick' markets to develop. Finally, transactions costs of recontracting may be prohibitive.

Even a zephyr of realism blows down the house of cards consisting of a proposition that real equilibrium is invariant against what Tobin (1980) calls the public debt aspects of social insurance.

References include Barro, 1974, 1984; Carmichael, 1982; Feldstein, 1974; Nagatani, 1981; Samuelson, 1958 and Tobin, 1980. Nagatani deploys the overlapping generations model of Samuelson (1958) to show that centrally co-ordinated pension plans may be necessary for Pareto superior allocations; compare Nagatani (1981, pp. 194–202).

3(b) An Example from the USSR

Birman (1983) argues that, 'in order to restore the stimulative rôle of earnings, money accumulations by the population must be liquidated'.

Thus, becaused of repressed Soviet inflation, 'total savings are approaching annual wages . . . and almost exceed the level of [Soviet] retail trade'. Nominal incomes substantially exceed the total nominal value of goods that can be purchased: 'in short the people's savings are forced on them'. Why strive to increase earnings when one's liquid assets exceed one year's consumption expenditure and are growing?

A Dynamic Model of Birman's Analysis. The rate of change of liquid asset accumulation($\dot{\zeta}$) is inverse to the energy of the labour force (ε): $\dot{\zeta}$ increases as output falls short of its norm. And the energy of the labour force decreases as liquid asset accumulation (ζ) increases. There results a relation in canonical form:

$$\dot{\zeta} = f(\zeta); \qquad f'(\zeta) > 0 \tag{11.1}$$

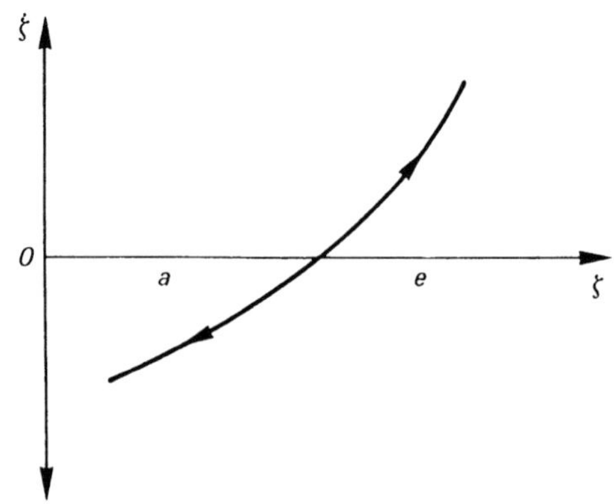

FIGURE 8.3 *Phase diagram for equation (11.1)*

Initially, in Figure 8.3 the system is observed at '*e*'; and things are getting worse. But instability can be exploited: when at '*e*', the system is in a sort of unstable 'low equilibrium growth trap' (see Nelson, 1956; and Branson, 1979, pp. 487–90). And the equivalent to a 'big push' towards a virtuous circle of growth could be a violent shove to '*a*': enough liquid assets would then be wiped out for the energy of the labour force to be intensified enough for real growth to run ahead of liquid asset accumulation.

8.5 CONCLUDING REMARKS

The monetary dimension of fiscal policy is based on residues of financial assets left from public sector borrowing. Similarly, financial intermediary liabilities, central to conventional monetary theory, are residues of lending.

The literature of monetary theory is dualistic. In its classical and neoclassical aspect, it stretches an impermeable membrane between the theory of real economic action and that of the determination of nominal values. In its dynamical aspect, it seeks to discover monetary sources of trends and fluctuations in real economic action. Dennis Robertson, consciously in the path of Thornton, was clear that the importance of 'money' was for fluctuations, not comparative statics; or recall Pigou's *veil of money*. Keynes's *Treatise* is sound on this point; but the *General Theory* oscillates between anti-classical statics and the analysis of fluctuations – and, indeed, short of reinterpretation, emphasizes the former (see Burstein, 1975). Professor Tobin's work picks up the 'anti-classical statics' themes of the *General Theory* – seeking linkage between monetary and real action under *placid* conditions.

Consensus among 'Keynesians' and 'classicals' exists on at least one point: monetary upheavals, or convulsions, affect real economic action, sometimes profoundly.

9 Three Topics in the Monetary Theory of Closed Systems

9.1 PRELIMINARY REMARKS

Two of the three topics have been 'neglected' because of faulty underlying conceptualisation. The third, 'substitution and complementarity, etc.' belongs to the book's core; and should be deepened.

Gallons of ink have been spilled on real balance effects and on inside/outside money. The reader will demand that a claim of 'faulty conceptualisation' be spelled out.

9.2 REAL BALANCE EFFECTS

I argued in Burstein (1968) that the *burden of the money supply* makes more sense than positive real balance effects: why do so many who accept Barro's arguments about public debt insist that heaps of soiled paper should be perceived as collective wealth? Model consistency of microperception is surely violated by such a result. Model consistency *does* require that Agent χ_1 take into account the strategies of Agents $\chi_2, \ldots, \chi_n$ for deployment of their liquid claims. In a crude counterpart to the proper game, χ_1 may find that the 'goods smörgasbord' has been picked clean by the time she is ready to choose from it; she may end up with a fistful of worthless currency.

The Model of Tobin (1980): Pigou and Fisher on Deflation and Debt

Bringing into play Irving Fisher's version of wealth effects of price changes, shared by the Chicago School of the time, Tobin (1980, pp. 10–11) writes:

When nominal prices and wages are deflated, debt service is a higher proportion of debtors' incomes . . . Bankruptcies and defaults . . . transmit the distress of debtors to their creditors . . . Debtor [s] . . . give priority to restoration of financial structure above real investment.

Maybe Leontief is right that sufficient deflation would make existing coins capable of buying the whole GNP. It would also make existing debts an astronomical multiple of the GNP.

We cast Tobin's argument into algebra; and then obtain comparative statics results in the usual way.

System 1 is in *ISLM* form; but income (Y) is fixed at Y^*:

$$\left.\begin{aligned} Y^* &= A + f(p, r) \qquad (1.1) \\ M &= L(p, r; Y^*) \qquad (1.2) \end{aligned}\right\} \text{System 1}$$

System 1 is to be solved for $(\bar{p}, \bar{r}; Y^*)$. Gradients of *IS* and *LM* are obtained by partial differentiation of equations (1.1) and (1.2).

$$0 = f_p dp + f_r dr \qquad (1.3)$$

$$0 = L_p dp + L_r dr \qquad (1.4)$$

Therefore,

$$dr/dp = -f_p/f_r \qquad (IS) \qquad (1.5)$$

$$dr/dp = -L_p/L_r \qquad (LM) \qquad (1.6)$$

System 1

The reduced form of System 1 displays the relationship between the equilibrium price level and autonomous expenditure:

$$\left.\begin{aligned} &\bar{p} = \phi(A) \qquad (1.7) \\ &\partial\bar{p}/\partial A < 0 \quad \text{for } \phi'(A) < 0 \qquad (1.8) \end{aligned}\right\} \text{System 1}$$

Inequality (1.8) exhibits Fisher's case: equilibrium requires that the stimulus supplied by an increase in autonomous expenditure be offset by the *contractive* effect of lower prices. The necessary condition for Inequality (1.8) is:

$$|L_p f_r| < |f_p L_r| \qquad (1.9)$$

That is,

$$|f_p/f_r| > |L_p/L_r| \qquad (1.10)$$

System 1

The slope of IS must exceed that of LM: 'the effect is so great that *IS* is steeper than LM and the comparative statics of monetary and fiscal policy are reversed.' (Tobin, 1980, p. 15.) In particular, as we have seen, expansionary fiscal policy leads to a lower equilibrium price level.

System 2 and Its Explication

$$\left.\begin{aligned} A + f(p, r) &= g(p, w) \qquad (2.1) \\ M &= L(p, r) \qquad (2.2) \end{aligned}\right\} \text{System 2}$$

The wage unit is denoted as w. And $dA = dM = 0$. How does the wage unit affect aggregate demand?

$$\left.\begin{aligned} &(f_p - g_p)dp + f_r dr = g_w dw \qquad (2.3) \\ &L_p dp + L_r dr = 0 \qquad (2.4) \\ &\Delta = (f_p - g_p)L_r - L_p f_r \qquad (2.5) \end{aligned}\right\} \text{System 2}$$

'f_p' is pivotal for the determinant's sign: $f_p > 0$ in the Fisher case; $f_p < 0$ in the Pigou case. And planned output is an increasing function of the price level; and a decreasing function of the wage unit.

Equations (2.6) and (2.7) concern the sign of the determinant:

$$[(+)-(+)][(-)]-(+)(-) = ? \qquad \textit{Fisher case} \qquad (2.6)$$

$$[(-)-(+)][(-)]-(+)(-) = (+) \qquad \textit{Pigou Case} \qquad (2.7)$$

(If f_p is sufficiently positive, the determinant is negative in the Fisher case.)

$$d\bar{p}/dw = g_w L_r/\Delta = (+)/\Delta \qquad (2.8)$$

$$d\bar{r}/dw = -L_p g_w/\Delta = (+)/\Delta \qquad (2.9)$$

In the Pigou case, a reduction in the wage unit leads to lower prices and interest rates. So wage cuts must be expansionary:

$$d[f(\cdot)] = f_p dp + f_r dr = (-)(-)+(-)(-) = (+) \qquad (2.10)$$

In the strong Fisher case,

$$\Delta < 0; d\bar{p}/dw < 0; d\bar{r}/dw < 0$$

How does a wage cut affect aggregate demand? The higher price level supplies stimulus; the higher interest rate will be contractive. If the latter effect, measured by f_r, is powerful enough, wage cuts lead to lower equilibrium output.

A flat IS curve? When an IS-type relation is constructed in (r, p) space, its slope, in the strong Fisher case, must be positive. At 'very high' price levels, the price effect becomes so powerful that it swamps out the influence of the interest rate.

System 3 and its Explication

In System 3, the interest rate is pegged. And, at the level of naïveté of the modelling of Section 9.2, we had just as well assume that there is a 'liquidity trap'; then LM can be jettisoned.

$$A + f(p, r^*) = g(p, w) \tag{3.1}$$

For: $dA = 0$; $r = r^*$

$$d\bar{p}/dw = g_w/(f_p - g_p) \tag{3.2}$$

In the Pigou case,

$$d\bar{p}/dw = (-)/[(-)-(+)] = (-)/(-) = (+) \tag{3.3}$$

In the Fisher case generally

$$d\bar{p}/dw = (-)/[(+)-(+)] = (-)/(?) = (?) \tag{3.4}$$

In the strong Fisher case, f_p is so large that

$$d\bar{p}/dw = (-)/(+) = (-) \tag{3.5}$$

Summarising, in the Pigou case, wage cuts must stimulate aggregate demand. Then,

$$df(\cdot) = f_p dp = (-)(-) = (+) \tag{3.6}$$

And in the strong Fisher case wage cuts also stimulate aggregate demand:

$$df(\cdot) = f_p dp = (+)(+) = (+) \tag{3.7}$$

In general the strong Fisher case wage cuts may depress aggregate demand because higher prices force up interest rates. This channel of influence is blocked off in System 3, a liquidity trap variant of the model – indeed a variant in which the real rate of interest is pegged for *any* reason.

Concluding Remark on Real Balance Effects

The thrust of the Leontief parable, permitting a coin to purchase national output, leads to the possibility of chaos in a monetary economy.

Each agent, able to exercise immense buying power, can wipe the table clean. In the absence of a 'balance of terror', panic buying would be endemic. Hyperinflation may alternate with hyperdeflation.

9.3 INSIDE MONEY AND OUTSIDE MONEY

9.3.1 The Value of the Services of Money and Seigneurage Profit

(See Pesek and Saving, 1967. Also Patinkin, 1969; Johnson, 1969a, 1969b; Gurley and Shaw, 1960; Makinen, 1977, pp. 156–60; and Harris, 1981, pp. 30–42.)

L'affaire Pesek and Saving can be resolved only if the controlling propositions of the theory of value are properly understood.

In the solution of the collective dual problem, the shadow price of (paper) money should be *zero*: destruction of a unit of paper money would not affect the real value of the problem. But, if the *social contrivance*, 'money', were abandoned, the real value of the economy's resources would shrink dramatically.

Since the contribution to social wealth of additional paper money is *nil*, a scenario in which the money industry increases its profits by issuing more money must be analysed by the theory of *distribution* (including *economic rent*); *not* by the theory of production. The régime of property rights assignment will determine the proportion of social benefit imputable to a product that its producers can appropriate. In the theory of money, in contrast, say, to that of knowledge-based products, the mass of benefit is invariant against the seigneurage régime (see Burstein, 1984). The proper problem concerns the optimal level of real monetary services, a quantum not accurately measured by seigneurage profit.

The Spielberg Phenomenon. Analysis of a process that absorbs insignificant real resources (that has insignificant opportunity cost), *and* which generates large additions to real output, makes it easy to see that Pesek and Saving (1967) and Johnson (1969a, b) confuse creation of monopoly rent, or quasi rent, with creation of social wealth. Of course, rents are *charges* against the economy, just as the *j-th* agent's cash holdings are a charge against other agents.

Phantasisers and Physiocrats. The concoctions of Steven Spielberg, the legend of Mohammed Ali, and all the stuff of which dreams are made, contribute to national product just as does the value added by the laundry trade or cultivation of the land. And it is useful to visualise these latter, pseudo-physiocratic producers as comprising an economy trading with the phantasy-makers – rather as the industrial sector traded with the pure service sector in Chapter 6. The bootstrap quality of the 'phantasy trade' doubtless contributes to its glamour: its members create economic value out of the air. In a psychadelic limit, the 'physiocrats' might trade all their tangible product to the phantasy-makers and live on gossamer *délices;* physiocrats would become transmogrified into lotus eaters.

Paper money, including chequeable claims against financial institutions, also creates value 'out of the air'. And it yields seigneurage profit. Nor is it inconceivable that the opportunity to 'issue' more demand deposits increases the net worth of the banking system. We have reached the domain of Pesek and Saving.

9.3.2 The 'Pesek and Saving' Controversy

Makinen (1977, pp. 255–8) writes:

> The grant of monopoly to create bank money means that, when the right is exercised, the bank will acquire an equal value of assets which yield the going rate of interest . . . If one assumes that bank money can be produced at no cost, the bank's net worth is then equal to the capitalized or present value of its interest receipts or income.
>
> The mere possession of the monopoly right increases the net worth of society, for it represents an asset for its owners for which *there is no offsetting liability on any balance sheet in the society* (emphasis supplied).
>
> A decrease in commodity prices will increase the real value of this component of net worth and will be one source of the Pigou Effect.

The argument capsulated by Makinen contains two fallacies. The first concerns the real balance effect in general: at the least, this concept contradicts rational expectations. The second, more germane for the moment, concerns confusion of seigneurage profit, a charge on society, with the value created by the 'money producers'.

The italicised phrase simply is wrong: there *is* a charge on society: the shareholders of the banks have increased the value of their claims on a pool of produce not augmented by issue of additional paper money.

The Pesek–Saving argument leads to the following *reductio ad absurdum*. Say that product X_i, now produced under perfect competition, becomes monopolised. There will be no offsetting liability on any balance sheet: there may appear to be a positive wealth effect; *and* social wealth and welfare will decrease.

9.4 SUBSTITUTION AND COMPLEMENTARITY AMONG FINANCIAL ASSETS

Four examples, in roughly ascending order of difficulty are studied (see Tobin, 1961; Leijonhufvud, 1968; and Tobin, 1982b). In the first there are three assets: zero-yield money; government bonds; equities. After a temporary tax increase, leading to a public sector surplus, government debt retirement causes the stock of bonds to fall. In Example 1a, bonds and equities are substitutes; in Example 1b, complements. In Examples 1a and 1b, money is substitutional with other assets; but in Example 1c, money and equities are complements.

In Example 2, but not in Example 1, the price level is endogenous so that real quantities of bonds and money, as well as equities, are endogenous. In Example 2, a temporary public sector deficit is covered by monetary issue.

Example 3 contains three assets: central bank credit, traded in the equivalent to a federal funds market; government bonds; equities. Once again a fiscal episode is stipulated – thus avoiding a complexity posed by an open-market operation, requiring that an increase in central bank credit be offset by a decrease in government debt.

Examples 2 and 4 imitate each other: in each, the price level is endogenous; and is given for Examples 1 and 3.

Example 1a. The public are to be induced to reduce their bond holdings. This will be accomplished by lower bond rate, together with a higher yield on equities.

System 4 both demonstrates the points just made and establishes a paradigm for the continuing work of Section 9.4.

$$\left.\begin{aligned} f(r,\zeta) &= M \qquad (4.1)\\ g(r,\zeta) &= B \qquad (4.2)\end{aligned}\right\}\text{System 4}$$

Holdings of the three assets are to exhaust a budget constraint (see

Tobin, 1982b, for a discussion of this point). Bond and equity yields are represented by (r, ζ). Differentiation yields:

$$f_r dr + f_\zeta d\zeta = dM \tag{4.3}$$

$$g_r dr + g_\zeta d\zeta = dB \tag{4.4}$$

$$\Delta = \begin{vmatrix} (-) & (-) \\ (+) & (-) \end{vmatrix} = (+) - (-) = (+) \tag{4.5}$$

$$d\bar{r}/dB = \begin{vmatrix} (0) & (-) \\ (1) & (-) \end{vmatrix} /(+) = (+)/(+) = (+) \tag{4.6}$$

$$d\bar{\zeta}/dB = \begin{vmatrix} (-) & (0) \\ (+) & (1) \end{vmatrix} /(+) = (-)/(+) = (-) \tag{4.7}$$

The combined effect of lower bond yield and higher equity yield makes the public content with a smaller stock of government debt. (Alternatively, a reduction in the stock of government debt requires, in equilibrium, lower bond yield and higher equity yield).

Example 1*b*. Where the matrix of equation (4.5) is (ξ_{ij}), ξ_{22} now is positive rather than negative: higher equity yield increases demand for bonds, *ceteris paribus*. Because of the sign switch, the sign of the determinant becomes ambiguous:

$$d\bar{\zeta}/dB = \begin{vmatrix} - & 0 \\ + & 1 \end{vmatrix} /(?) = (-)/(?) \tag{4.8}$$

If ξ_{22} is positive enough, the sign of the determinant becomes negative so that:

$$d\bar{\zeta}/dB = (-)/(-) = (+) \tag{4.9}$$

Assume that $dB > 0$. The public are induced to hold the larger stock both because own yield is higher and the yield on complementary equities is higher.

Example 1*c*. Complementarity of money and equities might be justified along lines taken by Tobin (1958). Assume – *pace* the correct analysis of Chang *et al.* (1983) – that optimal risk management calls for cash to increase with equity positions. Then the fall in bond yield reduces the opportunity cost of holding the cash component of the equity/cash bundle.

Example 2. This example concerns the non-neutrality of changes in the monetary base or the stock of government debt in a monetary/fiscal theory.

If an increase in money supply leads to higher prices, the real stock of government debt will decline. So Example 2 is sucked into the field of Example 1. It follows that:

> The only neutral way to engineer a change in the quantity of money. . . is trivial; it is to decree a scalar change in the monetary unit of account. . . It is trivial and neutral because it applies not just to the currency but to all assets and debts denominated in the unit of account. (Tobin, 1980, p. 32)

Modigliani–Miller theorems of public debt – effectively neutralising it – finesse Tobin's argument. (See Wallace, 1981a; Leijonhufvud, 1968 and Burstein, 1963, pp. 204–10.) And it follows that the theory of money properly is a monetary/fiscal one: 'Radcliffe' and Gurley and Shaw earn a kudos. (See Chick, 1977, chapter 4.)

Example 3. Tobin (1982b) explains that asset models can be open so that total holdings described by the model are not subject to a global budget constraint. This is the path taken by Example 3 – in which the equivalent to federal funds rate is q; H is central bank credit; and $\phi(q, r, \zeta)$ determines excess demand for equities.

$$f(q, r, \zeta) = H \tag{5.1}$$

$$g(q, r, \zeta) = h(r, B) \tag{5.2}$$

$$\phi(q, r, \zeta) = 0 \tag{5.3}$$

It is necessary to introduce a *valuation function* for bonds, i.e. $h(r, B)$: the value of the stock of bonds, discounted at rate r, is endogenous.

Differentiating around an equilibrium point,

$$f_q dq + f_r dr + f_\zeta d\zeta = dH \tag{5.4}$$

$$g_q dq + g_r dr + g_\zeta d\zeta = h_r dr + h_B dB \tag{5.5}$$

$$\phi_q dq + \phi_r dr + \phi_\zeta d\zeta = 0 \tag{5.6}$$

$$\begin{vmatrix} f_q & f_r & f_\zeta \\ g_q & g_r - h_r & g_\zeta \\ \phi_q & \phi_r & \phi_\zeta \end{vmatrix} = \Delta \tag{5.7}$$

Since the sign of the determinant is ambiguous, the effect of an increase in the real monetary base on the cost of capital is ambiguous.

A rather outré script is now written. Potential substitution is neglected – as are off-diagonal elements other than ϕ_q and f_ζ, which are positive. Central bank credit and equities are *complements.*

(The controlling matrix is not symmetrical. In the corresponding consumer problem, if income effects can be neglected, (X_{rs}) is symmetrical by Young's theorem; otherwise not. See Samuelson, 1947, 1983, pp. 141 and 187; also Sokolnikoff, 1939, pp. 87–90.)

Along lines suggesting German practice, the public prefer to hold shares indirectly. Banks obtain resources to buy shares by selling deposits. And, of course, central bank credit is complementary with bank liabilities.

Ambiguity dominates:

$$\begin{vmatrix} + & 0 & + \\ 0 & + & 0 \\ + & 0 & + \end{vmatrix} = (+)-(+) = (?) \tag{5.8}$$

$$d\bar{\zeta}/dH = \begin{vmatrix} + & 0 & + \\ 0 & + & 0 \\ + & 0 & 0 \end{vmatrix} /(?) = (-)/(?) \tag{5.9}$$

Now stipulate that complementarity is so strong that the determinant is surely negative. Then

$$d\bar{\zeta}/dH = (-)/(-) = (+) \tag{5.10}$$

And

$$d\bar{q}/dH = \begin{vmatrix} + & 0 & + \\ 0 & + & 0 \\ 0 & 0 & + \end{vmatrix} /(-) = (+)/(-) = (-) \tag{5.11}$$

An increase in the supply of central bank credit leads to a lower federal funds rate so that the yield of a central bank/equity package falls – as does the demand price for a share. The required return on capital increases.

It can fairly be concluded that – once portfolio analysis is inserted into the model – effects of monetary/fiscal policy on the cost of capital may be impossible to ascertain *a priori.* The reader can work out other permutations.

Example 4. If an increase in central bank credit leads to a higher price level, the real value of the stock of bonds will fall. (For given values of B and r, the nominal value of the stock of bonds is $h(B^*, r^*)$. It follows that, when prices of goods are flexible, insight into the system's behaviour can be gained by operating the model under the assumption that an increase in the quantity of central bank credit is accompanied by a reduction in the stock of bonds – ignoring price level change. And equities and central bank credit are to be unrelated in demand; whilst central bank credit and bonds, as well as bonds and equities, are substitutes. Equation (5.12) displays the structure of the resulting systemic determinant:

$$\Delta = \begin{vmatrix} + & - & 0 \\ - & + & \ominus \\ 0 & \ominus & + \end{vmatrix} \tag{5.12}$$

And,

$$\Delta = (+)[(+)-(+)]-[(-)(-)] = (?)-(+) = (?) \tag{5.13}$$

The encircled elements in equation (5.12) concern substitution between bonds and equities. If such substitution is especially strong, the determinant is negative. Assume this is the case.

Recalling that $dH > 0$ and $dB < 0$,

$$d\bar{q} = \begin{vmatrix} + & - & 0 \\ - & + & - \\ 0 & - & + \end{vmatrix} /(-) = (-)/(-) = (+) \tag{5.14}$$

(The numerator of the second term has the same sign structure as the systemic determinant but is based on a different Jacobian.)

An increase in central bank credit requires that the equivalent to the federal funds rate *increase*. The reader of Chapter 3 will not find this result weird: if portfolio managers are to be induced to hold more of some asset, it must become more attractive to hold!

As for the effect on bond yield,

$$dr = \begin{vmatrix} + & + & 0 \\ - & - & - \\ 0 & 0 & + \end{vmatrix} /(-) = [(+)(-)-(-)(+)]/(-)$$

$$= (-)+(+)/(-) = (?)/(-) \tag{5.15}$$

Nor will the reader of Chapter 3 find *this* result weird. Only relative yields matter in models of this sort; one has to go all the way back to the determinants of the real productivity of capital to 'nail down' the interest rate structure in equilibrium.

The equity yield is better determined, but fundamentally ambiguous:

$$d\zeta = \begin{vmatrix} + & - & + \\ - & + & - \\ 0 & \ominus & 0 \end{vmatrix} /(-) = [(+)(-) - (-)(-)(-)]/(-)$$

$$= [(-)+(+)]/(-) = (?)/(-) \quad (5.16)$$

Attention is called to the circled element. If substitution between bonds and equities is particularly strong (if the demand price for equities is strongly affected by the bond yield):

$$d\zeta = (+)/(-) = (-) \quad (5.17)$$

Equation (5.17) implies that an increase in the monetary base leads to a lower cost of capital. (The monetary base change may be achieved by an open-market operation or a temporary budget deficit accompanied by an increase in the general price level in equilibrium.) In a two-asset model, it is quite acceptable for yields on bonds *and* on central bank credit to increase – the former relatively more – for the public to be induced to hold relatively more bonds.

Part III
The Theory of Money in Open Economies

10 Some Theory of the Open Macroeconomy

10.1 A KEYNESIAN SYSTEM WITHOUT CAPITAL FLOWS

10.1.1 Crowding Out in an Open Keynesian Model

The only adjustment mechanism of the hyper-keynesian scheme that follows is based on expansion and contraction of domestic production; adjustment via terms of trade, for example, is ignored.

Let

$$\begin{aligned} f(y, r) &= \text{private sector demand,} \\ G &= \text{public spending,} \\ X &= \text{exports,} \\ \psi(y) &= \text{imports.} \end{aligned}$$

The Model

$$\left.\begin{aligned} f(y, r) + G^0 + X^0 &= y + \psi(y) && (1.1) \\ L(y, r) &= M && (1.2) \\ X^0 &= \psi(y) && (1.3) \end{aligned}\right\} \text{System 1}$$

Comments on the Model

(1) The right-hand side of equation (1.1) determines aggregate supply.
(2) Equation (1.3) requires that export demand determine the equilibrium level of output so that $d\bar{y}/dX^0 = 1/\psi'(y)$.
(3) A degree of freedom must be surrendered: M is to be endogenous.
(4) The model is to be solved for $[\bar{r}, \bar{y}, \bar{M}]$ relative to $[X^0, G^0]$.

Operating the Model. Multipliers are obtained by differentiation of the system in the neighbourhood of the solution $-d\bar{y}/dG = 0$ (!).

$$\left.\begin{aligned}(1-f_y+\psi_y)dy-f_r dr &= dG^0+dX^0 && (1.4)\\ L_y dy+L_r dr-dM &= 0 && (1.5)\\ \psi_y dy &= dX^0 && (1.6)\\ \Delta &= \psi_y f_r && (1.7)\end{aligned}\right\}\text{System 1}$$

$$\left.\begin{aligned}d\bar{y}/dX^0{}_{dG^0=0} &= f_r/f_r\psi_y = 1/\psi_y && (1.8)\\ d\bar{y}/dG^0{}_{dX=0} &= 0/\Delta = 0(!) && (1.9)\end{aligned}\right\}\text{System 1}$$

Explaining equation (1.9)

$$\left.\begin{aligned}\begin{vmatrix}1 & -f_r & 0\\ 0 & L_r & (-1)\\ 0 & 0 & 0\end{vmatrix} &= 0 && (1.9a)\\ d\bar{r}/dG^0 &= -\psi_y/\psi_y f_r = (-1)/(-) = (+) && (1.10)\end{aligned}\right\}\text{System 1}$$

Conclusions. Since $d\bar{y}/dG^0 = 0$ and $d\bar{r}/dG^0 = (+)$, $d\bar{r}/dG^0 = (-)$. There is *crowding out* in a strictly keynesian economy; and the multiplier is zero. Fiscal policy affects the rate of interest, but not the equilibrium level of output.

10.1.2 A Dynamic Version of a Keynesian System Without Capital Flows

Let

λ = the trend rate of growth of exports,
r = the real rate of interest,
τ = the terms of trade,
$\phi(\tau, r)$ = imports,
X_0 = the initial level of exports,
$X_0/y_0 = x'$ = the initial proportion borne by exports to output,
$i(\cdot)$ = the proportion borne by investment to output,
g = the proportion borne by public spending to output,
$v(r, \omega)$ = the capital/output ratio,
ω = the real wage rate,
Ω = the rate of taxation,

$c(r, \Omega)$ = the proportion borne by consumption of domestic goods to output.

(Relevant functions are homogeneous: scale does not affect the above ratios.)

System D is driven by export growth, in turn based on the rate of growth of the global economy. The only important difference between Systems D and 1 is that, in the former, the trade-off is between public spending and consumption, not investment: the proportion of output devoted to capital formation is subordinated to the overall growth rate required by export performance.

System D

$$X_0 e^{\lambda t} = \phi(\tau, r) \quad \text{(D.1)}$$

$$\lambda = i(r)/v(r, \omega) \quad \text{(D.2)}$$

or

$$i(r) = \lambda v(r, \omega) \quad \text{(D.2a)}$$

(Equations D.1, D.2 and D.2a: System D)

If $\omega = \omega^*$, equations (D.1) and (D.2) comprise an independent recursive system. Equation (D.2) determines $\bar{r}$. Upon plugging $r = \bar{r}$ into equation (D.1), $\bar{\tau}$ is determined.

Aggregate demand for goods must equal aggregate supply:

$$1 = x' + i(\bar{r}) + g + c(\bar{r}, \Omega) \quad \text{(D.3)}$$

Taking g to be policy determined:

(1) $\bar{\Omega}$ becomes determined;
(2) there is a 1:1 trade-off between consumption and public spending. The tax rate increases with public spending:

$$dg = [\partial c/\partial \Omega]\, d\Omega\text{: } d\Omega/dg = (-)[1/(-)] = (+)$$

If the interest rate obeys a global norm, so that $r = r^*$, a degree of freedom must be regained: let the real wage rate conform to λ. Since $\partial v/\partial \omega > 0$, $\partial \omega/\partial \lambda < 0$.

By way of three final observations: (1) λ is analagous to Harrod's *natural rate of growth* (see Allen, 1967, chapter 11)–but the natural rate of growth, determined in a closed economy by the growth rate of the labour force and its productivity, will not bind an open economy (in which, of course, inward and outward migration make the rate of growth of the labour force endogenous); (2) the tax rate, Ω, is the critical fiscal policy variable, validating decisions taken on public spending; (3) monetary policy plays no rôle.

10.2 MACROSYSTEMS WITH CAPITAL FLOWS

10.2.1 A Small Open Economy

(Settlement of current account deficits by transfer of official reserves is not considered.)

The level of employment is determined by the condition that the marginal productivity of labour equals its marginal disutility; the real wage equals labour's marginal physical product. Fiscal policy determines allocation of output between private and public ends. The law of one price determines prices of goods; and interest rates are determined in world markets so that $i = i(r^*)$. Real holdings of foreign and domestic monetary, and other assets are determined by asset preferences: monetary policy affects nothing real.

Traded and Non-Traded Goods. If prices of non-traded goods are sticky and price adjustment is incomplete, monetary changes affect real activity. Thus, in the early stages of a monetary expansion, the exchange rate may fall more than domestic prices rise so that real wages fall: demand for labour may increase.

In general, perfectly elastic demand for exports assures that *sans* price stickiness there cannot be involuntary unemployment – so long as workers accept the real wage necessary to induce exporters to offer enough jobs.

10.2.2 A Larger Economy: *sans* a Full Employment Stipulation

The Model

$$\left.\begin{aligned} f[y, r, G, x(\tau, y)] - j(\tau, y) &= y \qquad (2.1) \\ j(\tau, y) - x(\tau, y) &= \Phi(\tau, r, y) \qquad (2.2) \end{aligned}\right\} \text{System 2}$$

Unknowns: (y, τ)
Parameter: G
Constant: r

Solve for $(\bar{y}, \bar{\tau})$ relative to (G^*, r^*)

Comments on the Model

(i) The variables are defined in real terms. Thus $\Phi(\cdot)$ defines real capital inflow.

(ii) The economy is a price-taker in capital, but not in goods, markets.
(iii) Once demand for money is stipulated, an appropriate quantity of unborrowed reserves (for example) must be supplied.
(iv) If a decrease in 'tau' is accompanied by widespread belief that it will rebound towards its original level, 'our' interest rate can fall: repatriated funds will appreciate in the measures of their origin.

Comparative Statics

$$\left.\begin{aligned}(1-f_y-f_x x_y+j_y)dy-(f_x x_\tau-j_\tau)d\tau &= f_r dr+f_G dG \quad (2.3)\\ (\phi_y+x_y-j_y)dy+(x_\tau-j_\tau+\phi_\tau)d\tau &= -\phi_r dr \qquad (2.4)\end{aligned}\right\}\text{System 2}$$

The Jacobian matrix is of the form

$$\begin{bmatrix} + & + \\ - & [(-)+\phi_\tau] \end{bmatrix}$$

If ϕ_τ is neglected, the determinant's sign is ambiguous: $(-)-(-) = (?)$. If expectations are elastic enough, so that ϕ_τ is positive enough, the determinant is positive. Say that ϕ_τ is large enough for the term to which it belongs to be positive. Then $d\bar{y}/dG$ and $d\bar{\tau}/dG$ are positive: incremental capital inflow will be accompanied by deterioration of the current account; domestic savings will increase by less than public expenditure. If expectations are inelastic enough: $d\bar{y}/dG = (+)$; $d\bar{\tau}/dG = (-)$. An increase in government spending may be accompanied by an improvement in the current account (always assuming that demand for exports is price elastic), and so by increased capital *outflow*: income will then increase enough to generate incremental savings in excess of the increase in public spending. (The statement is conditional because the income effect on the current account may exceed the terms-of-trade effect even if the determinant is negative.)

Another response to elastic expectations is issue of *foreign-denominated bonds*: issuers expect to repay by selling 'local currency' for foreign currencies on maturity. In fact $\phi(\cdot)$ determines *ex ante* the excess of tenders of foreign 'currency' for our promises to pay later in our 'currency' *and* in 'foreign currency' and *vice versa.* (A subset of relevant assets/liabilities may be called *money.*)

Speculation; Bubbles. If expectations are regressive, an increase in the foreign exchange value of the *j*-dollar leads to fear of capital loss–deterring capital inflow. And *j*-dollar appreciation stimulates capital inflow if expectations are elastic. Elastic expectations can lead to *bubbles*. Bubbles lead their own lives; and their deaths are not foreseeable. Bubbles thrive on 'greater fool' theories: the fact that an asset is overpriced may make it *more* attractive. And, if expectations are elastic, an increase in the *j-th* public sector borrowing requirement, leading (in one channel of analysis) to appreciation of the *j*-dollar, may incite a bubble in the *j*-dollar market.

Section 10.4 explains how, in the upshot, bubbles aside, floating exchange rates may 'exhibit the fluctuations typical of stock prices rather than goods prices' (Branson, 1983, p. 61, citing Frenkel, 1981; see also Dornbusch, 1983, especially p. 20).

Rational Expectations. Are the expectations formed in System 2 model consistent? The murky answer makes a point: since static models cannot generate forecasts, there is no way to check expectations against model performance. In general, rational expectations logic is violated: expectations hardly can be consistent with forecasts that cannot be extracted from the model!

True, the case where $\partial\phi/\partial\tau = 0$ finds System 2 obedient to rational expectations: if a shift in data leads to a permanent change in the exchange rate, '$\partial\phi/\partial\tau = 0$' correctly implies that the market all along expected this to happen.

10.2.3 A Larger Economy: with a Full Employment Stipulation

System 2 must be rearranged. Differentiation around an equilibrium point of the resulting System 3 leads to:

$$\left.\begin{aligned}
&f_r\,dr + [f_x x_\tau - j_\tau]\,d\tau = (1 - f_y - f_x x_y + j_y)\,dy - f_G\,dG && (3.1)\\
&\phi_r\,dr + [x_\tau - j_\tau + \phi_\tau)]\,d\tau = (-\phi_y + j_y - x_y)\,dy && (3.2)\\
&\Delta = (-)\,[(-) - (+) + (\phi_\tau)] - [(+)\,(-)] && (3.3)\\
&\Delta = (+) \text{ if } \phi_\tau < \beta, \text{ a positive number} && (3.4)\\
&\Delta = (-) \text{ if } \phi_\tau > \beta && (3.5)
\end{aligned}\right\}\text{System 3}$$

Take $\phi_\tau < \beta$: $\Delta = (+)$: $d\bar{r}/dG = (+)$; $d\bar{\tau}/dG = (+)$. An increased public sector borrowing requirement leads to higher interest rates and foreign-exchange appreciation. (Of course, $\phi_\tau = 0$ belongs to this case.)

Take $\phi_\tau > \beta$: $\Delta = (-)$: $d\bar{r}/dG = (+)$; $d\bar{\tau}/dG = (-)$. An increased public sector borrowing requirement leads to higher interest rates and foreign-exchange *depreciation.* And, since the current account will be more favourable, there will be net capital *outflow.* The crowding-out effect of an increase in public spending will be twofold: room must be found for increased exports as well as increased public spending. The upshot contradicts widespread belief that the large American federal budget deficits *circa* 1981–4 were responsible for appreciation of the dollar *and* that foreign-exchange rate expectations are highly elastic. The model implies either that these expectations are not that elastic or that the marked rise in the dollar primarily resulted from shifts in asset preferences – as was claimed by Treasury Secretary Donald Regan. Indeed, if elastic expectations are assumed, the model implies that federal deficits have braked the rise of the dollar caused by asset-preference shifts – and indeed the massive increase in the supply of US Government securities must have done so to some extent (see Chapter 11).

As for interest rates, for $dG = (+)$, interest rates must rise enough for domestic expenditure to contract enough for increased public spending *and* exports to be accommodated. Capital-market effects of higher public sector borrowing requirements are the greater.

The scheme violates *Rational Expectations.* No mechanism assures that the expectation that terms of trade will continue to improve, or deteriorate, is correct. The model lacks proper dynamics – a fault often papered over with 'impact effect' cover.

A Dynamical Model Flowing from Sections 10.2.2 *and* 10.2.3

$$\dot{\eta} = \phi(\eta, \rho) \tag{1}$$

$$\dot{\rho} = \psi(\eta, \rho) \tag{2}$$

The foreign exchange rate is denoted η; the growth rate of the real economy, ρ. And four comments are called for. (1) $\partial\phi/\partial\rho < 0$: the higher the growth rate, the greater the excess supply of the economy's currency. (2) $\partial\phi/\partial\eta < 0$: the higher the foreign exchange rate, the greater the excess supply of the economy's currency – under inertial expectations. (3) $\partial\psi/\partial\rho = (?)$: the accelerator can play dirty. (4) $\partial\psi/\partial\eta < 0$: growth is deterred by an overvalued currency.

Procedure. Set the left-hand sides of equations (1) and (2) equal to zero – going on to solve for the rest point. And redefine the unknowns so that $z = \eta - \bar{\eta}$ and $q = \rho - \bar{\rho}$.

$$\dot{z} = f(z, q) \qquad 0 = f(0, 0)$$
$$\dot{q} = g(z, q) \qquad 0 = g(0, 0)$$

Stability depends on the properties of the Jacobian's determinant:

$$\begin{vmatrix} f_z & f_q \\ g_z & g_q \end{vmatrix}$$

10.2.4 Introduction of an Interest Parity Principle *cum* Speculation

If a German contemplates transferring funds to New York, he most likely will reckon the results on a Deutschmark scale. Interest rate differentials *and* expected changes in foreign exchange rates will count. If transfers are *covered*, the upshot can be more or less certain – US dollars would be sold forward and DM bought forward simultaneously with spot sales of DM and purchases of dollars.

(System 5, but not System 4, conforms to Rational Expectations.)

System 4: A Full Employment System (more strictly, 'the level of employment is given').

$$\left.\begin{aligned} r - r^* &= \zeta && (4.1) \\ \zeta &= \psi(\lambda) && (4.2) \\ f(r, y^*) + x(\lambda, \zeta) - j(\lambda, \zeta) + G &= y^* && (4.3) \end{aligned}\right\} \text{System 4}$$

The currency's *forward discount* is ζ; and its spot rate, λ. And $\psi(\lambda)$ concerns expectations of future spot rates. (To repeat, here expectations are not 'rational'.)

Solve for $(\bar{r}, \bar{\lambda}, \bar{\zeta})$ relative to $G = G^*$. Differentiating around the solution point:

$$\left.\begin{aligned} dr \qquad - d\zeta &= 0 && (4.4) \\ \psi'(\lambda)\, d\lambda \qquad - d\zeta &= 0 && (4.5) \\ (j_\lambda - x_\lambda)\, d\lambda - f_r\, dr + (j_\zeta - x_\zeta)\, d\zeta &= dG - (1 - f_y)\, dy^* && (4.6) \end{aligned}\right\} \text{System 4}$$

The signs of the Jacobian matrix are:

$$\begin{pmatrix} 0 & (+) & (-) \\ (+) & 0 & (-) \\ (+) & (+) & (-) \end{pmatrix}$$

The $x_{3,3}$ element is to be negative: expectations are to be inertial (inelastic).

Explaining how terms like $d\bar{\lambda}/dG$ are obtained, the determinant, Δ, is obtained, qualitatively, as follows: $(-)(+)[(-)-(-)]+(-)=(?)$. The determinant is negative if $|j_\zeta - x_\zeta| > |f_r|$. In a smallish, very open economy, $\partial x/\partial\zeta$ is apt to be large so that the determinant is negative.

$$d\bar{\lambda}/dG = \begin{vmatrix} 0 & + & - \\ 0 & 0 & - \\ + & + & - \end{vmatrix} /(-) = (-)/(-) = +$$

$$d\bar{r}/dG = \begin{vmatrix} 0 & 0 & - \\ + & 0 & - \\ + & + & - \end{vmatrix} /(-) = (-)(+)/(-) = (+)$$

$$d\bar{\zeta}/dG = \begin{vmatrix} 0 & + & 0 \\ + & 0 & 0 \\ + & + & + \end{vmatrix} /(-) = (-)(+)(+)/(-) = (+)$$

The rate of interest, the exchange rate and the discount on the exchange rate all increase for $d(G) = (+)$.

Bridge Passage to System 5. Equations (4.2) and (4.5) imply highly inertial expectations. But for a persistent discount on the j-dollar to conform to optimal forecasting and, indeed, a market capable of learning from experience, some force must persistently exert itself against the j-dollar. Perhaps the *j-th* economy is to have faster money growth than the rest of the world.

Recalling the remarks introducing Section 10.2.4, the German investor is properly concerned with the DM effects of a decision to transfer funds to New York and then repatriate them to Frankfurt; not with purchasing-power parity.

System 5: Obeying Rational Expectations

Preliminary Comments

(1) It follows from equations (5.1) and (5.2) that the real rate of interest, $\hat{r}$, is determined by global conditions.

(2) Equation (5.3), fully explained in Section 10.3, concerns long-run equilibrium relations between foreign-held debt, real growth and the current account of the balance of payments.

Let

λ = the foreign exchange rate, here equivalent to terms of trade,
z = the proportion borne by foreign debt to GNP or GDP (y),
ρ = the economy's secular real rate of growth,
ξ = the proportion borne by capital inflow to y,
x, j = the proportions borne by exports and imports to y,
ζ = the forward discount on the economy's currency,
π, π^* = the economy's inflation rate; that of the rest of the world,
v = the capital/output ratio,
r, r^* = nominal interest rates 'here' and 'abroad',
$\hat{r}$ = the real rate of interest.

Remark. The system's simplistic technology leads to: $i/v = \rho$

$$r - r^* = \zeta \quad (5.1)$$
$$\zeta = \pi - \pi^* \quad (5.2)$$
$$\hat{r} + [j(\lambda, \rho) - x(\lambda)]/z = \rho \quad (5.3)$$
$$\rho = [s(\hat{r}) - g + [j() - x()] - rz]/v \quad (5.4)$$

(5.1)–(5.4): System 5

System 5 determines $(\bar{r}, \bar{\zeta}, \bar{\rho}, \bar{\lambda})$, relative to $(g^*, z^*, v, \hat{r}, \pi^*)$ in ways about to be explained. ($g = G/y$.)

(1) The system is dichotomised: real variables are determined by real forces; nominal ones by 'nominal' forces.
(2) Equations (5.3) and (5.4) determine $(\bar{\rho}, \bar{\lambda})$ relative to $(g^*, z^*, v, \hat{r})$. Equations (5.1) and (5.2) comprise a subset that can be solved recursively. Since the inflation rate is treated instrumentally, the forward discount pops out of equation (5.2) – permitting equation (5.1) to be solved for $\bar{r}$. And it is worth repeating that Rational Expectations, requiring fulfillment of equation (5.2), impose the globally determined real rate of interest, $\hat{r}$, on the $j-th$ economy.
(3) Satisfaction of equation (5.2) assures that the forward discount necessary for interest parity is consistent with correct forecasting.
(4) Equations (5.3) and (5.4) are based on the 'foreign balance' equilibrium condition: *capital inflow equals the current-account deficit.* So the amount of finance available for private sector capital formation is: *net internally supplied finance (s-g) plus net capital inflow* $[j - x - debt\ service = j - x - \hat{r}z]$. And $\rho = i/v$. See equation (5.4) . . . Equation (5.3) is the subject of Section 10.3.

(5) Demand for our real debt by the rest of the world is described by the *point* $(\hat{r}, z^*)$.
(6) The proof that the real growth rate (ρ) in long-run equilibrium is a decreasing function of the proportion of output absorbed by the tacitly unproductive public sector runs along the following lines.

Finance available for capital formation must equal i and is equal to $s-g+j-x-\hat{r}z^*$.

It is established in Section 10.3 that in long-run equilibrium: $j-x=(\rho-\hat{r})z^*$.

Therefore: $i=s-g+\rho z^*$. And, under the simplistic technology: $\rho=i/v$. So: $i=[v/(v-z^*)]\,[s-g]$: $di/dg = -v(v-z^*)$.

The capital/output ratio (v) must exceed the foreign debt/output ratio (z^*) if we are not to be bankrupt: i.e. foreign debt must not exceed total capital. Any degree of net equity assures that: $v>z^*$. *Ergo*, $di/dg<0$ *in long-run equilibrium!*

10.3 RELATIONSHIPS IN LONG-RUN EQUILIBRIUM BETWEEN FOREIGN-HELD DEBT, REAL GROWTH, THE CURRENT ACCOUNT, ETC.: THE 'BRAZIL' PROBLEM

In a properly specified long-run equilibrium, the ratio of real foreign debt to other real magnitudes is constant: foreign debt grows at the balanced growth rate, ρ.

Let

z = the proportion borne by foreign debt to y,
r = the rate of interest,
ρ = the long-run growth rate of the economy,
ξ = the proportion borne by capital inflow to y.

System 6: where equation (6.1) is the *fundamental relationship*

$$r+\xi/z=\rho \tag{6.1}$$

$$(\rho-r)z=\xi \tag{6.2}$$

$$rz=-\xi=x-j \qquad (\text{for } \rho=0) \tag{6.3}$$

(1) The left-hand side of equation (6.1) measures the rate of growth of

the stock of foreign-held debt. (Capital inflow measures the increase in principal.)

(2) Equation (6.3) shows that, for $\rho = 0$, the export surplus must equal annual interest cost.

(3) If the interest rate exceeds the growth rate, there must be an export surplus. The following example strengthens this result. Try: $z = 0.8$; r = 0.12; $\rho = 0.2$. Debt service charges are 9.6 per cent of y; and principal is permitted to growth at 2 per cent per annum. So a current account surplus equal to 7.6 per cent of y is consistent with long-run equilibrium.

(4) For $\rho > r$, and $z > 0$, long-run equilibrium requires a current-account deficit.

(5) For $z < 0$, the current account is in deficit in long-run equilibrium – cf. Britain c. 1910.

Brazil

The collapse, *c.* 1982–4, of the international credit of Argentina, Mexico and Brazil, *inter alios*, has been a major economic, and geopolitical, event – partly because of over-exposure of international banks.

For some years, Brazil easily financed current account deficits incident to rapid real growth. Then a series of shocks, including the huge increases in the oil-price in 1973–4 and 1979, hit the Brazilian economy. Real rates of interest soared, causing debt service costs to reach unprecedented levels. The global forces besetting Brazil led to global recession: demand fell for Brazilian exports, partly because labour union and manufacturer pressure caused such Brazilian exports as steel to be restricted or barred in various markets. The upshot is illustrated by another arithmetic manipulation of equations (6.1) and (6.2):

> In phase one: $r = 0.03$; $\rho = 0.08$. The economy can meet interest cost by incurring fresh indebtedness; and it can increase principal by 5 per cent per annum. In phase two: $r = 0.12$; $\rho = 0.02$. Secular equilibrium requires an annual current-account surplus equal to 10 per cent of output; and in phase one was consistent with a current-account deficit equal to 5 per cent of output.

'Brazil' and the Transfer Problem

(See Johnson, 1958; Keynes, 1949-reprint; Ohlin, 1949-reprint;

Samuelson, 1952; Machlup, 1950; and Haberler, 1937 – summarised by Burstein, 1963, pp. 828–32, 837 and 839–40.)

Analysis of the *j-th* economy's foreign debt can be plugged into that of Reparations and the Transfer Problem. It is immaterial here whether the debt principal has been incurred voluntarily or not. As for the transfer problem:

> Why should there be a transfer problem? Acceptable changes in the terms of trade may not be able to achieve the necessary favourable current-account balance. Of course, the *j-th* country may be able to attract capital inflow. Indeed there were Allied loans to Germany during the 1920s. But to meet debt-service needs by borrowing more is to risk the wrath of God. . .
>
> Only one avenue may remain: development of a favourable current account through 'income effects.' If Country *j* were to contract its growth rate, while Country *k* grew relatively faster, and if marginal propensities to consume were high enough and foreign trade important enough, the addition to *j*'s crown of thorns (*k*'s laurels) might make possible a large-enough surplus in *j*'s current account to effect the transfer. (Burstein, 1963, pp. 826–9)
>
> If *j* turns itself into a wasteland and while *k* becomes a land of sybarites, fond of the delicacies concocted by *j*'s groaning masses, *j* can achieve as 'favourable' (!) a current account as may be called for. (Ibid., p. 829)

Afterword to Section 10.3

The *j-th* external finance requirement can be covered by sale of *i*-dollar denominated securities. Indeed that is what Brazil *et al.* did. The feasibility condition of Section 10.3 is indifferent to borrowings denominated in foreign measures instead of *j*-dollars. But effects on the exchange rates of the *j*-dollar *do* depend on whether bonds are sold *j*-dollar or *i*-dollar consideration. In the latter case, capital inflow does not depend on increased demand for *j*-dollars. But, following convention, we stipulate in Section 10.2 that the *j-th* external finance requirement is covered by sale of securities for *j*-dollar-denominated consideration (see Chapter 11, Sections 11.3 and 11.4).

10.4 INTERACTION OF OPEN ECONOMIES UNDER FLEXIBLE EXCHANGE RATES DETERMINED IN CAPITAL MARKETS

10.4.1 A Closed Economy Analogue: Leijonhufvud (1981)'s Wicksell Connection (see Chapter 6, Section 3)

Leijonhufvud (1981) points out that the model of Keynes's *Treatise* breaks down because it lacks a theory of output. Indeed, Keynes (1936) stresses this fact – and the *General Theory* does contain a theory of output.

The transition from the *Treatise* to the *General Theory* encompasses a transformation of Keynes's view of the *natural rate of interest*: hence Leijonhufvud's felicitous term, *The Wicksell Connection.*

> I am no longer of the opinion that the concept of a 'natural rate' of interest. . . has anything very useful or significant to contribute to our analysis. It is merely the rate of interest which will preserve the *status quo*. (Keynes, 1936, p. 243)

Leijonhufvud comments:

> The [Keynesian] sequence goes as follows. Assume an initial equilibrium. Some event reduces the marginal efficiency of capital. At impact, saving now exceeds *intended* investment at the initial levels of interest and income. This saving-investment gap, it is maintained, can have *no effect* on the rate of interest. [It] has to be closed altogether through income adjustment. (Leijonhufvud, 1981, p. 174)

For Leijonhufvud's *event*, read, 'events in the stock market (the gambling parlour of Chapter 12 of the *General Theory*) lead to an increase in the cost of capital'. Retain Leijonhufvud's analysis while moving the shock from the real sector to the bourse. The rate of interest generated by the bourse is transformed into a natural rate of interest by an appropriate decrease in output. The point to be carried out of Section 10.4.1 concerns ways in which real markets may respond, more or less passively, to changes in data generated by financial markets.

Reflecting further on the Wicksell Connection, recall from Chapters 3, 8 and 9 that a purely financial analysis of a system in which all nominal yields are freely competitively determined can determine no more than a set of *relative* yields, dual to a set of equilibrium portfolios. Productivity and thrift must determine absolute real rates of interest (see Epstein and Hynes, 1983).

10.4.2 Transition to the Open Economy Problem

The 'open' equivalent to the neurasthenic bourse of the *General Theory* is a quasi-exogenous process determining real rates of interest and foreign exchange rates in the *j-th* economy. To the extent that foreign exchange rate fluctuation is heavily influenced by fluctuation of supply and demand for assets in international financial markets, an economy operating under a floating-rate régime may behave like one whose wages and prices are not fully adapted to levels necessary for the equilibrium of a fixed-rate régime – unless its wages and prices are perfectly flexible. In other words, successful adaptation of open economies to asset-market events requires adequate wage–price flexibility. This upshot, so alien to orthodox paradigms for floating-rate régimes, and contradicting their *raison d'être*, is the most salient feature of the post-Bretton Woods world economy.

10.4.3 Proper Open Economy Problems

10.4.3.1 *A Very Simple Scheme in which Foreign Exchange Rates are Strictly Determined in Asset Markets.* The analogy to the Wicksell Connection is robust: foreign exchange rates are to be determined in asset markets so that prices of goods and services must adjust to exchange-rate fluctuations; and, since 'real trade' events are not to affect exchange rates, the system behaves like a classical fixed-rate system.

If prices were perfectly flexible, exchange-rate movements would not have real effects: domestic prices would float up and down, countering the motion of the exchange rate. But inertial prices, quoted in domestic units of account and influenced by embedded contracts, inelastic expectations, etc., make it inevitable that financial events affect real markets.

A Simple Sequence. The growth rate of the stock of *j*-dollars accelerates: the *j*-dollar depreciates – stimulating *J*'s exports and discouraging its imports. In time though, *J* prices will accelerate; and, as is explained in Section 10.5.4, the process may look like 'cost push'. In the upshot, workers may play 'catch up' so that the price level 'overshoots' in the train of 'wage inflation'. The *j-th* economy's pseudo-boom may give way to a pseudo-slump.

The sequence illustrates *stagflation.* Prices will continue to accelerate well into the slump; and an important contributor to an open economy's recovery from a slump is moderation of its inflation rate – stimulating exports and import substitution, surely if foreign exchange rates are autonomously determined in asset markets. Indeed, deceleration of prices likely will continue well into the recovery (see Hamada and Sakurai, 1978).

10.4.3.2 *A More Realistic Open Model.* It remains to incorporate feedback from the real economy into the exchange-rate formation process.

$$\left.\begin{aligned} \dot{\xi} &= \phi(\xi, q; \alpha) \qquad (7.1) \\ \dot{q} &= \psi(\xi, q; m) \qquad (7.2) \end{aligned}\right\} \text{System 7}$$

Let

α = the shift parameter for the foreign exchange market,
m = the rate of money growth, (α and m are fixed for the analysis),
ξ = the deviation of the foreign exchange rate from its equilibrium value,
q = the deviation of the inflation rate from its equilibrium value.

The origin for System 7 is the solution of

$$\left.\begin{aligned} \Phi(\xi', \pi; \alpha) &= 0 \qquad (7a.1) \\ \Psi(\xi', \pi; m) &= 0 \qquad (7a.2) \end{aligned}\right\} \text{System 7}$$

ξ' and π – the foreign exchange rate and the inflation rate – are measured relative to (0, 0); the origin for System 7 is $(\xi', \bar{\pi})$, the solution of System 7a. And $(\bar{\xi}', \bar{\pi})$ is to be a rest point for System 7–stability being studied in the usual way.

10.5 COMMUNICATION OF BUSINESS (TRADE) CYCLES BETWEEN ECONOMIES; STAGFLATION; ETC.

10.5.1 Introductory Comments: A Simple Model of Stagflation

The material of Sections 10.4 and 10.5 is in a way analytically trivial. Simply by tinkering with phases and frequencies of underlying generation functions, along with lag/delay structures, the implausible becomes plausible. Consider an example supplied by Mundell (1968), succinctly summarised by Swoboda (1983, pp. 94–5):

> a fiscal boom is transmitted abroad, whereas a monetary expansion at home increases income there but reduces it abroad. The reason is that a fiscal expansion that raises the domestic interest rate creates a capital inflow, a depreciation of the foreign currency, and an increase in net foreign exports. In contrast, a domestic monetary expansion induces a depreciation of the domestic currency, a capital outflow, and an increase in domestic net exports, the counterpart to which is a fall in foreign exports and output.

A Simple Model of Communication of Stagflation (See also Hamada and Sakurai, 1978.) A shift in, or disturbance to, asset preferences in world capital markets leads to depreciation of the *A*-dollar. Just as in Mundell's model, *A*-dollar depreciation stimulates economy *A* and depresses *B* in a two-economy world, especially if wages are sticky.

In time, inflation in *A* will erode the terms-of-trade advantage for its exports provoked by the initial shift or shock – perhaps pushing *A* into recession. And, by then, *B* may be experiencing lower inflation because of its recent recession.

For reasons embedded in the controlling lag structure, high inflation typically may be associated with recession and low inflation with boom conditions. The underlying theory is like that of expectations-augmented Phillips curves.

B may be stimulated by orders placed during *A*'s boom – and filled during the *A* recession. *B* prices may not accelerate until its boom is well along. Indeed *B* prices may accelerate only towards the end of *B*'s boom – and then continue to accelerate well into the ensuing recession (see Okun, 1981 and Eckstein, 1981). Thus, costs of production tend to fall during early stages of recoveries as physical capital and 'tenured' labour are better utilised; and unit costs increase well into recessions, as utilisation rates of capital and tenured labour fall. So Economies *A* and *B* may have identical growth and inflation norms; and cycles that are in counterphase. More complex possibilities, including *resonance*, are studied later in this section.

Finally, if the systems' motions are induced by vibrations of oscillators in continuous action, resulting data probably demand spectral analysis (see Yavorksy and Pinsky, 1975, vol. 2, chapter 49; and D'Abro, 1951, vol. 2, pp. 815–7).

10.5.2 Fixed and Flexible Exchange Rates and Transmission of Real Economic Fluctuations

'The fundamental argument for flexible exchange rates is that they would allow countries autonomy with respect to their use of monetary, fiscal and other policy instruments' (Johnson, 1973).

(For ways in which asset market events may disrupt the 'fundamental argument', see Branson, 1983; Dornbusch, 1983; and Swoboda, 1983.)

Following Allen (1967), the Canadian economy is to exhibit an *intrinsic oscillation*. The American economy has its own intrinsic oscillation. Ignore any effects of the Canadian oscillation on the American one, but note that the oscillation of Canadian output may have two components: an intrinsic one; and a *forced oscillation*, transmitted by the American economy. Stipulate that the forced oscillation is transmitted through the current account of the Canadian balance of payments: Canadian exports surge during upswings of the American economy, and sag during American downswings, and Canadian imports oscillate sympathetically with the Canadian economy. Now consider how foreign exchange fluctuation may, or may not, buffer the transmission process. (Potential buffers in fixed exchange régimes include credit and money supply policies and, of course, Hume's specie-flow mechanism.) When the American economy surges, the Canadian dollar will appreciate (to the extent the current account matters). Appreciation of the Canadian dollar will damp stimulative effects – based on income effects – of an American economic expansion on Canada. Reversing the thrust of the American engine, depreciation of the Canadian dollar will damp the resulting negative shock to the Canadian economy.

Rational Expectations

The scenario ignores unexploited opportunities for profit; it depicts a market that neglects opportunities to accumulate American (Canadian) dollars during booms (recessions) of the American economy. In a corrected scenario, exchange-rate fluctuations will be more moderate – the amplitude of the 'exchange-rate cycle' will be less. (We already have explained how flexible-rate régimes may become dominated by asset market influences.)

10.5.3 R. G. D. Allen's Model of Intrinsic and Forced Oscillations

'A great simplification is achieved by assuming that the intrinsic oscillation is regular, neither damped nor explosive . . . Then the differential equation of the model simplifies [to equation 8.1]' (Allen, 1967, p. 347, compare chapter 18.2, pp. 347–50).

$$(v-s)D^2 Y + sY = (D+1)A(t) \tag{8.1}$$

The solution of the homogeneous form ($A = 0$) is

$$Y = B\cos(\omega t - \varepsilon) \tag{8.2}$$

($\omega = \sqrt{[s/(v-s)]}$, where v and s are the capital-output ratio and the propensity to save.)

Allen's 'exogenous oscillation in autonomous expenditure' (the oscillation of the American economy) is written as

$$A(t) = \eta\cos(\alpha t) \tag{8.3}$$

The amplitude and period of the exogenous oscillation are η and α.

Attention shifts to the forced oscillation in Y; in particular to comparison of it with that of $A(t) = \eta\cos(\alpha t)$. The amplitude of the forced oscillation well may exceed that of the exogenous one. In general, the resulting composite cycle in Y will have a longer period than that of the intrinsic cycle. And the forced oscillation will have a larger amplitude than that of the exogenous oscillation.

Allen concludes with some discussion of *resonance*: 'As the period of the forced oscillation tends to equal the period of the intrinsic oscillation, the amplitude of the oscillation in output gets indefinitely large' (Allen, 1967, pp. 349–50).

10.5.3.1 *Relation to Friedman's Formal Analysis* (cf. Chapter 5). Reconciling Allen's analysis to Friedman's, assume that the intrinsic oscillation is subject to stochastic shock. Then convert Allen's autonomous oscillation into the equivalent of the stabilising expenditures of Friedman's authority. The authority wants to induce a composite oscillation with lower amplitude and, perhaps, a longer period than the intrinsic one. Poor correlation of 'stabilising' with intrinsic (including stochastic) expenditures makes the former counterproductive. And the resonance problem persists.

10.5.4 Stagflation, Cost-Push Inflation, etc. in a Régime of Dirty Floating: A British Example

(See Cuthbertson, 1979, esp. pp. 130–6.)

In régimes of dirty floating, authorities, although not formally committed to defend specific pars, intervene in foreign exchange markets.

10.5.4.1 *Mr Heath's Fate.* Mr Edward Heath, British Prime Minister, 1970–4, denied responsibility for British inflation, insisting that it was imported: rising prices of imports, measured in sterling, were his government's fate, not its fault. And, indeed, inflation often looks cost-based – however speciously.

Figure 10.1 sketches a correct analysis.

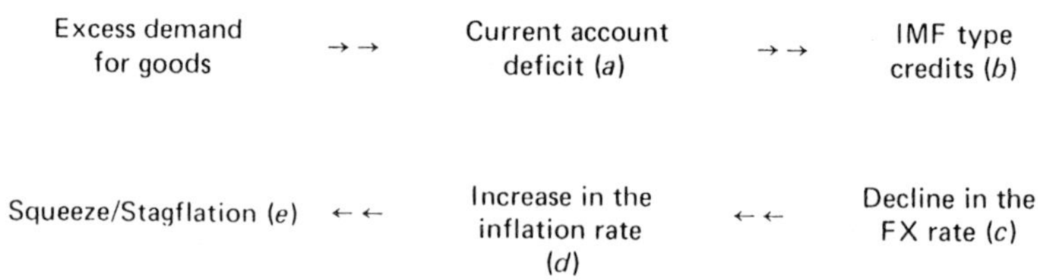

FIGURE 10.1 *Schematic account of a British inflation process*

Comments are keyed to the diagram.

(a) Fiscal policy became expansive, and was validated by a passive monetary policy. True, the value of recently discovered North Sea oil deposits shot up because of the 1973 oil shocks: expansive policy could more easily be financed.

Massive increases in consumption expenditure led to current-account deficits easily financed by external borrowing. Imported supply floated up to meet intensified demand; in early stages of expansionary policy, disequilibrium in goods markets was avoided.

(b) Capital inflow supported sterling.

(c) Rapidly increasing external British debt began to alarm creditors and potential creditors. Indeed, the British Government became concerned about its mounting external debt. It became prudent, if not mandatory, to abandon efforts to support sterling by borrowing foreign exchange. Prescient speculators who sold sterling short, and held on, scored heavily.

Interpolation. Offers to sell sterling forward – offers requiring that nothing more than security deposits be put up – can sink spot sterling. The *interest parity* can be sustained only if a spot currency follows its forward rates down. See Keynes (1923, 1930), Einzig (1961) and Spraos (1959) – as well as Burstein (1963, pp. 262–5).

An ingenious scheme for supporting the *j*-dollar by offering other currencies for it forward was explained by Keynes (1923); and was rather hesitantly tried by the Kennedy Administration in spring 1961. The theory of such operations was searchingly analysed by Spraos (1959).

(d) The imported inflation chimera came into play. Depreciation of sterling led to higher prices of imports; the upshot looked like cost-push. Controlling lags characteristically are complex and erratic; and indeed are hard to identify.

Remark. Inflation concerns rising, not higher, prices. A sustained increase in the British inflation rate here would require *continuing* depreciation of sterling. The scheme explains episodes, not secular trends.

(e) The *dénouement* is reached: stagflation! Real wages eroded as prices increased, that is as effects of sterling depreciation worked their way through pipelines. Labour unrest followed. Mr Heath's confrontation with the miners led to his fall.

10.5.4.2 *General Comments on Stagflation in Open Economies.* Balance-sheet effects of current-account deterioration in the wake of expansionary policies will finally alarm authorities – and the IMF! They may slash public spending, raise taxes, squeeze liquidity, raise Bank Rate (importantly to attract capital inflow or deter outflow), etc. Output may fall. Unemployment will increase. And inflation will persist for some time: lags are erratic and long; inflation expectations may be inertial. Resulting data will defy orthodox models – unlikely to take proper account of controlling lags.

10.5.4.3 *Epilogue: France.* Events in France, following the election of M. Mitterrand in 1981, but engendered in part during the reign of M.

Giscard d' Estaing, mirrored the British story – and indeed moved faster to a more dramatic economic conclusion. The Mitterrand Government, soon after coming to power, operated a *closed* Keynesian model. It soon became clear that even a Keynesian model as simple as System 1 would have been a much better choice. Recall the principal implications of System 1:

(1) real growth is strictly bounded by the current account of the balance of payments;
(2) expansive fiscal policy is nugatory as a stimulus to real growth.

Strong fiscal stimulus supplied by the French Government led to the collapse of the French current account and the franc. Huge support operations, contributing to an unprecedented level of foreign-held debt, failed to prop up the franc. In a few months the French economy went through the 'cycle' of Figure 10.1. Stagflation persisted into autumn 1984 (the time of writing).

10.6 CODA TO CHAPTER 10: AN EXERCISE IN OPEN-SYSTEM DYNAMICS

A scheme of Tobin (1975) is applied to a problem in open macroeconomics.

Let

y = output,
z = aggregate demand,
τ = terms of trade.

(1) The current account is determined by $\phi(y,\tau)$ and $z = f(y,\tau)$.
(2) Assume that wages and prices are sticky, and the foreign exchange régime flexible, so that τ proxies the exchange rate of the j-dollar.
(3) The world economy is closed; terms-of-trade change is not available to the world!

The Model: System 9

$$\left.\begin{aligned} \dot{y} &= \lambda[f(y,\tau) - y] && (9.1) \\ \dot{\tau} &= \mu[\phi(y,\tau)] && (9.2) \end{aligned}\right\} \text{System 9}$$

Now make a linear approximation to the system in the neighbourhood of its rest point, stipulated to be unique. Switch the origin to $(\bar{y}, \bar{\tau})$ so that the variables of System 10 – (y', τ') – are deviations of output and terms of trade from $(\bar{y}, \bar{\tau})$.

$$\left.\begin{aligned} \dot{y}' &= \alpha y' + \beta \tau' \qquad (10.1) \\ \dot{\tau}' &= \gamma y' + \delta \tau' \qquad (10.2) \end{aligned}\right\} \text{System 10}$$

Common economic reasoning suggests the coefficients are negative. If the absolute value of β – by way of example – is large, the determinant of the coefficient matrix is negative, along with the trace $(\alpha + \delta)$. And the complementary eigenvalues are complex with negative real parts – so that the phase portrait displays stable foci, that is, an attracting spiral (see Figure 10.2, along with Arrowsmith and Place (1982), especially pp. 50–2).

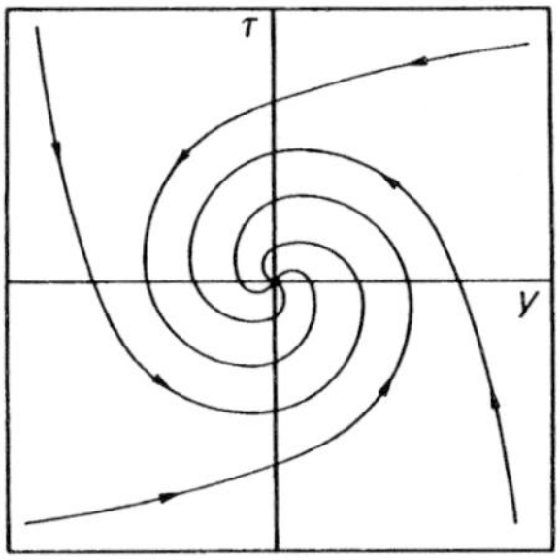

FIGURE 10.2 *The phase portrait of system 10 (as specified)*

11 Some Pure Theory of Money in an Open Macroeconomy

Two principal themes are developed in a number of ways. The first, encompassing *quasi banking*, concerns how the *j-th* money supply may become endogenous. The second concerns properties of a sophisticated debt-denomination and discharge process in which choice of measure is open so that contracts might call for the *j*-dollar equivalent to a basket of currencies to be paid over at date *t*.

11.1 THE QUANTITY THEORY OF MONEY IN AN OPEN ECONOMY

11.1.1 Preliminary Comments

Girton and Roper (1978) make a striking point. The received notion of the quantity theory follows Irving Fisher: the principal model concerns a closed economy whose price level is a function of the quantity of money made available by its authorities; causality runs from money to prices. J. Laurence Laughlin, following Hume, opted for an open model in which perceived causality in the *j-th* economy runs from prices to money so that its quantity of money is determined by liquidity preference: its authorities exercise no control over its quantity of money; or its prices; or its interest rates. Abstracting from the capital account, quantities of money in the open model are adjusted by Hume's *specie-flow mechanism:* deviations of actual from desired aggregate monetary holdings trigger changes in current accounts of the balance of payments: for example, an excess of actual over desired holdings stimulates expenditure, leading to current-account deterioration and so to specie outflow – until portfolio imbalance is corrected. And *vice versa par contre.*

In the open model, the purchasing power of specie in the long run is determined by its cost of production (cf. Chapter 4):

> The proportion between the value of gold and silver and that of goods of any other kind depends . . . [only] . . . upon that between the quantity of labour which is necessary . . . to bring . . . gold and silver to market, and that which is necessary . . . to bring thither . . . other . . . goods. (Adam Smith, *Wealth of Nations*, Everyman's Library edition (1910, 1970), vol. 1, p. 293)

Global excess demand for specie (say gold) leads to falling wages and prices – reckoned in gold – and to higher rates of gold production, until equilibrium is restored. The mechanism is asymmetrical: once the purchasing power of gold falls so low that gold production cannot be justified, further wage/price increases do not affect gold production, already nil. But the model remains self-correcting: excess supply of gold is drained by inflation's attrition of the real value of gold stocks.

11.1.2 Mathematical Illustrations

11.1.2.1 *A Simple Mathematical System*

(In System 1, 'gold' and 'money' are used interchangeably.)

Let

M_j = the money supply of the *j-th* economy,
M^* = the global supply of money,
y_j^* = real activity of the *j-th* economy,
α_j = a shift parameter measuring the intensity of the *j-th* liquidity preference,
p = the global price level, parametric for the *j-th* economy,
$L^j(\cdot)$ determines demand for money in the *j-th* economy. (Parameters include (y_j^*, M^*, α_j))

$$\left.\begin{array}{lr} L^j(\alpha_j, p, y_j^*) = M_j \qquad j = 1, 2, \ldots, n & (1.1) \\ \sum M_j = M^* & (1.2) \end{array}\right\} \text{System 1}$$

The $n+1$ equations determine $(\overline{M}_j, \overline{p})$.

The reduced form of System 1 is System 1R.

$$\left.\begin{array}{lr} \overline{M}_j = \phi^j(\alpha, M^*, y^*),\ j = 1, 2, \ldots, n & \\ \quad (\alpha \text{ and } y^* \text{ are vectors.}) & (1R.1) \\ \overline{p} = \psi^j(\alpha, M^*, y^*) & (1R.2) \end{array}\right\} \text{System 1R}$$

It is to be shown that: $\partial \bar{p}/\partial \alpha_j < 0$; $\partial \bar{p}/\partial M^* > 0$; $\partial \bar{M}_r/\partial \alpha_j > 0$; $\partial \bar{M}_r/\partial \alpha_j < 0$.

It is instructive first to develop informal proofs of the key comparative statics results.

$\partial \bar{p}/\partial a_r < 0$. (The law of one price prevails.) *The* global price level will fall if liquidity preference increases in the *r-th* economy. Demand for money having increased in the *r-th* economy, and not fallen anywhere, there must be global excess demand for money. Lower commodity prices increase the real money-supply.

$\partial \bar{p}/\partial M^* > 0$. Think of the discovery of gold in America in the sixteenth century: the Spanish current account went into deficit until global monetary equilibrium became restored. When the system regains its rest-point (in an appropriately defined space), the global price level will have increased *pro rata* with the global money supply. Gold will be distributed over the world in the same proportions as before.

$\partial M_r/\partial a_r > 0$. The proposition is that an increase in liquidity preference in the *r-th* economy leads to its holding a larger proportion of the global money supply. Historically, Indian and French holdings of precious metals have relatively exceeded Scotland's, for example. And Western price movements have been affected by shifts in Oriental asset preferences.

Differentiating around a solution point,

$$(\partial L^j/\partial \alpha_r)\,d\alpha_r + (\partial L^j/\partial p)\,dp = dM_j \qquad j = 1, 2, \ldots n$$
$$\sum dM_j = 0$$

We assume that $d\alpha_r > 0$ and that $d\alpha_s = 0 (s \neq r)$. It follows that $d\bar{p} < 0$. If $d\bar{p} = 0$, demand for gold will be higher in the *r-th* economy and lower nowhere. If $d\bar{p} > 0$, demand for gold will be higher everywhere. (Partial derivatives of demand for money (gold) with respect to liquidity preference and the price level are positive.) So $d\bar{p} < 0$ is necessary. Then demand for gold will be lower in economies $1, 2, \ldots, r-1, r+1, \ldots n$. But the sum of gold holdings must be unchanged: ergo (!), $\partial \bar{M}_r/\partial \alpha_r > 0$.

$\partial \bar{M}_s/\partial \alpha_r < 0$. This proposition just has been proved.

11.1.2.2 *A More Formal Method of Proof.* A three-economy case is perfectly general. Differentiate around the solution point: the following set of linear equations results.

$$d\bar{M}_1 - (\partial L^1/\partial p)\,dp = (\partial L^1/\partial \alpha_1)\,d\alpha_1$$
$$d\bar{M}_2 - (\partial L^2/\partial p)\,dp = 0$$

$$d\bar{M}_3 - (\partial L^3/\partial p)dp = 0$$

$$d\bar{M}_1 + d\bar{M}_2 + d\bar{M}_3 = 0$$

The four-by-four matrix of left-hand side coefficients, 'organised by sign', is:

$$\begin{bmatrix} + & 0 & 0 & - \\ 0 & + & 0 & - \\ 0 & 0 & + & - \\ + & + & + & 0 \end{bmatrix}$$

Its determinant is positive. Solving for $d\bar{p}/d\alpha_1$: $-(\partial L^1/\partial \alpha_1)/(+) = (-)$.

The signs of the following determinants must be ascertained in order to solve for changes, in equilibrium, in money (gold) stocks in the first and second economies relative to a change in liquidity preference in the first.

$$\begin{vmatrix} + & 0 & 0 & - \\ 0 & 1 & 0 & - \\ 0 & 0 & 1 & - \\ 0 & 1 & 1 & 0 \end{vmatrix} = A = (+)$$

$$\begin{vmatrix} 1 & + & 0 & - \\ 0 & 0 & 0 & - \\ 0 & 0 & 1 & - \\ 1 & 0 & 1 & 0 \end{vmatrix} = B = (-)$$

$$\partial \bar{M}_1/\partial \alpha_1 = A/(+) = (+)$$

$$\partial \bar{M}_2/\partial \alpha_1 = B/(+) = (-)$$

11.1.2.3 *Extension of Matrix-Method Approaches to the Open Version of the Quantity Theory of Money.* An increase in the global quantity almost surely would not be equiproportionately distributed *ab initio.* Thus initial influxes of gold and silver, discovered in America in the sixteenth century, flowed into Spanish coffers; when the process had run its course, initial relative holdings largely were restored. Clower and Burstein (1960) studied a related problem, posed by Archibald and Lipsey (1958): can there be a unique absorbing state in a space defined by proportions of the global stock of money held be various agents?

Two techniques are displayed. One is based on differential equations; the other on Markov chain analysis.

Differential Equations

$$\dot{x}_1 = -(a_{12}+a_{13})x_1 + a_{21}x_2 + a_{31}x_3 \quad (1a.1)$$
$$\dot{x}_2 = a_{12}x_1 - (a_{21}+a_{23})x_2 + a_{32}x_3 \quad (1a.2)$$
$$\dot{x}_3 = a_{13}x_1 + a_{23}x_2 - (a_{31}+a_{32})x_3 \quad (1a.3)$$

Define row vector (x). For a non-trivial rest point to exist, it is necessary that $det A = 0$: the problem can be solved up to a factor of proportionality. (Cf. $xA = 0$.)

Indeed A is *singular*: there is row (i.e. linear) dependence. Add rows (1) and (2); multiply the sum by (-1); the result is row (3).

The proportion of specie held in economy (1) that will flow out to economy (2) over a unit interval is a_{12}:$a_{12}x_1$ is the periodic rate of outflow from economy (1) when its specie stock is x_1. For inflow, coefficients are assigned minus signs. In equilibrium, aggregate inflow and outflow are balanced at each node.

Markov Chain Theory (Sources include Kemeny, Snell and Thompson, 1957, chs. 4 and 7; Kemeny and Snell, 1962, chs. 5 and 6 and appendices; and Burstein, 1968, pp. 224–5 (where an application is made to a bank deposit grid).)

Stating important concepts:

(1) A stochastic matrix is a square matrix with row sums of unity
(2) A row vector is called a probability vector if it consists of non-negative components summing to unity
(3) The probability vector (t) is a fixed point of the transformation tP, *i.e.* $t = tP$. P is a transition matrix; t is an absorbing state
(4) The stochastic matrix P is *regular* if all its elements are positive. Any regular matrix is *ergodic*.
(5) If P is a regular stochastic matrix, $P^n \to T$ as $n \to \infty$.
(6) Each row of T is the same probability vector t. If p is any probability vector, $pP^n \to t$ and t is the unique fixed point probability vector of P.

Our problem conforms to the above criteria:

$$P = \begin{bmatrix} a_{11} & a_{12} & a_{13} \\ a_{21} & a_{22} & a_{23} \\ a_{31} & a_{32} & a_{33} \end{bmatrix}$$

Interpret a_{ii} as the proportion of specie holdings of the *i-th* economy that will be retained during the period. Of course, $\sum_j a_{ij} = 1$. And (p) is a row vector of proportions of the global specie stock held at each of the three nodes; the elements of (p) sum to unity. The set of proportions will be pP after the first transition; pP^2 after the second; . . . ; and pP^n after the n-th. As $n \to \infty$, $pP^n \to t$ so that $tP = t(!)$.

11.1.3 Properties of Paper/Specie Systems

11.1.3.1 *General Analysis.* (See Chapter 2, Section 2.1. Also see Wallace (1981b) for a development of the problem along different lines.) Adam Smith analysed paper-money issue by British-American colonies and diffusion of bank money in Scotland and England. System 2 obtains one of his results.

$$\left.\begin{aligned} &L(\alpha^*, \hat{p}^*, y^*) = M^* && (2.1) \\ &M^* = z + q^*; dz^* = -dq^*(!) && (2.2) \end{aligned}\right\} \text{System 2}$$

Let

y = a parameter indexing the economy's real activity,
α = a parameter measuring the intensity of liquidity preference,
$\hat{p}$ = the global price level, parametric for a given economy,
z = the economy's gold holdings,
q = the supply of paper money, issued by the government, and measured in gold,
M = the money-holding of the economy.

Equation 2.2 implies that paper and gold are *perfect substitutes*: a unit increase in paper emission drives out a unit of gold.

The model operates recursively: upon values for y, $\hat{p}$ and α being specified, M^* emerges. Plug M^* into equation 2.2 and take a decision on q: z^* pops out. The monetary authorities can determine the paper component of the equilibrium quantity of money, but not its total. So to speak domestic credit expansion, but not 'foreign assets', is under the authorities' control.

Preface to System 3. Paper and gold are *not* perfect substitutes. Recalling colonial American experience, stipulate that paper issue is inconvertible but that external payments must be made in gold.

$$\left.\begin{aligned} &x = f[E(\dot{p}/p), \hat{p}, y] && (3.1) \\ &z = g[\qquad\qquad] && (3.2) \end{aligned}\right\} \text{System 3}$$

New Symbols. Let

x = the quantity of incovertible paper issue, measured in gold,
p = the price of a unit of paper issue relative to a gold numéraire,
$E(\dot{p}/p)$ = the expectation of the time-rate of change of p (proxy to a functional).

$E(\dot{p}/p)$ is determined by the expected evolution of money growth. Upon $E(\dot{p}/p)$ becoming established, x and z are determined. The real equilibrium quantity of paper money (*i.e.* its gold value) is *not* policy-determined.

Seigneurage profit can be defined as the gold value of a steady rate of sale of paper money – recalling from Chapter 7 that demand is unit-elastic relative to the profit-maximising depreciation rate.

An n-Economy 'Mixed Money' Model

$$\left.\begin{array}{lll} \phi^j(y,\hat{p},m) = x_j & j = 1, 2, \ldots, n & (4.1) \\ \psi^j(\cdot) = z_j & j = 1, 2, \ldots, n & (4.2) \\ \sum z_j = z^* & & (4.3) \end{array}\right\} \text{System 4}$$

y and m are n-vectors; m measures growth rates of paper issues. The system contains $2n+1$ equations in the unknowns $(z_1, \ldots, z_n)$, $(x_1, \ldots, x_n)$ and $\hat{p}$. Since seigneurage profits will be sensitive to m_r relative to m' (a n-1 vector excluding m_r), the model ideally would deal explicitly with the game played by oligopolist currency writers; but, for the sake of simplicity, m_r is a parameter.

At this level of abstraction, System 4 entails an inflation problem only trivially. Transactors may contract in units scaled on 'gold' – or relative to an infinite variety of currency cocktails. Agents hold variegated liquid asset balances; and contract in synthetic units of account, varying from transaction to transaction. Competition among currency writers assures, if there are enough depreciation averters, that there will be at least one non-depreciating currency.

System 4 is *not* a monetary approach to the balance of payments. Thus there is no reason for transactors in the *j-th* economy to formulate contracts in the *j-th* unit of account: during the German hyperinflation of the 1920s, the pound sterling effectively became a money of account; and cigarettes have served as money in similar circumstances.

Finally, it is important to avoid a confusion that besets Hayek (1976). Only transactions costs impose intersection of the unit of account and currency-choice ideas: for example, transactors preferring US dollars as money of account may arrange to discharge debt by tender of French francs.

11.1.3.2 *Adam Smith's Analysis.* In the *Wealth of Nations*, Adam Smith develops both the perfect and imperfect substitution cases – after characteristically remarking that: 'the substitution of paper in the room of gold and silver money, replaces a very expensive instrument of commerce with one much less costly and sometimes equally convenient' (Everyman's Library ed., 1910, 1970, vol. 1, p. 257.)

As for perfect substitution:

> But as the quantity of gold and silver, which is taken from the currency, is always equal to the quantity of paper which is added to it, paper money does not necessarily increase the quantity of the whole currency. (Ibid., p. 289)

Smith goes on to discuss discounts of paper currency against gold (cf. ibid., p. 293) – and thus intersects our imperfect substitution case.

11.1.3.3 *Illustration from History: Eighteenth Century British America.* There was confusion in eighteenth-century North America, as there is now, between 'shortages' of transactions balances and 'high' interest rates on loans (see Burstein, 1966 and Smith, 1984). And it seemed sinister to many that borrowers should be able to obtain real assets by issuing paper, especially if the paper exercised legal tender power.

Spontaneous and contrived forces led to substitution for specie balances. Spontaneous forces led to creation of a flimsy liquidity structure based on a mass of private paper which, repeatedly endorsed, became means of payment. The immense volume of trade credit, much of it represented by negotiable instruments, became a prime circulating medium. (See Braudel, 1979, 1984, discussed below Section 11.1.3.4. A more sophisticated, and extensive, system of this sort was contrived in sixteenth-century Antwerp.)

Contrivance led to the first sustained significant issues of fiat paper money in the West, and the first anywhere since China abandoned it in the fifteenth century (see Toynbee, 1954, pp. 307–17). These fiat issues led to a system of freely floating exchange rates. Determinants of premia (discounts) included preferences for foreign (*v.* domestic) goods, states of confidence in local authorities and rumours about often nebulous attitudes in London towards colonial paper issues. Similar factors determined fluctuation in the *exchange on Hamburg* during the British Restriction on specie payments from 1797 to 1821 (see Viner, 1937 and Hawtrey, 1950).

11.1.3.4 *Illustration from History: Sixteenth Century Antwerp.* Braudel explains that Antwerp's supply of money was 'inadequate': 'some fictional paper money had somehow to be invented' (Braudel, 1984, p. 155).

> Settlements in both directions, whether payments or receipts, were effected by the letter obligatory . . . and the letter was the [negotiable] property of its holder . . . Thus debts and credits circulated on the market, creating an extra form of currency with the advantage that it could cancel itself out in the miraculous reckoning known as the *scontro*, the clearing house or *rescontre* as it was called in Holland. (Braudel, 1984, p. 155)

And Braudel goes on to suggest (at p. 157) that comparable procedures existed in earlier centuries in 'Ghent, Bruges and Ypres – not to mention Florence, Lucca and Milan.'

It is especially interesting that the clearing-union model of Chapter 1, Section 1.3 has been anticipated for so many centuries. And one frets that the research programmes of monetary theorists have been flawed: prevailing paradigms are too simplistic to account for say fourteenth-century financial practice!

11.1.3.5 *Concluding Observations, Section* 11.1.3. (1) If paper is a perfect substitute for specie, then, along lines developed in System 2, paper issue in the *j-th* economy will drive out specie 1:1. And global effects will be like those following a decrease in liquidity preference in the system of Section 11.1.2.

Transforming the analysis, think of effects in a small open economy of an increase in domestic credit expansion. (See below; also Parkin, 1982, chapter 39.) The quantity of money will not be affected: foreign exchange reserves (devisen reserves) will fall 1:1 with the increase in domestic credit.

(2) The general case of imperfect substitution is modelled by System 3. Its flavour is that of Friedman's inflation tax.
(3) Assume that paper issue is by fiat. A fundamental principle of monetary theory can be extracted along the following lines. Authorities can control the nominal, but not the real, volume of their issue. Indeed, in models as simple as those under immediate study, monetary events have real consequences only to the extent to which wage–price flexibility is imperfect. And we recall Lerner (1952, pp. 384–5): 'Wage and price rigidity is an essential property of money: . . . any money . . . cured of wage and price rigidity would not be able to survive as money.'

11.2 DENATIONALISED MONEY

Consider an open system in which each economy has its own official money of account and legal tender currency, but in which agreements everywhere are cast up in various monies of account. All economies are on fiat paper standards; and exchange rates float freely. The quantity of money in the *j-th* economy becomes difficult to define: the aggregate value of *monies* varies from day to day with exchange rates and shifts in textures of liquid asset holdings – in whatever metric is selected.

Agents will not be indifferent towards textures of monetary balances: for one thing currency choice is sensitive to expected appreciation or depreciation in foreign exchange markets; for another, credit transactions in goods markets lead to open positions in various currencies that affect the risk attributes of a given portfolio of liquid claims (positive and negative).

Turning to the system's *adjustment process*, in Italy there may be excess demand for dollar assets, and excess supply of lira ones: the price of dollar exchange ('devisen') will increase in a lira measure; and Italy's current account may become more favourable. Another effect of a positive shift in Italian demand for US dollar balances is substitution of lira for dollars in the United States – analogously to the way in which an increase in specie preference in the *j-th* economy led to increased specie holdings there, and reduced ones everywhere else, in System 1.

Equilibrium requires that prices, in the lira measure, rise *partout*; and that prices, in the dollar measure, fall. And dollar exchange will rise in the foreign exchange markets. In the new equilibrium, Americans will want to hold less wealth in dollar-denominated assets and more in lira ones.

Denationalised Money and Public Debt Management

So far we have stayed on familiar ground – studying how shifts in asset preferences can dominate foreign exchange rate movements; and observing that, under neutral expectations, if secular monetary expansion is more rapid in the *j-th* economy, the *j*-dollar will steadily depreciate against the *k*-dollar. Now we plunge into fresh perplexes.

Tightening up analogies between national monetary/fiscal authorities and corporate treasurers, assume that there is substantial excess demand for *j*-dollars; and that French authorities seek to raise x million *FF* to cover a public sector borrowing requirement. It becomes attractive to the Ministre des Finances to issue *j*-dollar denominated securities; although the proceeds well may be paid in French francs at currently prevailing exchange rates.

Two Development Passages Concluding Section 11.2

(i) Section 11.4 explains that forward positions in various 'currencies' are not captured by money supply measures. A forward contract entitling one to z French francs in sixty days has the essential properties of a French franc time deposit and may be more liquid. One's obligation to pay x US dollars for *FFz* drains one's liquidity in the way comparable bank liabilities drain bank liquidity. The vendor of the French francs is 'drained' in the same way; and his claim to US dollars in future is as liquid as an American time deposit.

It makes no more sense to cancel out the *FF*/$ positions in aggregative financial accounting than to cancel out monetary liabilities of banks: banks *do* owe what depositors own. The purchaser of the *FF* has gained liquidity, as has the mirror image transactor. The upshot simply illustrates the theory of gains from trade.

Nor do ordinary money supply measures track, say, net US dollar positions of US residents – who may have sold forward US dollars for forward rights to foreign currencies; in effect reducing their US dollar positions by selling quasi time deposits, buying foreign-denominated quasi time deposits with the proceeds, i.e. swopping one futurity for another.

Extra-National Creation of j-Dollars. So far we have assumed that $-*j* liquid asset supply is endemic to the *j-th* economy, an assumption feebly propped up by efforts of governments to thwart the natural mechanisms of markets. But in globally free financial dealing, a London office of the Midland Bank would create chequeable French franc accounts in exchange for, say, US-dollar-denominated deposits: 'currency competition' would go much farther than Klein and Hayek take it.

If French banks (effectively part of the public sector) contract their credit, French money supply, as ordinarily measured, will contract. But, in a régime of free financial dealing, Frenchmen, seeking *FF* loans, could turn to Citibank; and the residue of resulting loans would comprise *FF* monetary assets in the form of Citibank liabilities.

It would be prudent for Citibank then to increase its holdings of *FF*-denominated assets, e.g. government stock close to maturity: it might offer US dollar deposits for *FF* assets. Small changes in relative rates of return would induce the global public to make the relatively small switches required. Or Citibank could buy put options, assuring *FF* values of US dollar, sterling, *DM*, *etc.* assets (see below).

(ii) In finance, compositions of the bundles of securities offered by treasurers importantly are functions of perceived asset preferences of buyers (portfolio managers): if the public come to prefer short-dated bonds, companies will borrow shorter. To an increasing extent, bundles of securities offered by national treasuries obey this maxim.

It must appeal to the Finance Minister of *Z* to get off an issue of *z*-dollar stock when preference for '*z*-dollars' strengthens. Or if the Finance Minister regards weaker preference for '*z*-dollars' to be transitory, he may issue *j*-dollar-guaranteed securities instead; planning to refund into *z*-dollar-denominated issue when the market returns to normal.

Concluding the analysis, *j*-dollar-denominated securities issued by governments *A*, *B*, . . . *I*, *K* . . . have significant monetary properties. So, at this level of abstraction, the supply of basal *j*-dollar stocks is beyond the suzerainity of the *j-th* government. In particular, the global supply of government securities, denominated in *j*-dollars, will respond elastically to fluctuations in intensities of preferences for such securities. This result must be unsatisfactory from the point of view of open-loop monetary control.

11.3 TOWARDS A THEORY OF QUASI BANKING

We develop a 'Swiss franc' case. There may be a kernel of verisimilitude: substantial volumes of Swiss francs are held as investments.

Section 11.3.1 operates on the assumption that 'Swiss franc' paper is only generated by 'Swiss' sources. Section 11.3.2 is pitched to a higher level of generalisation: 'Swiss francs' may be generated *partout*. Section 11.3.3 is pitched still higher.

11.3.1 Properties of a Currency Dedicated to Liquid Asset Holding, but not to Vehicular Uses (See McKinnon, 1979, for a discussion of the vehicular role of the US dollar)

Klein (1974a) supplies a context. A major source of income for the *j-th* economy is seigneurage profit. In a steady state, seigneurage profit is measured by the yield of the mass of stock acquired with the proceeds of *j*-dollar sales; in a growth state, or when an 'inflation tax' (really a depreciation tax) can be levied (so that there is replacement demand), profit can be augmented (see Chapter 7).

The exchange rates of the *j*-dollar will be determined by shifting asset preferences, together with actual and expected rates of growth of *j*-dollar issue, relative to other such rates.

Two points emerge:

(i) Along lines developed by Klein (1974a) and Hayek (1976), 'Swiss' authorities will seek a profit-maximising expansion path of 'Swiss' issue. And they will seek optimal credibility. In the real stochastic world, their best efforts will fail to prevent substantial, erratic foreign exchange rate fluctuation; and they will often regret their strategic choices.
(ii) The 'Swiss' will most likely not use their 'franc' as their commercial unit of account.

The first point has been adequately explained; but some elaboration of the second is required.

Recalling a central conclusion of Chapter 10: when exchange-rate formation is dominated by asset-market events, the real economy can become a dog wagged by its asset-market tail; the real economy must adapt to erratically vibrating exchange rates.

Turning to the modalities of choice of commercial units of account, the analysis runs along the lines of Section 11.6 ('Optimal Currency Zones'). It is surely desirable in the real Swiss world that the Swiss franc's exchange rate against the DM does not vibrate erratically. At least in theory, the problem can be solved by finessing the Swiss franc; by drafting commercial agreements in fictitious units; thus assuring minimised effective foreign exchange oscillation.

11.3.2 Consequences of Denationalisation of the *j*-Dollar

In principle, at this level of abstraction, a commitment to deliver Swiss francs forward can be made by anyone, anywhere – as can a commitment to deliver a stock 'on call' over a stated interval; or, more tenuously, 'naked options', risking exigent need to come up with a stock one does not have, that gets called away, can be written (see Section 11.3.3).

So, up to a point, increased demand for Swiss franc denominated assets can be met out of thin air.

> *When Lord Cooper was right, he said, 'Definitely Lord Cooper'; when he was wrong, 'Up to a point.'*
> *' . . . Capital of Japan? Yokohama isn't it?'*
> *'Up to a point, Lord Cooper.'*
>
> Evelyn Waugh, *Scoop* (London: Chapman and Hall; 1948, uniform ed., p.13. First published, 1938)

Postponing discussion of possible need to *deliver* stocks on the contract date or during the call period, notice that, typically, forward transactors do not hedge particular risks. Rather they seek to enhance their liquidity. If successful they are less likely to need fresh supplies of spot Swiss francs. Normally contracts would be settled without delivery.

If forward dealing possibilities were unbounded, actual liquid asset stocks would not comprise active constraints on our problem. But the 'Swiss franc' model *is* bounded – for reasons that suggest a US dollar model may *not* thus be bounded.

The Size of the Market and Liquidity. (See Telser, 1981; Working 1948; Working, 1962.)

Telser (1981, p. 1) stresses monetary properties of futures contracts: 'An organized futures market facilities trade among strangers. The correct explanation [for its emergence] is closely related to why we conduct trade using money instead of by barter.' Perhaps even more important for us, he develops analogies from futures market clearing houses to banks:

> [A price] squeeze resembles a run on a bank . . . [Unlike a bank] the clearing house . . . always has assets that match exactly in timing its

> liabilities. Nevertheless, an unexpectedly large demand for delivery by the buyers of futures contracts accompanies an unexpectedly large increase in the spot price for deliverable supplies during the delivery month. So there is said to be a price squeeze.
>
> (Telser, 1981, p. 14)

Futures transactions in thin foreign exchange markets can be destabilising: short covering of 'Swiss francs' could provoke demand exceeding the entire stock of 'Swiss' government securities and money, however defined. In a related context, Telser (1981) explains that the controlling rationale usually requires that only a few futures contracts be written. Indeed, sometimes the best that even an organised futures market can do is to post 'fair' loss-limitation rules during crises.

Long-standing real world Swiss, Japanese and German hostility to use of their 'currencies' as international stores of value is thus easy to understand; as is the fact that markets for international stores of value have been highly concentrated. The predominance of the dollar has been based on the exceptional liquidity of US dollar denominated securities – resulting from the vast, deep markets for United States securities.

11.3.3 Monetisation of Assets *en Général* by Forward, Futures and Options Markets in Closed and Open Economies

Glossary

> A *forward contract* is for deferred delivery of a given quantity . . . at a given price between the two parties named in the contract . . . Forward contracts are in fact more common than futures contracts and are the ancestors of futures contracts. This is the vital point. (Telser, 1981, p. 5)

> A *futures contract* is a financial instrument traded on an organized futures market such that all contracts of the same maturity date are perfect substitutes for each other . . . The validity of a futures contract is independent of the identities of the buyer and seller. It is a creation of the organized exchange and its clearing house. A futures contract is . . . fungible . . . A given futures contract stands on its own almost in the same sense as currency. (Ibid., p. 5)

> A *call option* is an option to buy a specified number of shares at any time within the contract period at a stated price (the option price) . . . A *put option* gives the holder the right to sell a specified number of shares at a fixed price any time within the contract period. (Malkiel and Quandt, 1969, p. 7)

Discussion

Theme

In a closed or open economy, *j*-dollar liquidity can be created by anyone willing to buy a long asset forward or sell a put-option on a long asset. Such transactions do not in principle require spot payment of consideration. And underlying risks are like those of a bank. If forward and options markets are well developed, risks are easily manageable.

Development

The seller of a put option makes himself liable to have say a long security *put* to him. *He sells liquidity; his liability to have a stock put to him creates liquidity for the option's buyer.* And observe that a set of forward sales, appropriately matched by purchases, can, virtually rheostatically, generate phased maturities that may lead to a position virtually indistinguishable from one obtained by option deals – if markets are developed fully enough.

The procedures just explained can convert thirty-year paper into 'money'. They permit a portfolio manager asymptotically to approach that epitome of liquidity, (Alexander) Pope's father: 'Pope's father, . . . when he retired from business, carried a chest of guineas with him to his villa at Twickenham and met his household expenses from it as required' (Keynes, 1936, p. 221).

An Open Economy Example. The *j-th* economy may operate quite strictly in a *j*-dollar metric. Now assume that liquidity of *j*-nationals begins to drain away; perhaps a boom is not fed by the monetary authorities. As a result, there will be increased demand for put options – not only for options on \$-*j* stock, but also for options to put securities nominally worth *y* *i*-dollars for *x* *j*-dollars. Wider spreads will induce higher volumes of options writing. The open economy process is isomorphic with the closed economy one, and flows from the same principal source: distribution of the banking function over a continuous field enables infusions of liquidity to be supplied by quasi banks as well as banks; and balance-sheet displacement for 'infusers' may be miniscule.

Recapitulation and Further Development of Four Points Contained in Section 11.3

(i) Although, for the most part, options transactors will not stand for delivery, squeezes do occur. Development of this point explains the international predominance of the US dollar. In the enormous, thick US dollar markets, pressures on option writers and forward transactors are easily absorbed: writers have recourse to trillions of dollars worth of dollar assets held throughout the world; squeezes can be averted by tiny shifts in global asset portfolios.

(ii) The banking function becomes uniformly distributed over a continuous field instead of being concentrated at a few nodes. The prime function of a bank is to exchange its highly liquid liabilities for less liquid, often virtually unmarketable, assets. 'Nodal', closely regulated, banks are perceived to expand and contract their balance sheets in discrete steps, responding to discontinuous official stimuli. The quasi banks of the theory continuously expand and contract in profit-seeking response to stimuli received from the market. As a result, money supply, however defined, evolves in a closed-loop sytem.

Universal quasi banking leads to efficient markets in liquidity. In primitive financial markets, it often is impossible to transfer liquidity from the *r-th* to the *s-th* portfolio. Liquidity constraints on the *r-th* programme may be slack (inactive) so that corresponding shadow prices are zero, while liquidity constraints on the *s-th* programme may be active so that corresponding shadow prices are 'high'; but sales of the *r-th* liquidity capacity may be blocked in imperfect markets. As financial markets deepen and expand, such sales become routine: quasi banking equates shadow values of liquidity constraints at a common margin – through options writing, forward dealing, etc.

(*A Conjecture.* Physical delivery is precluded by contracts controlling trades in industrial share averages. Equivalent quasi-banking dealing leads to more perfect international markets in liquidity: trading then is uninhibited by fears of delivery squeezes. And in such quasi-banking dealing the US dollar would lose much of its edge.)

(iii) In régimes of quasi banking, expansionary episodes can be triggered by the *avilability* of liquidity (by liquidity *in posse*) even if monetary statistics are neutral. And liquidity (*in posse*) can drain away because of changes in market sentiment even if monetary statistics are neutral. I developed a theory along similar lines (in Burstein, 1963, pp. 716–18) in connection with ways in which *cumulative Wicksellian processes* may unfold without money supply initially changing. And, indeed, interest-rate forecasts are based on projections of planned demand for finance – obviously not picked up by current flow-of-funds reports.

> Open lines of credit at bank rate permit firms to bid for goods. They anticipate borrowing after contracts are closed. They will fail to obtain the goods. Prices will rise. They will borrow after all – in order to maintain their real cash balances. (Burstein, 1963, p. 717.)

Wicksellian *deflation* is interestingly asymmetric with Wicksellian inflation. (Again see Burstein, 1963, pp. 716–18.) The problem is neatly closed up by Leijonhufvud (1981) in his 'Wicksell Connection'.

(iv) As a result of modern innovations, supplies of liquidity tend to be functions of demand for liquidity. It may be easier to work out effects of liquidity supply responding elastically to demand-shifts by developing a model in which supply is strictly exogenous; cf. a model based on Friedman's (1974a) theory of nominal income in a closed system.

Let

m = the growth rate of the monetary base as determined by the Rule,
q = the growth rate of nominal income,
α = a shift parameter; $\partial\pi/\partial\alpha > 0$.

The Relation

$$\pi_t = m + f\{\alpha - \int_0^t [q(\tau) - m]d\tau\} \qquad f(0) = 0; \quad f' > 0$$

Remarks. If $\alpha \neq 0$, a force induces acceleration. But, under strictly open-loop monetary control, the force becomes dominated by effects of a cumulative liquidity drain (if $\alpha > 0$) or liquidity infusion (if $\alpha < 0$). In the long run, nominal income is locked into the unaccelerated path, $q = m$. The thrust of Section 11.4.3 is that rapidly developing innovations in financial markets, engendering closed-loop responses, erode this rather compelling result.

11.4 DOMESTIC CREDIT EXPANSION

11.4.1 Mechanics

> It is convenient to make a distinction between an increase in the money supply and domestic-credit expansion . . . In a closed economy $\Delta M = DCE$ and this also is the case if the over-all balance of payments is exactly in balance, leaving the *foreign assets* of the central bank unchanged. However, if ΔFA is positive, money supply will increase by more than domestic-credit expansion, and, if ΔFA is negative, ΔM will be less than *DCE*. (Newlyn and Bootle, 1978, p. 26)

In the conventional paradigm, if an open system has a positive current account, foreign assets are sold to banks who in turn sell them to the central bank for its credit. Such transactions increase money supply but not *DCE* – although subsequent increases in the monetary liabilities of the banks (and so in money supply) are accompanied 1:1 by domestic-credit expansion. Similarly, foreign assets are purchased from banks, and transmitted to foreigners, in the wake of a current-account deficit – decreasing money supply, but not *DCE*; although subsequent decreases in the monetary liabilities of the banks (and so in money supply) are accompanied 1:1 by contraction of *DCE*.

In 1977 Britain had to meet conditions in order to get credit from the *IMF*; cf. the traumatic Chancellor's letter of intent. The principal condition concerned *DCE:*

> It is not known why the authorities adopted *DCE* as a target, but it is clear that the *IMF* favours it [!] . . . If the authorities' goal is some value for the Balance of Payments, then a *DCE* target always will be superior to a money-supply target . . . Since (broadly speaking) *DCE* equals the change in money supply plus the balance of payments deficit, given the maintenance of the target value for *DCE*, any change in the balance of payments . . . will cause an equal and opposite change in the money supply. (Newlyn and Bootle, 1978, p. 176).

Say that money and *DCE* have been growing at a target rate of x^* per cent per annum and that the current account has been in balance. Now the current account is to go into surplus: for money growth of x^*, DCE growth will be $x^{**} < x^*$. For the *DCE* target to be met, money growth must increase. If the current account deteriorates, so that the central bank is drained of foreign assets, money growth must fall below x^* for the x^* *DCE* target to be hit.

Supplement to Section 11.4.1: *A Mathematical Illustration of the DCE Model for a Small Open Economy on Fixed Exchage*

Let

m_j = the growth rate of the j-th money supply,
m^* = the secular growth rate of global money supply (perhaps that of a metallic reserve stock),
λ_j = the proportion borne by the *j-th* money stock to the global money stock (in a common measure),
λ_j^* = the equilibrium value of λ_j.

The Model in General Form

$$m_j = m^* - f(\lambda_j - \lambda_j^*) \quad (1)$$

$$\dot{\lambda}_j = g(m_j - m^*) \quad (2)$$

The Model in Linear Form

$$m_j = m^* - \alpha(\lambda_j - \lambda^*{}_j) \quad (3)$$

$$\dot{\lambda}_j = \beta(m_j - m^*) \quad (4)$$

Differentiating equation (3):

$$\dot{m}_j = -\alpha\dot{\lambda}_j \quad (5)$$

Substituting from equation (5) into equation (4):

$$\dot{m}_j = -\alpha[\beta(m_j - m^*)] \quad (6)$$

Stability is assured since $d\dot{m}_j/dm_j = -\alpha\beta < 0$. Figure 11.1 shows this graphically.

When growth of the *j-th* money stock has been 'too fast', the *j-th* economy will lose foreign exchange reserves, leading to curtailment of monetary expansion. Obviously, the mass of the *j-th* money stock at date *t* cannot be controlled by the *j-th* monetary authorities.

11.4.2 DCE and the Currency School

Monetary controversies seem to enjoy eternal life. The *DCE* debate is hard to distinguish from the bullionist/anti-bullionist debate following the Restriction of specie payments imposed by the Bank of England in 1797. 'The bullionists argued . . . that a circulation exceeding in amount

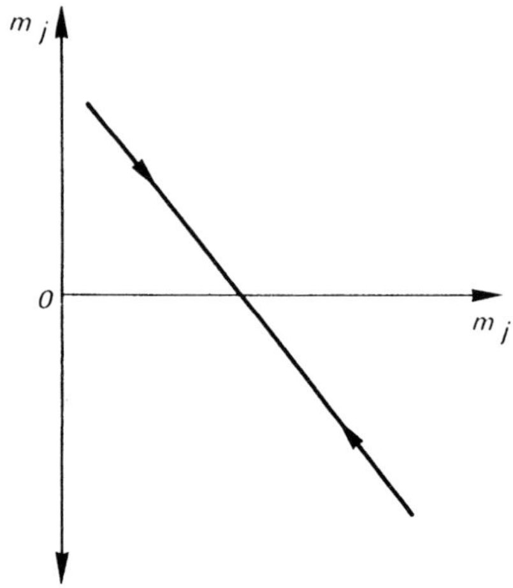

FIGURE 11.1

what, under otherwise like conditions could have been maintained under a metallic standard was in excess' (Viner, 1937, p. 125).

Anti-bullionists argued that depreciation of the paper pound, measured by the Exchange on Hamburg, was not because of intrinsic 'over issue', but rather because of the pressures of heavy military remittances abroad and large grain importations. Their argument was specious: it does not satisfy a criterion based on money supply behaviour under metallic standards. '[I]t was primarily because under the paper standard the English currency was not contracted as it necessarily would have contracted under a metallic standard that the foreign remittances resulted in such a marked depreciation of the paper pound on the exchanges' (Viner, 1937, p. 145).

Bullionist philosophy became embedded in the doctrine of the Currency School, whose triumph over the Banking School was enshrined in Peel's Act in 1844.

Peel's Act (the Bank Charter Act of 1844) embodied the *currency principle* requiring that a mixed currency operate like a purely metallic one: money supply growth was to be sensitised to the balance of payments. Viner's description of Bank operations under the Palmer Rule of 1832 shows that the domestic credit expansion criterion of the IMF is a clone of the currency principle:

> An influx of gold from abroad would thus act to increase the note circulation by a corresponding amount; an efflux of gold or a demand

> for coin for internal circulation would result in a corresponding decrease in note circulation. The internal circulation, specie plus paper, would thus remain constant unless acted upon by external gold movements. (Viner, 1937, p. 225).

(The Act of 1844 did little more than sever the banking and note issue departments of the Bank of England. From our restricted point of view, the 1832 and 1844 principles are the same.)

11.4.3 What is Money?

The great Banking School/Currency School debate continues to define the theory of monetary policy. The following snippet from perhaps the most monumental post-1844 eruption perhaps tells all: 'the factor which monetary policy should seek to influence or control is something that reaches beyond what is known as the "supply of money". It is nothing less than the state of liquidity of the whole economy.' ('Radcliffe', 1959, p. 357).

(Also see Chick, 1977.) Of course, a principal theme of Chapter 11 has been that innovations may make it infeasible for monetary policy to control *any* 'factor'.)

The 1844 debate concerned a *de facto* definition of money that excluded bank deposits. The perpetual debate concerns definitions of money excluding *X*. J. S. Mill's comments remain pointed:

> [In] late years, an artificial limitation on the issue of bank notes has been regarded . . . as an expedient . . . [against] . . . speculation; and this opinion received the recognition and sanction of the legislature by the Currency Act of 1844 . . . Though . . . bank notes [have] a greater power over prices than is possessed by bills or book credits, we have not found reason to think that this superior efficacy has much share in producing the rise in prices which accompanies a period of speculation, nor consequently that any restraint applied to this one instrument can be efficacious, to the degree which often is supposed in moderating either that rise or the recoil which follows it . . . [And then] there is a fourth form of credit transactions, by cheques on bankers, and transfers in a banker's books, which is exactly parallel in every respect to bank notes, giving equal facilities to an extension of credit, and capable of acting on prices quite as powerfully. (J. S. Mill, 1940, reprint, pp. 536–7)

From its inception, the theory of money has been unable to define its object of study!

Words strain,
Crack and sometimes break, under the burden,
Under the tension, slip, slide, perish
Decay with imprecision, will not stay in place
Will not stay still.

T. S. Eliot, *Burnt Norton*,
from *Four Quartets* (New York:
Harcourt Brace, 1943)

11.5 A PROPER DYNAMIC MODEL

The real rate of interest is determined globally; and foreign trade is ruled by a law of one price. Variables include the real wage rate and the rate of real growth – whose growth rates are y_1 and y_2. Parameters include natural rates of growth of the real wage rate and output – y_1^* and y_2^*. Equations (4.1) and (4.2) have the particular solution (y_1^*, y_2^*).

$$\dot{y}_1 = b_{11}(y_1 - y_1^*) + b_{12}(y_2 - y_2^*) \tag{4.1}$$

$$\dot{y}_2 = b_{21}(y_1 - y_1^*) + b_{22}(y_2 - y_2^*) \tag{4.2}$$

Transform the origin to $(0, 0) = (y_1^*, y_2^*)$ so that $y_1' = y_1 - y_1^*$ and $y_2' = y_2 - y_2^*$. Equations (4.3) and (4.4) follow.

$$\dot{y}_1' = b_{11}y_1' + b_{12}y_2' \tag{4.3}$$

$$\dot{y}_2' = b_{21}y_1' + b_{22}y_2' \tag{4.4}$$

The system comprising equations (4.3) and (4.4) is *simple*. (See Arrowsmith and Place, 1982, Chapter 2.) It has the solution (0, 0). The determinant being assumed to be non-zero, stability depends on the roots of the quadratic characteristic equation. If the coefficients comprising Matrix B are

$$B = \begin{bmatrix} -0.2 & 0.3 \\ -0.1 & -0.4 \end{bmatrix}$$

the eigen values (roots) are a conjugate complex pair with negative real parts. The system then is stable: its phase diagram then displays stable foci (see Arrowsmith and Place, 1982, p. 51).

11.6 OPTIMAL CURRENCY ZONES

11.6.1 Preliminary Comments

When will a common unit of account minimise variance of regional income, prices or some other variable X? Consider an economic domain. Points belonging to it that are coloured red share a particular unit of account – and belong to subset R. Violet point p does not belong to R. If the variance of X, reckoned at each point belonging to R, would fall if p were to join R, p should join R (relative to a variance-minimisation criterion). Next consider red point q. If q were removed from R, the variance of X, reckoned at each point belonging to R, would fall: the criterion calls for the removal of q from R. Boundaries constructed in this way are unlikely to conform to political ones. (The difficult line of reasoning leading to a rigorous set of criteria belongs to the theory of the core.)

11.6.2 Macroeconomic-Policy-Based Criteria

In the 1960s the 'optimal currency zone' idea was absorbed by the then fashionable 'optimal stabilisation policy' idea.

> In a currency area comprising different countries with national currencies, the pace of employment in deficit countries is set by the willingness of surplus countries to inflate. But in a currency area comprising many regions and a single currency, the pace of inflation is set by the willingness of central authorities to allow unemployment in deficit regions. (Mundell, 1961)

If the trade cycles of two members of a currency zone are in counterphase, a policy directed towards cooling off at one point will exacerbate unemployment at the other.

Mundell goes on to discuss *factor mobility*. If factors are not mobile between two points and if, so to speak, the economic temperatures of the points change oppositely, a macropolicy intended to stabilise one point will destabilise the other. Perfect factor mobility would assure even heat distribution; and make uniform macropolicy more attractive.

Finally, Mundell (1961) makes an argument that both recalls Section 11.3 and anticipates Section 11.6.3:

> Markets for foreign exchange must not be so thin that any single speculator (perhaps excepting central banks) can affect the market prices; otherwise the speculation argument against flexible exchange rates would assume weighty dimensions.

11.6.3 Microtheoretical-Based Argument

After Irish independence the Irish pound remained tied to the British pound for some time. The economic reasons must have been compelling.

Assume, counterfactually, that Irish exports substantially went to British markets *and* that the Irish and British pounds floated against each other. Then Irish pound proceeds of exports might fluctuate substantially. And, to the extent that wage bargains were stickily set in Irish pounds, exporters' net proceeds would fluctuate still more erratically. Indeed, their variance might be dominated by currency rate fluctuations, so that Irish exporters, if they could not purchase cheap insurance, willy-nilly would be currency speculators. Nor would so thin a market work smoothly: only a few futures contracts could be written efficiently (see Telser, 1981).

After Ireland joined the Common Market (EEC), the links between Irish and British currency were severed. (A proximate cause was Britain's refusal to join the European currency 'snake'.) Since Irish trade drifted towards the continent after Ireland joined the EEC, the 'variance minimisation' hypothesis is supported both by the Irish-British currency link, while it lasted, and the severance.

Effects of Choice of Metric. Say that, on average, producers in region z competitively sell their outputs on British, French, American and German markets in fairly stable value-weighted proportions. If these markets are dominated by their national currencies, socioeconomic stability will be promoted by expressing wage bargains in Pfolmars, even if Pfolmar-denominated debt is ordinarily discharged by z-dollar tenders.

The European Currency Unit (ECU).

> The *European Currency Unit (ECU)*, a composite of nine Common Market members' currencies, . . . offers a more stable hedge against the dollar than any other single European currency . . . The ECU's

success may be partly due to the fact that all of its currencies are in a homogeneous trading area. The SDR mixes currencies from around the world. (Peter Truell, *The Wall Street Journal*, 1983)

Not for the first time, Life imitates Art.

Bibliography

Alchian, A. (1977) 'Why Money?', *Journal of Money, Credit and Banking*, vol. 9, p. 133.

Allen, R. G. D. (1938) *Mathematical Analysis for Economists* (London: Macmillan).

Allen, R. G. D. (1956) *Mathematical Economics* (London: Macmillan).

Allen, R. G. D. (1967) *Macro-Economic Theory: A Mathematical Treatment* (London: Macmillan).

Allias, M. (1966) 'A Restatement of the Quantity Theory of Money', *American Economic Review*, vol. 56, p. 123.

Allingham, M. G. and M. L. Burstein (eds) (1976) *Resource Allocation and Economic Policy* (London: Macmillan).

Archibald, G. C. and R. G. Lipsey (1958) 'Monetary and Value Theory: A Critique of Lange and Patinkin', *Review of Economic Studies*, vol. 26, p. 1.

Argy, V. and M. G. Porter (1972) 'The Forward Exchange Market and the Effects of Domestic and External Disturbances under Alternative Exchange Rate Systems', IMF *Staff Papers*, vol. 19, p. 503.

Arrow, K. J. (1978) 'The Future and the Past in Economic Life', *Economic Inquiry*, vol. 16, p. 157, reprinted in K. J. Arrow, *Collected Economic Papers, General Equilibrium* (vol. 2) (Oxford: Basil Blackwell).

Arrowsmith D. K. and C. M. Place (1982) *Ordinary Differential Equations* (London: Chapman & Hall).

Bagehot, W. (1873) *Lombard Street* (London: Kegan Paul).

Bailey, M. J. (1968) 'Comment: Optimal Monetary Growth', *Journal of Political Economy*, vol. 76, p. 874.

Bailey, M. J. (1971) *National Income and the Price Level: A Study in Macroeconomic Theory*, 2nd ed. (New York: McGraw-Hill).

Baily, M. N. (1978) 'Stabilization Policy and Private Economic Behaviour', *Brookings Papers on Economic Activity*, no. 1.

Barro, R. J. (1974) 'Are Government Bonds Net Wealth?', *Journal of Political Economy*, vol. 82.

Barro, R. J. (1976) 'Rational Expectations and the Rôle of Monetary Policy', *Journal of Monetary Economics*, vol. 2, p. 1.

Barro, R. J. (1984) *Macroeconomics* (New York: John Wiley).

Baumol, W. J. (1967) 'Macroeconomics of Unbalanced Growth: The Anatomy of Urban Crises', *American Economic Review*, vol. 57, p. 415.

Bewley, T. (1980) 'The Optimum Quantity of Money', in Karaken and Wallace (eds) (1980) pp. 49–82.

Birman, I. (1983) 'Will Andropov Purge the Passbooks', *Wall Street Journal* (21 March).

Black, F. (1970) 'Banking and Interest Rates in a World Without Money: The Effects of Uncontrolled Banking', *Journal of Bank Research*, vol. 1, p. 9.

Blaug, M. (1978) *Economic Theory in Retrospect*, 3rd ed. (Cambridge: Cambridge University Press).

Blinder, A. S. and R. M. Solow (1973) 'Does Fiscal Policy Matter?', *Journal of Public Economics*, vol. 2, p. 319.
Blinder, A. S. and R. M. Solow (1974) *The Economics of Public Finance* (Washington: The Brookings Institution).
Bodin, J. (1606) *The Six Books of a Commonweale* (London).
Bomberger, W. A. and G. E. Makinen (1980) 'Indexation, Inflationary Finance and Hyperinflation', *Journal of Political Economy*, vol. 88, p. 505.
Branson, W. H. (1979) *Macroeconomic Theory and Policy*, 2nd ed. (New York: Harper & Row).
Branson, W. H. (1983) 'Economic Structure and Policy for External Balance', IMF *Staff Papers*, vol. 30, p. 39.
Braudel, F. (1984) *The Perspective of the World* (New York: Harper & Row), Siân Reynolds, tr., vol. 3 of F. Braudel, *Civilization and Capitalism, 15th–18th Century*, first published as *Le Temps du Monde* (Paris: Librarie Armand Colin, 1979).
Breckenridge, S. P. (1903) *Legal Tender* (Chicago: University of Chicago Press).
Bresciani-Turroni, C. (1937) *The Economics of Inflation* (London: Allen & Unwin).
Bridgman, P. W. (1927) *The Logic of Physics* (New York: Macmillan).
Brunner, K. and A. H. Meltzer (1972) 'Money, Debt and Economic Activity', *Journal of Political Economy*, vol. 80, p. 951.
Buchanan, J. (1958) *Public Principles of Public Debt* (Homewood, Ill.: Richard D. Irwin).
Buiter, W. H. (1977) 'Crowding Out and the Effectiveness of Fiscal Policy', *Journal of Public Economics*, vol. 7.
Buiter, W. H. (1980) 'The Rôle of Economic Policy After the New Classical Macroeconomics' (Cambridge, Mass.: National Bureau of Economic Research, Working Paper No. 580), reprinted in D. Currie and D. A. Peel (eds) *Contemporary Economic Analysis* (Beckenham, Kent: Croom Helm).
Burmeister, E. (1980) *Capital Theory and Dynamics* (New York: Cambridge University Press).
Burstein, M. L. (1963) *Money* (Cambridge, Mass.: Schenkman).
Burstein, M. L. (1966) 'Colonial Currency and Contemporary Monetary Theory: A Review Article', *Explorations in Entrepreneurial History* (2nd series), vol. 3, p. 220.
Burstein, M. L. (1968) *Economic Theory: Equilibrium and Change* (London: John Wiley).
Burstein, M. L. (1975) 'Some More Keynesian Economics', *Economic Inquiry*, vol. 13.
Burstein, M. L. (1976) 'Economic Theory and Political Strategy – Cambodia', in Allingham and Burstein (eds) (1976) pp. 61–71.
Burstein, M. L. (1978) *New Directions in Economic Policy* (London: Macmillan).
Burstein, M. L. (1982) 'Stock Flow Analysis', in D. Greenwald (ed.) *Encyclopedia of Economics* (New York: McGraw-Hill) pp. 899–902.
Burstein, M. L. (1984) 'A Theory of the Diffusion of Knowledge-Based Products: Applications to Developing Economics', *Economic Inquiry*, vol. 22, pp. 612–633.
Bushaw, D. W. and R. W. Clower (1957) *Introduction to Mathematical Economics* (Homewood, Ill.: Richard D. Irwin).

Cagan P. (1956) 'The Monetary Dynamics of Hyperinflation', in M. Friedman, (ed.) (1956) *Studies in the Quantity Theory of Money* (Chicago: University of Chicago Press).

Campbell, C. D. and G. C. Tullock (1954) 'Hyperinflation in China, 1937–1949', *Journal of Political Economy*, vol. 62.

Carlson, K. M. and R. W. Spencer (1975) 'Crowding Out and Its Critics', Federal Reserve Bank of St Louis, *Review*, vol. 57.

Carmichael, J. (1982) 'On Barro's Theorem of Debt Neutrality: The Irrelevance of Net Wealth', *American Economic Review*, vol. 72, p. 202.

Chandler, L. V. (1953) *The Economics of Money and Banking*, rev. ed. (New York: Harper & Row).

Chang, W., D. Hamberg, and J. Hirata (1983) 'Liquidity Preference towards Risk is a Demand for Short-Term Securities – Not Money', *American Economic Review*, vol. 73, p. 420.

Chick, V. (1977) *The Theory of Monetary Policy*, rev. ed. (Oxford: Basil Blackwell).

Christ, C. F. (1968) 'A Simple Macroeconomic Model with a Government Budget Constraint', *Journal of Political Economy*, vol. 76.

Cipolla, C. M. (1956) *Money, Prices and Civilization in the Mediterranean World: Fifth to Seventeenth Century* (Princeton: Princeton University Press).

Clower, R. W. (1967) 'A Reconsideration of the Microfoundations of Monetary Theory', *Western Economic Journal*, vol. 6, p. 1.

Clower, R. W. (1968a) 'Stock-Flow Analysis', *International Encyclopedia of the Social Sciences* (New York: Crowell, Collier & Macmillan) pp. 273–77.

Clower, R. W. (1968b) 'Comment: The Optimal Growth Rate of Money', *Journal of Political Economy*, vol. 76, p. 876.

Clower, R. W. (1969) 'What Traditional Monetary Theory Really Wasn't', *Canadian Journal of Economics*, vol. 2, p. 299.

Clower, R. W. and M. L. Burstein (1960) 'On the Invariance of Demand for Cash and Other Assets', *Review of Economic Studies*, vol. 28.

Clower, R. W. and P. Howitt (19??) The Transactions Theory of the Demand for Money: A Reconsideration', *Journal of Political Economy*, vol. 86, p. 449.

Cuthbertson, K. (1979) *Macroeconomic Policy, etc.* (London: Macmillan).

D'Abro, A. (1951) *The Rise of the New Physics*, vol. 2 (New York: Dover Pub.).

David, P. A. and J. L. Scadding (1974) 'Private Savings, Ultranationality, Aggregation and "Dennison's Law"', *Journal of Political Economy*, vol. 82, p. 225.

Diamond, P. A. (1965) 'National Debt in a Neoclassical Growth Model', *American Economic Review*, vol. 55, p. 1126.

Dornbusch, R. (1976) 'The Theory of Flexible Exchange Rate Régimes and Macroeconomic Policy', *Scandinavian Journal of Economics*, vol. 78, p. 255.

Dornbusch, R. (1983) 'Flexible Exchange Rates and Interdependence', IMF *Staff Papers*, vol. 30, p. 3.

Eckstein, O. (1981) *Core Inflation* (Englewood Cliffs, N. J.: Prentice-Hall).

Einaudi, L. (1952) 'The Theory of Imaginary Money', reprint appearing in *Enterprise and Secular Change* (Homewood, Ill.: Richard D. Irwin).

Einzig, P. (1961) *A Dynamic Theory of Forward Exchange* (London: Macmillan).

Eisner, R. and P. J. Pieper (1984) 'A New View of the Federal Debt and Budget Deficits', *American Economic Review*, vol. 74, p. 11.

Eltis, W. A. and P. J. N. Sinclair (eds) (1981) *The Money Supply and the Exchange Rate* (Oxford: Clarendon Press).

Epstein, L. G. and J. A. Hynes (1983) 'The Rate of Time Preference and Dynamic Economic Analysis', *Journal of Political Economy*, vol. 91, p. 665.

Evans, P. (1984) 'The effects on Output of Money Growth and Interest Rate Volatility in the United States', *Journal of Political Economy*, vol. 92, p. 204.

Fama, E. F. (1980) 'Banking in the Theory of Finance', *Journal of Monetary Economics*, vol. 6, p. 39.

Farrer (Lord) (1898) *Studies in Currency* (London).

Feldstein, M. (1974) 'Social Security, Induced Retirement and Aggregate Capital Accumulation', *Journal of Political Economy*, vol. 82.

Feldstein, M. (1980) 'Fiscal Policies, Inflation and Capital Formation', *American Economic Review*, vol. 70, p. 636.

Fetter, F. W. (1965) *The Development of British Monetary Othodoxy, 1797–1875* (Cambridge, Mass.: Harvard University Press).

Fischer, S. (ed.) (1980) *Rational Expectations and Monetary Policy* (Chicago: University of Chicago Press).

Flexner, J. T. (1965) *George Washington: The Forge of Experience, 1731–1775* (Boston: Little, Brown).

Flood, R. P. and P. M. Garber (1984) 'Gold Monetization and Gold Discipline', *Journal of Political Economy*, vol. 92, p. 90.

French, A. P. (1968) *Special Relativity* (New York: Norton).

Frenkel, J. (1981) 'Flexible Exchange Rates, Prices and the Rôle of "News": Lessons from the 1970s', *Journal of Political Economy*, vol. 89, p. 665.

Friedman, B. (1978) 'After the Phillips Curve', Federal Reserve Bank of Boston.

Friedman, M. (1942, 1953) Discussion of the Inflationary Gap', *American Economic Review*, vol. 32, p. 334, reprinted, with some changes in his *Essays in Positive Economics* (Chicago: University of Chicago Press, 1953).

Friedman, M. (1944, 1953) 'Lange on Price Flexibility and Full Employment: A Methodological Criticism', *American Economic Review*, vol. 36, pp. 613–31.

Friedman, M. (1948, 1953) 'A Monetary and Fiscal Framework for Economic Stability', *American Economic Review*, vol. 38, pp. 245–64 – reprinted in Friedman (1953), pp. 133–56.

Friedman, M. (1951a, 1953) 'Commodity Reserve Currency', *Journal of Political Economy*, vol. 59, p. 203 – reprinted in Friedman (1953).

Friedman, M. (1951b, 1953) 'The Effects of a Full-Employment Policy on Economic Stability: A Formal Analysis', in Friedman (1953), pp. 117–32 – originally published as 'Les effets d'une politique de plein emploi sur la stabilité économique: analyse formelle', *Économie Appliquée*, vol. 4 (1951), pp. 441–56.

Friedman, M. (1956) Introduction to M. Friedman (ed.) *Studies in the Quantity Theory of Money* (Chicago: University of Chicago Press).

Friedman, M. (1962) *Price Theory: A Provisional Text* (Chicago: Aldine Press).

Friedman, M. (1968a) 'The Rôle of Monetary Policy', *American Economic Review*, vol. 58, p. 1.

Friedman, M. (1968b) 'Money: Quantity Theory', in D. L. Sills (ed.), *International Encyclopedia of the Social Sciences* (New York: Crowell, Collier & Macmillan) vol. 10, pp. 432–46.

Friedman, M. (1969) *The Optimal Quantity of Money and Other Essays* (Chicago: University of Chicago Press).
Friedman, M. (1974a) 'A Theoretical Framework for Monetary Analysis', in R. J. Gordon (ed.) (1974) *Milton Friedman's Monetary Framework: A Debate with His Critics* (Chicago: University of Chicago Press), pp. 1–62.
Friedman, M. (1974b) 'Reply to Tobin', in R. J. Gordon (ed.) (1974), p. 137*ff*.
Friedman, M. (1977) 'Nobel Lecture, Inflation and Unemployment', *Journal of Political Economy*, vol. 85, p. 451.
Friedman, M. (1984a) 'Financial Futures Markets and Tabular Standards', *Journal of Political Economy*, vol. 92, p. 165.
Friedman, M. (1984b) 'The Taxes Called Deficits', *Wall Street Journal*, 26 April.
Friedman, M. and A. J. Schwartz (1963) *A Monetary History of the United States* (Princeton: Princeton University Press for the National Bureau of Economic Research).
Frisch, H. (1983) *Theories of Inflation* (New York: Cambridge University Press).
Frydman, R. and E. S. Phelps (1984) '*Rational Expectations' Examined* (New York: Cambridge University Press).
Girton, L. and D. Roper (1978) 'J. Laurence Laughlin and the Quantity Theory of Money', *Journal of Political Economy*, vol. 86, p. 599.
Girton, L. and D. Roper (1981) 'Theory and Implications of Currency Substitution', *Journal of Money, Credit and Banking*, vol. 13, p. 12.
Gordon, R. J. (ed.) (1974) *Milton Friedman's Monetary Framework: A Debate with his Critics* (Chicago: University of Chicago Press).
Gordon, R. J. (1976) 'Recent Developments in the Theory of Inflation and Unemployment', *Journal of Monetary Economics*, vol. 2, p. 185.
Gordon, R. J. (1984) *Macroeconomics*, 3rd ed. (Boston: Little, Brown).
Greenfield, R. L. and L. B. Yeager (1983) 'A Laissez Faire Approach to Monetary Stability', *Journal of Money, Credit and Banking*, vol. 15, p. 302.
Gurley, J. G. and E. S. Shaw (1960) *Money in a Theory of Finance* (Washington: The Brookings Institution).
Haberler, G. (1937, 1964) *Prosperity and Depression*, 5th ed. (London: Allen & Unwin).
Hadjimichalikakis, M. (1982) *Monetary Policy and Modern Money Markets* (Lexington, Mass.: Lexington Books).
Hahn, F. H. (1966) 'Equilibrium Dynamics with Heterogeneous Capital Goods', *Quarterly Journal of Economics*, vol. 80.
Hahn, F. H. (1980) 'Discussion' appearing in Karaken and Wallace (eds) (1980), pp. 83–96.
Hahn, F. H. (1982) *Money and Inflation* (Oxford: Basil Blackwell).
Hamada, K. and M. Sakurai (1978) 'International Transmission of Stagflation under Fixed and Flexible Exchange Rates', *Journal of Political Economy*, vol. 86, p. 877.
Hammond, B. (1957) *Banks and Politics in the United States* (Princton: Princeton University Press).
Harris, L. (1981) *Monetary Theory* (New York: McGraw-Hill).
Harrod, R. F. (1939) 'An Essay in Dynamic Economics', *Economic Journal*, vol. 49.
Harrod, R. F. (1948) *Towards a Dynamic Economics* (London: Macmillan).
Hawtrey, R. G. (1947) *The Gold Standard in Theory and Practice*, 5th ed. (London: Longmans, Green).

Hawtrey, R. G. (1950) *Currency and Credit*, 4th ed. (London: Longmans, Green).

Hayek, F. A. (1976) *Denationalization of Money* (London: Institute of Economic Affairs).

Hicks, J. R. (1938 and 1946) *Value and Capital*, 1st and 2nd eds, (Oxford: Clarendon Press).

Hicks, J. R. (1955) 'Economic Foundations of Wage Policy', *Economic Journal*, vol. 65.

Hicks, J. R. (1966) *Introduction* to J. R. Hicks (ed.) *D. H. Robertson, Essays in Monetary Economics* (London: Collins).

Hicks, J. R. (1967) *Critical Essays in Monetary Theory* (Oxford: Clarendon Press).

Howitt, P. (1974) 'Stability and the Quantity Theory', *Journal of Political Economy*, vol. 82, p. 133.

Hurst, J. W. (1973) *A Legal History of Money in the United States, 1774–1970* (Lincoln, Neb: University of Nebraska Press).

James, J. A. and R. E. Sylla (1980) 'The Changing Nature of the American Public Debt 1690–1835', Proceedings of the 9th Colloque International (Sept. 1978), published by the Crédit Communal de Belgique, pp. 243–73.

Johnson, H. G. (1958) *International Trade and Economic Growth* (London: Allen & Unwin), see esp. 'The Transfer Problem and Exchange Stability'.

Johnson, H. G. 1(1961) 'The General Theory After Twenty Five Years', *American Economic Review*, vol. 51, p. 1.

Johnson, H. G. (1967) *Essays in Monetary Theory* (London: Allen & Unwin) ch. 4.

Johnson, H. G. (1969a) 'Pesek and Saving's Theory of Money and Wealth: A Comment', *Journal of Money, Credit and Banking*, vol. 1, p. 535.

Johnson, H. G. (1969b) 'Inside Money, Outside Money, Income, Wealth and Welfare in Monetary Theory', *Journal of Money, Credit and Banking*, vol. 1, p. 30.

Johnson, H. G. (1973) *Further Essays in Monetary Theory* (Cambridge: Mass.: Harvard University Press), see 'The Case for Flexible Exchange Rates, 1969'.

Kaldor, N. (1960) *Essays on Economic Stability and Growth* (London: Duckworth).

Kaldor, N (1970) 'The New Monetarism', *Lloyds Bank Review*, no. 97.

Kamien, M. I. and N. L. Schwartz (1981) *Dynamic Optimization* (New York: North-Holland).

Karaken, J. and N. Wallace (eds) (1980) *Models of Monetary Economics* (Minneapolis, Minn.: Federal Reserve Bank of Minneapolis).

Kemeny, J. and J. Snell (1962) *Mathematical Models in the Social Sciences* (Boston: Ginn) chs 5, 6 and appendices.

Kemeny, J., J. Snell and G. Thompson (1957) *Introduction to Finite Mathematics* (Englewood Cliffs, N. J.: Prentice-Hall).

Kemmerer, E. W. (1937) *Money* (New York: Macmillan).

Keynes, J. M. (1921) *A Treatise on Probability* (London: Macmillan).

Keynes, J. M. (1923) *A Tract on Monetary Reform* (London: Macmillan).

Keynes, J. M. (1930) *A Treatise on Money*, 2 vols (London: Macmillan).

Keynes, J. M. (1936) *The General Theory of Employment, Interest and Money* (London: Macmillan).

Keynes, J. M. (1940) *How to Pay for the War* (London: Macmillan) – reprinted in E. Johnson and D. Moggridge (eds) (1972) *Essays in Persuasion* (London: Macmillan).

Keynes, J. M. (1949, reprint) 'The German Transfer Problem', in H. Ellis and Metzler, L. (eds) *Readings in the Theory of International Trade* (Homewood, Ill.: Richard D. Irwin for the AEA).

Kindleberger, C. P. (1978) *Manias, Panics and Crashes* (New York and London: Basic Books and Macmillan).

Klein, B. (1974a) 'The Competitive Supply of Money', *Journal of Money, Credit and Banking*, vol. 6, p. 423.

Klein, B. (1974b) 'Competitive Interest Payments on Bank Deposits and the Long Run Demand for Money', *American Economic Review*, vol. 64, p. 931.

Knapp, G. F. (1924) *The State Theory of Money* (London: Macmillan).

Kydland, F. E. and E. C. Prescott (1977) 'Rules Rather Than Discretion: The Inconsistency of Optimal Plans', *Journal of Political Economy*, vol. 85, p. 473.

Laidler, D. (1984) 'Misconceptions about the Real Bills Doctrine: A Comment on Sargent and Wallace', *Journal of Political Economy*, vol. 92, p. 149.

Laidler, D. and M. Parkin (1975) 'Inflation: A Survey', *Economic Journal*, vol. 85, p. 741.

Lange, O. (1944) *Price Flexibility and Full Employment* (Bloomington, Ind.: The Principia Press).

Leijonhufvud, A. (1968) *On Keynesian Economics and the Economics of Keynes* (New York: Oxford University Press).

Leijonhufvud, A. (1981) *Information and Coordination* (New York: Oxford University Press).

Lerner, A. P. (1952) 'The Essential Properties of Intertest and Money', *Quarterly Journal of Economics*, vol. 66 – reprinted in his *Essays in Economic Analysis* (London: Macmillan, 1953).

Lerner, E. (1956) 'Inflation in the Confederacy, 1861–1865', in Friedman (ed.) (1956), pp. 163–75.

Lucas, C. M. *et al.* (1977) 'On the Federal Funds Market', Federal Reserve Bank of New York *Quarterly Review* (Summer), pp. 33–48.

Lucas, R. E. (1972) 'Expectations and the Neutrality of Money', *Journal of Economic Theory*, vol. 4, pp. 103–24.

Lucas, R. E. (1975) 'An Equilibrium Model of the Business Cycle', *Journal of Political Economy*, vol. 83, pp. 113–44.

Lucas, R. E. (1976) 'Econometric Policy Evaluation: A Critique', in K. Brunner and A. Meltzer (eds) *The Phillips Curve and Labour Markets* (Amsterdam: North-Holland – supplement to the *Journal of Monetary Economics*, pp. 19–46.

Lucas, R. E. (1977) 'Understanding Business Cycles', *Journal of Monetary Economics* (supp.), vol. 5.

Lucas, R. E. (1981a) 'Tobin and Monetarism: A Review Article', *Journal of Economic Literature*, vol. 19, p. 558.

Lucas, R. E. (1981b) *Studies in Business Cycle Theory* (Cambridge, Mass.: MIT Press).

Machlup, F. (1950) *International Trade and the National Income Multiplier* (Philadelphia: Blakiston).

Makinen, G. E. (1977) *Money, the Price Level and Interest Rates: An*

Introduction to Monetary Theory (Englewood Cliffs, N. J.: Prentice-Hall).
Malkiel, B. G. and R. E. Quandt (1969) *Strategies and Rational Decisions in the Securities Option Market* (Cambridge, Mass.: MIT Press).
Mann, F. A. (1953, 1971) *The Legal Aspects of Money*, 2nd and 3rd eds (London: Oxford University Press).
Marshall, A. (1887) 'Remedies for Fluctuations of General Prices', reprinted in A. C. Pigou (ed.) (1925) *Memorials of Alfred Marshall* (London: Macmillan) pp. 188–211.
Marshall, A. (1923) *Money, Credit and Commerce* (London: Macmillan).
Marty, A. L. (1968) 'The Optimal Growth Rate of Money', *Journal of Political Economy*, vol. 76, p. 860.
McCallum, B. T. (ed.) (1980) *Rational Expectations, Journal of Money, Credit and Banking*, part 2 of vol. 12.
McCallum, B. T. (1984) 'Are Bond Financed Deficits Inflationary?: A Ricardian Analysis', *Journal of Political Economy*, vol. 92, p. 123.
McKinnon, R. I. (1979) *Money in International Exchange: The Convertible Currency System* (New York: Oxford University Press).
McLaughlin, A. (1962) *The Confederation and the Constitution, 1783–1789* (New York: Collier).
Metzler, L. A. (1948) 'Three Lags in the Circular Flow of Income', in L. A. Metzler *et al*, *Essays in Honour of Alvin, H. Hansen* (New York: Norton).
Metzler, L. A. (1949) 'The Transfer Problem Reconsidered', in L. A. Metzler and H. Ellis (eds) *Readings in the Theory of International Trade* (Philadelphia: Blakiston).
Metzler, L. A. (1951) 'Wealth, Saving and the Rate of Interest', *Journal of Political Economy*, vol. 59, p. 93.
Mill, J. S. (1940 reprint) *Principles of Political Economy*, Ashley (ed.) (London: Longmans, Green) book III, ch. 12, Part 6, pp. 536–7.
Mints, L. A. (1945) *A History of Banking Theory* (Chicago: University of Chicago Press).
Mises, L. von (1953) *The Theory of Money and Credit* (New Haven, Conn.: Yale University Press).
Modigliani, F. (1964) 'Long Run Implications of Alternative Fiscal Policies and the Burden of National Debt', in J. Ferguson (ed.) *Public Debt and Future Generations* (Chapel Hill, N. C.: University of North Carolina Press).
Modigliani, F. (1977) 'The Monetarist Controversy or, Should We Foresake Stabilization Policies?', *American Economic Review*, vol. 69, p. 1.
Modigliani, F. and L. Papademos (1981) 'The Structure of Financial Markets and the Monetary Mechanism', (unpublished).
Mundell, R. A. (1961) 'A Theory of Optimum Currency Areas', *American Economic Review*, vol. 51, p. 657.
Mundell, R. A. (1968) *International Economics* (New York: Macmillan) esp. ch. 12.
Mussa, M. (1976) 'The Exchange Rate, the Balance of Payments and Monetary and Fiscal Policy under a Régime of Controlled Floating', *Scandinavian Journal of Economics*, vol. 78, p. 229.
Muth, J. (1961) 'Rational Expectations and the Theory of Price Movements', *Econometrica*, vol. 29, p. 315.

Nagatani, K. (1981) *Macroeconomic Dynamics* (Cambridge and New York: Cambridge University Press).

Nelson, R. R. (1956) 'A Theory of the Low Equilibrium Trap in Underdeveloped Countries', *American Economic Review*, vol. 46.

Newlyn, W. T. and R. P. Bootle (1978) *Theory of Money*, 3rd ed. (Oxford: Clarendon Press).

Niehans, J. (1978) *The Theory of Money* (Baltimore: Johns Hopkins Press).

Nussbaum, A. (1957) *A History of the Dollar* (New York: Columbia University Press).

Obstfeld, M. and K. Rogoff (1983) 'Speculative Hyperinflations in Maximizing Models: Can We Rule Them Out?', *Journal of Political Economy*, vol. 91, p. 675.

Ohlin, B. (1949) 'The Reparation Problem: A Discussion', in Metzler and Ellis (eds) (1949).

Okun, A. M. (1981) *Prices and Quantities* (Washington: Brookings Institution).

Ostroy, J. M. (1973) 'The Informational Efficiency of Monetary Exchange', *American Economic Review*, vol. 63, p. 597.

Parkin, M. (1982) *Modern Macro-Economics* (New York: Prentice-Hall).

Patinkin, D. (1956, 1965) *Money, Interest and Prices,* 1st and 2nd eds (New York: Harper & Row).

Patinkin, D. (1961) 'Financial Intermediaries and the Logical Structure of Monetary Theory', *American Economic Review*, vol. 51, p. 95.

Patinkin, D. (1969) 'Money and Wealth', *Journal of Economic Literature*, vol. 7, p. 1140.

Pesek, B. P. and T. R. Saving (1967) *Money, Wealth and Economic Theory* (New York: Macmillan).

Phelps, E. S. (1961) 'The Golden Rule of Accumulation: A Fable for Growthmen', *American Economic Review*, vol. 51, p. 538.

Phelps, E. S. (1968a) 'Money Wage Dynamics and Labour Market Equilibrium', *Journal of Political Economy*, vol. 76, p. 678.

Phelps, E. S. (1968b) 'Comment on the Optimal Growth Rate of Money', *Journal of Political Economy*, vol. 76, p. 881.

Phelps, E. S. (1973) 'Inflation in the Theory of Finance', *Swedish Journal of Economics*, vol. 75, p. 67.

Poole, W. (1970) 'Optimal Choice of Monetary Policy Instruments in a Simple Stochastic Macro Model', *Quarterly Journal of Economics*, vol. 84, p. 197.

Poole, W. (1978) 'The Theory of Monetary Policy Under Uncertainty', in Teigen, R. L. (ed.) (1978) *Readings in Money, National Income and Stabilization Policy*, 4th ed. (Homewood, Ill.: Richard D. Irwin) pp. 327–33.

Radcliffe Committee (R. S. Sayers, principal author) (1959), Committee on the Working of the Monetary System, *Report* (London: HMSO).

Robbins, L. (1958) *Robert Torrens and the Evolution of Classical Economics* (London: Macmillan).

Robertson, D. H. (1926) *Banking Policy and the Price Level* (London: P. S. King).

Robertson, D. H. (1940) *Essays in Monetary Theory* (London: P. S. King).

Robertson, D. H. (1948) *Money* (London: Pitman).

Robertson, D. H. (1966, op. post.) *Essays on Money and Interest* (J. R. Hicks, ed.) (London: Collins).

Robinson, J. (1951) 'The Rate of Interest', *Econometrica*, vol. 19.

Robinson, J. (1947) *Essay in Marxian Economics* (London: Macmillan).

Robinson, J. (1974) *History versus Equilibrium* (London: Thames Polytechnic Papers in Political Economy).

Rueff, J. (1947) 'The Fallacies of Lord Keynes's General Theory', *Quarterly Journal of Economics*, vol. 61.

Rueff, J. (1948) 'Reply to Tobin', *Quarterly Journal of Economics*, vol. 62.

Salant, S. W. (1983) 'The Vulnerability of Price Stabilization Schemes to Speculative Attack', *Journal of Political Economy*, vol. 91, p. 1.

Samuelson, P. A. (1947, 1983) *Foundations of Economic Analysis*, 1st and 2nd eds (Cambridge, Mass.: Harvard University Press).

Samuelson, P. A. (1952) 'The Transfer Problem and Transfer Costs', *Economic Journal*, vol. 62. (See also *Economic Journal* vol. 64, 1954.)

Samuelson, P. A. (1957) 'Intertemporal Price Equilibrium: A Prologue to the Theory of Speculation', *Weltwirtschaftliches Archiv*', reprinted in his *Collected Scientific Papers*, vol. 3.

Samuelson, P. A. (1958) 'An Exact Consumption Loan Model of Interest with or without the Social Contrivance of Money', *Journal of Political Economy*, vol. 66.

Samuelson, P. A. (1967) 'Indeterminancy of Development in a Heterogeneous Capital Market with Constant Saving Propensity', in K. Shell (ed.) *Essays on the Theory of Economic Growth* (Cambridge, Mass.: MIT Press), reprinted in his *Collected Scientific Papers*, vol. 3.

Samuelson, P. A. (1968) 'What Classical and Neoclassical Monetary Theory Really Was', *Canadian Journal of Economics*, vol. 1, p. 1.

Samuelson, P. A. (1969) Nonoptimality of Money Holding Under Laissez Faire', *Canadian Journal of Economics*, vol. 2, p. 303.

Sargent, T. J. (1979) *Macroeconomic Theory* (New York: Academic Press).

Sargent, T. J. (1982) 'The Ends of Four Big Inflations', in R. E. Hall (ed.) *Inflation: Causes and Effects* (Chicago: University of Chicago Press for the National Bureau of Economic Research) pp. 41–97.

Sargent, T. J. and N. Wallace (1976) 'Rational Expectations and the Theory of Monetary Policy', *Journal of Monetary Economics*, vol. 2, p. 169.

Sargent, T. J. and N. Wallace (1981) 'Some Unpleasant Monetarist Arithmetic', Federal Reserve Bank of Minneapolis *Quarterly Review*, vol. 5, p. 1.

Sargent, T. J. and N. Wallace (1982) 'The Real Bills Doctrine versus the Quantity Theory of Money', *Journal of Political Economy*, vol. 90, p. 1212.

Sayers, R. S. (1957) *Central Banking After Bagehot* (Oxford: Clarendon Press).

Senior, N. (1830) *The Cost of Obtaining Money*, reprinted as no. 5 in the Scarce Tract Series published by the London School of Economics.

Sheffrin, S. (1983) *Rational Expectations* (New York: Cambridge University Press).

Shiller, R. J. (1978) 'Rational Expectations and the Dynamic Structure of Macroeconomic Models', *Journal of Monetary Economics*, vol. 4.

Smith A. (1776/1910/1970) *An Inquiry into the Nature and Causes of the Wealth of Nations*, 2 vols (London: Dent – Everyman's Library Edition, E. A. Seligman, ed.).

Smith, B. D. (1984) 'Money and Inflation in Colonial Massachusetts', Federal Reserve Bank of Minneapolis *Quarterly Review*, vol. 8, p. 1.

Sokolnikoff, I. S. (1939) *Advanced Calculus* (New York: McGraw-Hill).

Spraos, J. (1959) 'Speculation, Arbitrage and Sterling', *Economic Journal*, vol. 69.

Supel, T. M. and R. M. Todd (1984) 'Should Currency be Priced Like Cars?', Federal Reserve Bank of Minneapolis *Quarterly Review*, vol. 8, p. 3.

Swoboda, A. K. (1983) 'Exchange Rate Régimes and European–U. S. Policy Interdependence', IMF *Staff Papers*, vol. 30, no. 75.

Sylla, R. E. (1981) 'Monetary Innovations and Economic History', *Journal of Economic History*, vol. 41.

Telser, L. G. (1981) 'Why There Are Organized Futures Markets', *Journal of Law and Economics*, vol. 24, p. 1.

Temin, P. (1968) 'The Economic Consequences of the Bank War', *Journal of Political Economy*, vol. 76.

Temin, P. (1969) *The Jacksonian Economy* (New York: Norton).

Tinbergen, J. (1963) *On the Theory of Economic Policy*, 2nd ed. (Amsterdam: North-Holland).

Tobin, J. (1948) 'Comment on Rueff (1947)', *Quarterly Journal of Economics*, vol. 62, p. 763.

Tobin, J. (1952) 'Asset Holdings and Spending Decisions', *American Economic Review*, vol. 42.

Tobin, J. (1955) 'A Dynamic Aggregative Model', *Journal of Political Economy*, vol. 63, p. 103.

Tobin, J. (1958) 'Liquidity Preference as Behaviour Towards Risk', *Review of Economic Studies*, vol. 25, p. 65.

Tobin, J. (1961) 'Money, Capital and Other Stores of Value', *American Economic Review* (*Papers and Proceedings*), vol. 51, pp. 26–37.

Tobin, J. (1963) 'Commercial Banks as Creators of "Money" ', in D. Carson (ed.) *Banking and Monetary Studies* (Homewood, Ill.: Richard D. Irwin), pp. 408–19.

Tobin, J. (1965) 'Money and Economic Growth', *Econometrica*, vol. 33, p. 671.

Tobin, J. (1968) 'Notes on Optimal Monetary Growth', *Journal of Political Economy*, vol. 76, p. 833.

Tobin, J. (1974) 'Friedman's Theoretical Framework', in R. J. Gordon (ed.) (1974).

Tobin, J. (1975) 'Keynesian Models of Recession and Depression', *American Economic Review* (*Papers and Proceedings*), vol. 65, p. 195.

Tobin, J. (1980) *Asset Accumulation and Economic Activity* (Chicago and Oxford: University of Chicago Press and Basil Blackwell).

Tobin, J. (1982a) 'Financial Structure and Monetary Rules', *Tagung Geld Banken & Versicherungen*, vol. 2, Universität Karlsruhe.

Tobin, J. (1982b) 'Nobel Lecture', *Journal of Money, Credit and Banking*, vol. 14.

Tobin, J. and W. Buiter (1976) 'Long-Run Effects of Fiscal and Monetary Policy on Aggregate Demand', in J. L. Stein (ed.) *Monetarism* (Amsterdam: North-Holland) ch. 4 – reprinted as Cowles Foundation Paper no. 1, p. 437 (New Haven, Conn.: Yale University Press).

Townsend, R. M. (1978) 'Market Expectations, Rational Expectations and Bayesian Analysis', *International Economic Review*, vol. 19, p. 481.

Townsend, R. M. (1983) 'Forecasting the Forecasts of Others', *Journal of Political Economy*, vol. 91, p. 546.

Toynbee, A. J. (1954) *A Study of History*, vol. 7 (London: Oxford University Press for the Royal Institute of International Affairs).

Triffin, R. (1957) *Europe and the Money Muddle* (New Haven, Conn.: Yale University Press).

Triffin, R. (1961) *Gold and the Dollar Crisis*, rev. ed. (New Haven, Conn.: Yale University Press).

Viner, J. (1937) *Studies in the Theory of International Trade* (New York: Harper & Row).

Wallace, N. (1980) 'The Overlapping Generations Model of Fiat Money', in Karaken and Wallace (eds) (1980) pp. 49–82.

Wallace, N. (1981a) 'A Modigliani–Miller Theorem for Open-Market Operations', *American Economic Review*, vol. 71, p. 267.

Wallace, N. (1981b) 'A Hybrid Fiat-Commodity Monetary System', *Journal of Economic Theory*, vol. 25, p. 421.

Wallace, N. (1984) 'Some Choices for Monetary Policy', Federal Reserve Bank of Minneapolis *Quarterly Review*, vol. 8, p. 15.

Walters, A. A. (1971) 'Consistent Expectations, Distributed Lags and the Quantity Theory', *Economic Journal*, vol. 81, p. 273.

White, L. H. (1984a) 'Competitive Payments Systems and the Unit of Account', *American Economic Review*, vol. 74, p. 699.

White, L. H. (1984b) *Free Banking in Britain: Theory, Experience and Debate* (Cambridge: Cambridge University Press).

Wicksell, K. (1935) *Lectures on Political Economy*, vol. 2 (*Money*) (London: George Routledge) – English translation, edited and introduced by Lionel Robbins.

Wicksell, K. (1936) *Interest and Prices* (London: Macmillan) – a translation by R. F. Kahn of Geldzins und Güterpreise (Jena: Gustav Fischer, 1898).

Working, H. (1948) 'Theory of the Inverse Carrying Charge in Futures Markets', *Journal of Farm Economics*, vol. 30, p. 1.

Working, H. (1962) 'New Concepts Concerning Futures Markets and Prices', *American Economic Review*, vol. 52, p. 431.

Yavorsky, B. M. and A. A. Pinsky (1975) *Fundamentals of Physics* (Moscow: Mir Publishing Co.) 2 vols – translated by N. Weinstein.

Name Index

Subject Index